Double Vision

DOUBLE VISION

Perspectives on Gender and the Visual Arts

Edited and with an Introduction by
NATALIE HARRIS BLUESTONE

Madison ● Teaneck
Fairleigh Dickinson University Press
London and Toronto: Associated University Presses

Associated University Presses
440 Forsgate Drive
Cranbury, NJ 08512

Associated University Presses
25 Sicilian Avenue
London WC1A 2QH, England

Associated University Presses
P.O. Box 338, Port Credit
Mississauga, Ontario
Canada L5G 4L8

The paper used in this publication meets the requirements
of the American National Standard for Permanence of Paper
for Printed Library Materials Z39.48-1984.

Library of Congress Cataloging-in-Publication Data

Double vision : perspectives on gender and the visual arts / Natalie
Harris Bluestone, editor.
  p.   cm.
Includes index.
ISBN 0-8386-3540-7
1. Feminism and art.   2. Feminism and motion pictures.
I. Bluestone, Natalie Harris, 1931–
N72.F45D68   1995
704'.042—dc20   92-55110
                                                           CIP

PRINTED IN THE UNITED STATES OF AMERICA

For George
Amor omnia vincit

Contents

Introduction

NATALIE HARRIS BLUESTONE

[I]n the realm of academic investigation . . . "natural" assumptions must be questioned. . . . And it is here that the very position of woman as an acknowledged outsider . . . is a decided advantage.

—Linda Nochlin

THIS VOLUME AIMS TO PRESENT A TAPESTRY OF INTERWOVEN THEMES, WITH THREADS FROM many overlapping discplines. Two of the guiding principles have been doubleness and diversity. All the contributors to this volume share an experience of "double vision." As women scholars, curators, and teachers, they occupy a dual position. They are at the same time both inside the mainstream of their fields, and yet also outside the dominant group that has produced the bulk of the appreciated art of the past and controlled academic institutions and inquiry. All the writers also agree on the importance of clear thought and lucid writing, accepting the best mainstream standards of their disciplines. Feminist theorists in the past decades have often descried the general undervaluing of emotion by male philosophers and moralists. Some feminist writers about art have therefore advocated a discourse of feeling, the incorporation of poetic passages and aperçus into their work. The writers here, however, have all chosen the path of logic and analysis, rejecting the idea that these are pernicious male modes. But while they value the role of rational discourse, their positions as outsiders have led them to analyze topics previously overlooked, aspects of art and art production not seen by previous male scholars as problematic or valuable.

If the contributors share some common split in vision, they are otherwise markedly and intentionally diverse in their approaches and their conclusions. All would describe themselves as feminists, but they are diverse in their ideology. They represent a spectrum of feminist views, and even reject some of the tenets of what has become in the past twenty years almost a Feminist Establishment, complete with a "Who's Who?" and internecine and intergenerational quarrels. In age the contributors to this anthology span almost four decades. All of them are aware of the current issues and appreciative of the new information and insights feminists have produced. However, they hold disparate positions on such crucial issues as the existence of a female sensibility and the value of previous art done primarily by males. Some think there can be no progress without revolutionary change in the disciplines of art history and film criticism. Others see themselves as mainly opening up the dialogue to participants whose voices have been previously silenced.

The writers in this collection would agree that no "purely aesthetic," strictly formalist analysis of artworks is possible. Some find it important also to guard against the danger of feminist thinkers themselves promulgating an autocratic, narrowly proscribed discourse. They object when single-minded theorists cloud the viewer's vision, leading her away from the work rather than offering that added dimension which the good critic has always provided.[1] We are thus not only outside the mainstream male tradition, but as social historians and philosophers we are sometimes uncomfortably outside a growing mainstream feminist orthodoxy. For some, though not all of us, this perception of the dangers of excess zeal produces an uncomfortable further experience of double vision.

There is then purposely no single voice nor dominant vocabulary in this collection. While feminist film theorists talk of signs and signifiers, of decoding and deconstruction, others still find serviceable the earlier language and methods of their disciplines. There is, however, one characteristic all the writers share, and that is a desire to communicate the results of long-term interests, investigations, and research to as broad an audience as possible. Whereas most writers on feminism and art primarily address their feminist followers, the intent here has been to avoid "preaching to the faithful" alone. The hope is that innovative approaches and new details will be of interest not only to the already convinced specialist but also to the general reader.

★　★　★

The history of feminist art criticism beginning with and resulting from the ferment of the Women's Movement in the late 1960s has been divided into phases. We have progressed through an initial Retrieval Phase in which writers sought to discover all the previously overlooked female artists and to reclaim neglected artistic endeavors excluded from the fine arts. Then came a Gender Specific Phase which consisted of debates about whether there was a fundamental link between femaleness and certain kinds of art production and evaluation. The third stage consisted of a Litany of Oppression in which much important work was done to reveal the specifics of the obstacles and discrimination that women artists faced and which denied them the opportunities to make art. The latest stage has called for a Revolutionary Revamping of art history and criticism, a message, at least in embryo, present all along. These thinkers have demanded a shift in ideology and a total dismantling of the current power structure.

A mistaken model of phases of intellectual movements as strictly successive has led some to the idea that research, although it contains new information, can be anachronistic.[2] My own view is that there is room for repetition as well as for fresh insights on old subjects. I also believe that women do not speak in a single different voice, but instead in many voices. Some of the contributors to this volume share all of the assumptions of the fourth activist phase. That is, they assume: (1) The "genius" view of art history, a claim that the most worthwhile art has been made by uniquely gifted individuals, is both wrong, and insidiously designed to undervalue women. (2) Hierarchical thinking in general is undesirable since it creates spurious distinctions between "art" and "crafts," between sculpture and painting, history paintings and other genres, and is designed to undervalue women. (3) There is no such phenomenon as an "aesthetic" appreciation of an art work. Art can never be judged apart from the sociology of the times, specifically the class and gender ideology and prevalent power relations, which have always reflected the male domination characteristic of all known societies. (4) Visual art objects are signs, to be interpreted as such. Critical analyses of the works are to be "deconstructed," and some, influenced by movements in literary criticism, believe that the distinction between artistic work and critical "reading" is in large part illusory. (5) It is no longer enough to point out the obstacles women have faced in the past. Merely showing how women were denied such opportunities as access to nude models and entrance into studio apprenticeships, and, later, academies of art, is insufficient. Giving women access to these institutions and opportunities equal to those available to men for creating art is not enough. A radical restructuring of the ideologies underlying the evaluating and making of art is necessary.

Other contributors do not accept all these assumptions. Some are unwilling to abandon completely the idea of greatness in art. They are unwilling to discard the achievements of "doomdom," that is, the art and films of the DEWMs (*Dead European White Males*). Even though they recognize that many "masterworks" do indeed consist of offensive, demeaning portrayals of women's bodies and female sexuality, they still think it possible to admire other important qualities of these works. Some cling to standards that impede semiotic analysis, which resist what has been called our culture's pervasive "penchant for demystification." With regressive but steadfast conviction, they insist on the primacy of artistic creation over any kind of verbal analysis. They cling to the unfashionable idea "that the visual work of art is closer to the madness of inner life . . . a sacred madness."[3] Some of us resist the whole idea of "reading" a painting, just as we resist the term "visual literacy" out of an unwillingness to equate art objects to literary texts. Regardless of the terms we use for our analysis, we all nevertheless value the contributions of women thinkers to current ways of seeing.

Looking at paintings of rape we can no longer comment only on the flesh tones. We no longer see a sculpture like Giovanni Bologna's marble statue *The Rape of the Sabine Women* and consider it with complete neutrality, as we may once have done. The original two-figure bronze we learn "suggested ecstasy in the woman and represented a pas de deux."[4] But the sculptor said his composition could be the rape of Helen or of Proserpine or of a Sabine woman. Whatever. Feminist viewers of either sex—and of course there are many males who are ardent feminists—in considering either the early two-figure bronze or the later marble statue in which the woman has been given a "distraught" expression, would all point to the social implications of this concept of generic rape.

Clearly feminist thinking has already made decisive inroads. It would now be difficult to publish the overtly demeaning statements about women's genetic inferiority in artistic ability that were once commonplace. There are more women faculty members teaching about the visual arts and more women curators and educators in museums. And the pressure of students interested in women's studies has fostered the offering of courses about women painters, sexuality in modernist visual culture, women and film, in continuing education classes in small communities, as well as in the most elite institutions.

However, the subject of gender and art is still a very fertile field for investigation. There is much more to be said about the truncating of human potential that has resulted from the gender expectations expressed in the Nietzschean aphorism "men are to be warriors and women to give pleasure to warriors." The definition of masculinity that underlies endless paintings and sculpture representing dominance and submission has been almost as detrimental to the development of men's abilities and moral behavior as have the stereotypes of femininity. The competitive struggles of men, of the younger against the older, the stronger against the weaker, the native hero against the barbarian Other, the more cunning smaller against the witless larger—all have contributed to the limitation of men's possibilities. They have inhibited men's potential for peaceful, creative, constructive activity and satisfying egalitarian heterosexual and homosexual relationships.

In many of the most valued works of Western art a powerful sense of male struggle was expressed both iconographically and often even more forcefully in the formal qualities. But that tension between forces which constitutes their aesthetic strength both encouraged and reflected an ideology of masculine behavior that the world can no longer afford to approve. The reduction of the male nude to the biological status of a stag locking horns with another to be vanquished undoubtedly produced impressive art objects. But these endless Perseuses, Davids, Goliaths, Samsons, etc., also had an oppressive force. It is surely as difficult for male observers to recognize these portrayals as destructive of their capabilities as it was for centuries for women to recognize the damage done by the reinforcement of the Madonna-Whore stereotype in visual art.

All of the writers in this book share a conviction that investigations of such gender stereotypes are an important and fruitful enterprise. Yet this volume claims to show only a small segment of the kaleidoscope of possibilities that emerge once one looks at the visual arts through the prism of gender. No artificial attempt has been made to find a single thread that runs through every article. Ludwig Wittgenstein maintained that in attempting to define concepts in ethics and aesthetics, one should not look for a single set of defining characteristics possessed by each example subsumed under the concept. All the varied objects that we designate as art he says will bear only "family resemblances" to each other. So, too, the essays in this collection are connected only by the kind of loose resemblances that visually relate members of a family. Just as some, but not all, members of a family

might have the same chin or high forehead, some of the pieces in this book share the same theme—
e.g., concern with the portrayal of women in particular works. Others share only that common
desire to correct previous exclusions by orthodox male scholars. Thus the anthology is woven of
many strands, some of them overlapping, but there is no single cohesive principle, no doctrinaire
feminist stand. There is no figure in the carpet, nor picture in the tapestry, but only a collection of
investigations concerned in different ways with questions of gender.

★ ★ ★

Essays in this anthology represent different fields of inquiry including history of art and architecture, philosophy, early modern European social history, as well as film theory and criticism. The
first section of the collection is titled "The Eye of the Beholder: Gender, the Artist, and the Observer."
The two essays in this section point out the importance of considerations of gender to the meaning
and impact of the work of a single artist. The first essay by art historian Nancy Finlay sheds light
on an aspect of the animal paintings of the French artist Eugène Delacroix. A critic wrote at the turn
of the century that "to write adequately about Delacroix would be to relate the whole history of
modern art."[5] By highlighting one factor in this history, the artistic and literary merging of eros and
sadism, Finlay reveals previously neglected meanings in the work of Delacroix. As a historian she
has one view; as a female observer she has a kind of double vision. She sees how Delacroix's
ambivalent attitudes to women informed these paintings of animals killing animals and wild beasts
attacking women. An informal survey of contemporary female viewers suggests to Finlay that even
today women viewers miss a crucial sadistic, misogynist element in the work. She concludes that
the modern male viewer actually instinctively comes closer to the intended meanings of Delacroix's paintings.[6]

The second essay in this section makes female interpretations of an artist's work *the* central issue.
In my own contribution I explore women interpreters' views of the only known female sculptor of
the Renaissance, Properzia de' Rossi (1490–1530). Besides detailing and analyzing views of Properzia
I also include a metacritical discussion, an epistemological inquiry foreign to the tradition of art
history. That is, in discussing historical claims about Properzia and feminist objections to earlier
interpretations, I raise the philosophical issue of the objectivity or subjectivity of artistic judgments.
My aim is to reveal the hidden assumptions that I believe underlie critical evaluations of art. The
women writers I treat, like all critics, are decisively products of their historical periods, of the
prevalent theories of art and the social expectations of their times. And yet this does not entail the
complete relativism sometimes expressed in contemporary criticism.

I also question how fundamental the difference in gender is to the observer's vision of a work. Is
there indeed a "female gaze" distinct from that of the male who commissioned the work and was
generally the primary audience for whom the work was intended?[7] As women, the interpreters of
the work of Properzia all had a sense, explicitly expressed or not, of their position as outsiders. But
whether they see this sixteenth-century woman as romantic rebel, hopeless victim, or just another
sculptor depends largely on their context of interpretation.

Part Two of this volume is titled "Women as Patrons: Toward an Expanded Concept of Agency."
The two articles in this section by Christine Havice and Henrietta Startup both involve double vision
in that they too see a phenomenon previously overlooked by male researchers. No doubt their new
perspective stems from their awareness as women of the multiple roles women play. In Christine
Havice's informative synthesis of previous work, she shows how expanding our concept of agency,
of what is involved in the making of a work of art, adds to our knowledge of the origins of medieval
art as well as of women's history. As a medievalist and art historian she employs the painstaking
detailed methods of her discipline. But with double vision she also sees the pattern in what others
had previously seen only dimly, if at all.

In fact, Havice's awareness of the importance of the women who commissioned and provided ideas
for medieval artworks stems directly from the new awareness brought by the women's movement. In

the last three decades feminist scholars have focused on the unheralded contributions that women throughout history made to many different aspects of their societies. This rethinking of women's role is at the center of Havice's detailed investigations. She considers that the women who commissioned Books of Hours made an important contribution to the visual arts. Furthermore she sees the much-studied Hildegarde of Bingen and Christine de Pizan in a new light. As authors of works that required the provision of visual counterparts to their words, Havice shows both that they established the iconography of the images and must have participated in at least a supervisory manner in the actual process of creation.

The architectural historian and museum educator Henrietta Startup also writes about the little noted role of women as patrons. When she focuses on the architecture of the Arts and Crafts Movement, on the planning and execution of settlement houses in the late nineteenth and early twentieth century, she sees more than the work of the male architects. She has an added vision of the previously unseen. From her perspective women like May Morris, Emmeline Pethick-Lawrence, and Mary Simkhovitch, whose social aims, desires, and dreams shaped the arts and crafts culture, should not remain invisible. In her essay she shows how the ideas of these middle- and upper-class women—their convictions about the family, about egalitarianism, and about the importance of craft as a democratizing experience—guided the architects and influenced the final appearance of important public buildings.

The final section is titled "Societal Expectations: Messages about Gender in Painting and Film." The focus in Part Three is on the way in which images have conveyed the relations between men and women in different media and different periods. Sherrin Marshall, an early modern European historian who has concentrated on Dutch history, uses art objects as historical evidence to illuminate features of Dutch family life. As a feminist she is aware of how history has slighted the role of women. However, as an outsider she also questions the feminist assumption that all family life was male-dominated and that women are always to be seen as powerless and oppressed. In an earlier book on the Dutch gentry she focused on reciprocity as a key to understanding the society of the northern Netherlands.[8] In that work she concentrates on the interdependent relationships of the families she studies rather than on the achievement of individuals. "By 'changing the lens,'" she writes, "to include a wide range of historical sources . . . [w]e see that gentry women in early modern Netherlands . . . were often educated, and shared in a wide range of familial, political and social activities."[9] According to Marshall these women seem unaware of any "proper sphere" for women's activities. Dutch law and custom guaranteed them a great deal of independence and autonomy. Wives and husbands were frequently partners in the marital enterprise. She concluded that in gentry families "this emotional sharing was predicated on shared incomes and shared properties. Financial independence gave wives and widows legal, economic, and social clout."[10]

In Marshall's essay in this volume she focuses on the visual arts of the period. She shifts from the customary emphasis on the achievement of the great Dutch male artists to the messages about moderation and mutuality contained in the graphic expression of the seventeenth century. In an original investigation she demonstrates how the visual images accompanying the emblem literature of that period reveal the elements of balance she finds characteristic of the Dutch family of the time. The illustrations in these little known works, along with many of the more famous portraits from that era, represent the mutual importance and intertwined fate of husband and wife in seventeenth-century Dutch society.

The final two essays also deal with the relations between women and men, in this case in the distinctively twentieth-century medium of film. Feminist film theory has no doubt had the greatest impact to date on the study of visual phenomena. As the dominant movement in film criticism of the eighties, it has made many significant contributions to cinematic discourse. It has foregrounded patriarchal biases in mainstream production, particularly the role of scopophilia, or the "male gaze," as a strategy of domination. It has also shifted the emphasis away from the phallocentrism of Freudian psychoanalysis. Centering instead on applications of more recent theories by Jacques Lacan, feminists have shed light on the "specular spectator," the film audience as exemplifying a "mirror stage" parallel to that in child development. They have also given serious critical attention to independent women directors like Yvonne Rainer and Chantal Ackerman who are generally deprived of access to commercial screens. In doing so, they have attempted to break the mold of male hegemony, and have made a beginning in redeeming women from marginality and silence.

In "The Voice of the Other: Women in Third World and Experimental Film," Linda Dittmar suggests that silence can in fact be a positive value for women. Dittmar focuses on five films made at the margins of mainstream cinema. Here again the focus is on little-known work concerning people and issues generally ignored by film critics. Dittmar points out that all five of the films she discusses use women as their protagonists, and in various ways explore issues of repression and emergence through interactions among gender, race, and class. She argues for "readings that link gender to other disenfranchisements."

The original contribution of Dittmar's essay is in its focus on women's speech in the films she explores. She thus shifts the emphasis from the gaze to the ear, and therefore from Woman as object to women as subjects. She explores the connections between power and powerlessness revealed in the "talking pictures" she discusses, and shows how in all these films language itself becomes the territory through which struggles for emergence get enacted. These marginal films suggest that emergence is something that can happen in the auditorium. Both the films themselves, and Dittmar's own essay which she describes as "interventionist," link the critique of culture to the possibility of change.

The final essay in the volume describes the possibility of subversion that existed even in earlier Hollywood films. In a delightful analysis of three mass market films Julie Levinson shows how even routine studio products can "mutiny against hackneyed modes of gender representation." Levinson discusses three genre films, the "woman's weepie" *Stella Dallas, Bringing Up Baby,* and *The Man Who Shot Liberty Valance.* All three, she shows, are not quite as they seem; even the audience was meant to have "double vision."

Levinson describes how, in general, genre movies provide codified, predictable plots, characters, and characterizations. Gender delineations tend to be facile and stereotypical, with male and female lineaments drawn with broad strokes. But the films she discusses, while working within the familiar strictures of their respective forms, manage to challenge cliched generic and societal codes. They are "anomalous rebel texts," conventional in form but idiosyncratic in attitude.

Levinson shows how these films dissect and debunk the status quo and cleverly challenge us to rethink received notions of gender roles and behavior. While feminist critics are no doubt right about the destructive impact of most genre films, Levinson illustrates that rare cases do exist that can accommodate a pluralism of perspective. She finds it encouraging that popular culture is not always "a looming hegemonic monster" but has sometimes actually fostered reflection on the absurdity of gender stereotyping.

That such stereotyping is still prevalent in all aspects of the arts is undeniable. All the contributors to this volume share the conviction that sexism still persists in the institutions that make up the art world, in the academies, galleries, museums, systems of film finance, and art patronage. Nevertheless the number of women and men of good will who now attend to the gender concerns that characterize this anthology is increasing, and their viewpoints are gaining in influence. The goal of this volume is then twofold. It seeks to increase that influence by presenting original work of feminist writers about the visual arts, and it hopes also to contribute to an understanding of the diversity, complexity, and fertility of feminism itself.

Notes

1. Art historians, of course, often focus on only one aspect of artworks. However, even so gifted an observer as the British historian Griselda Pollock is in danger of leading viewers away from the works. In a lecture on "Toulouse-Lautrec and Misogyny" (at Harvard University in the Theory of the Image Series, 22 April 1992), Pollock stressed the psychopathology of the painter Toulouse-Lautrec, holding him up to her audience solely as an object for derision and ridicule. She described his debasement of women as compensa-

tion for his psychical impotence. Employing the concepts originally developed in film theory, Pollock focused on the fetishistic phallic elements in Toulouse-Lautrec's work. However, in using his paintings of lesbians to further her psychoanalytic and class analysis, she led the viewers away from an examination of the reproductions she actually showed. In comparing these paintings to the use of lesbian images in pornography, she failed to note the expressive and formal qualities that actually work against her view. The portrayal of two sleeping, fully covered lesbian women that she used to illustrate her thesis-ridden talk was neither a titillating nor a debasing image. For an alternative to Pollock's oversimplified view of this issue, see Roger Thomson's discussion in *Toulouse-Lautrec* (New Haven, Conn.: Yale University Press, 1991), pp. 428–35). Thomson points out that the painter's representations of lesbians "do not allow a consistent or unambiguous interpretation." For artists lesbianism was seen as an ironic contrast to bourgeois family values. While some of the paintings "imply a certain prurience on the artist's part" others appear almost sentimental and can be seen as images of affectionate partnership (p. 429). My general point is that when some feminists insist that all male artists' depictions of women are hegemonic and stem from psychopathology they sacrifice the richness and complexity of art.

2. See my discussion of this unfair criticism of Germaine Greer, below pp. 51, 63n.29.

3. Donald Kuspit, "Traditional Art History's Complaint Against the Linguistic Analysis of Visual Art," in *The Journal of Aesthetics and Art Criticism* (1987), p. 347. Kuspit offers a devil's advocate view of these reactionary tendencies in traditional art history. In my view, like Bilom on his donkey in the biblical parable, he comes to curse and ends by praising.

4. John Pope-Hennessy, *Italian High Renaissance and Baroque Sculpture* (New York: Random House, 1970), p. 53.

5. Julius Meier-Graefe. *Modern Art: The Struggle for Painting*, vol. 1 (1906, reprint in *Eugène Delacroix 1798–1863: Paintings and Drawings* (New York: Salander-O'Reilly Galleries, Inc., 1989), p. 77.

6. For another excellent analysis of the erotic elements of the work of a French painter, see Mary Sheriff's *Fragonard: Art and Eroticism* (Chicago: University of Chicago Press, 1990). Her analysis of the theme of conflicted emotions on multiple levels—the narrative, iconographic, allegorical, historical, and stylistic—are designed like the best of feminist criticism to enhance our understanding and appreciation of the work. She sees that there are instances when the "question of gender relations . . . needs a sophisticated analysis that will move us beyond the obvious division of female object-male viewer" p. 205, n. 110.

7. The psychologist and art educator Abigail Housen in her studies of over a thousand subjects has not succeeded in finding any "different voice" in female aesthetic understanding. Indeed she initially expected to discover basic differences of the sort some researchers claim to have found in the male and female approaches to moral judgment. However, although Housen has discovered differences in Aesthetic Stage based on familiarity and exposure to artworks, and even significant variables related to age, she has thus far found no significant gender differences that can be demonstrated in aesthetic development. Just as the psychologist Paiget noted no ultimate differences in intellectual development between boys and girls, Housen finds that gender does not seem to determine any of the basic aspects of aesthetic response. See Abigail Housen's "Research Studies on Gender and Aesthetic Development" (forthcoming), and, for a detailed account of the aesthetic stages she has used in her studies at Bard College and The Museum of Modern Art, "The Eye of the Beholder: Measuring Aesthetic Development" (Ed. D diss., Harvard University, 1983).

8. See *The Dutch Gentry, 1500–1650: Family, Faith, and Fortune* (New York: Greenwood Press, 1987). In this book Marshall used demographic and statistical information about 1,085 individuals, mostly from the province of Utrecht. To recreate family patterns and social relationships she supplemented her data with information from prenuptial and marriage contracts, wills, testaments, and letters.

9. Marshall, *Dutch Gentry,* p. 164.

10. Ibid.

Double Vision

Part One
The Eye of the Beholder: Gender, the Artist, and the Observer

1

Eros and Sadism: Delacroix's Depictions of Animals Eating People

NANCY FINLAY

T HE FRENCH ROMANTIC ARTIST EUGÈNE DELACROIX (1798–1863) IS BEST KNOWN TODAY FOR HIS large oil paintings, *The Massacres of Chios* (1824), *The Death of Sardanapalus* (1827) (figure 1.1), and *Liberty Leading the People* (1831), this last an image that has become an icon of revolution. Its recent appearance on postage stamps and book covers and its influence on the staging of the musical version of *Les Misérables* suggest that Delacroix's imagery retains much of its evocative power in the 1990s. Women are prominently featured in all three pictures. In *The Massacres of Chios* and *The Death of Sardanapalus,* they appear as the hapless victims of male violence; in *Liberty Leading the People,* the female personification of the goddess Liberty strides forward across the male corpses littering the barricade. The contrast between this active, bare-breasted heroine and the passive victims of the other two paintings suggests an ambivalent attitude toward women and their role that is not atypical of Delacroix's work as a whole. Delacroix's personal experience of women ranged from presumably passive studio models through the decidedly active and self-assertive George Sand (Baroness Aurore Dupin Dudevant, 1804–76), one of the most remarkable women of her age. A similar polarization is to be found in Delacroix's animal pictures, where man is sometimes shown as the victorious hunter, sometimes as the helpless victim of wild beasts. Such themes recur in drawings, prints, and paintings throughout the artist's career, beginning in the 1820s and continuing until the last decades of his life. The subject obviously held a strong attraction for him, a special fascination that led him to return to it again and again. A clue to what the fascination may have been lies in the response of modern viewers to these images of lions on the corpses of Arabs, of tigers and crocodiles assaulting Indian women. While female viewers tend to interpret such pictures simply as scenes of bloody carnage—"nature red in tooth and claw"—many male viewers find them sexually stimulating and provocative, a source of erotic pleasure not unlike that aroused by pornographic pictures and litera-ture.[1] A study of the nineteenth-century context of these works suggests that the man who instinct-ively recognizes the pornographic overtones of a painting such as the *Indian Woman Bitten by a Tiger* is probably closer to the artist's original intent than the woman who attempts to interpret the same image primarily in terms of a Darwinian struggle for existence.

Delacroix, of course, did not know of Darwin's *Origin of Species,* which was only published in 1859, and not translated into French until 1862, a year before the artist's death, but he was certainly familiar with popular versions of current scientific theories in which the concept of nature as a perpetual struggle gradually replaced the earlier Romantic vision of nature as an ideal state of har-mony. He was personally acquainted with the two important French scientists, Georges Cuvier and

Fig.1.1   Eugène Delacroix. The Death of Sardanapalus. *Oil on canvas. Paris, Musée
du Louvre.*

Etienne Geoffroy Saint-Hilaire, whose debate on taxonomy rocked the scientific community in the
1830s, permanently displaced man from his position near the top of the "great chain of being," and
laid the foundations for Darwinism.[2] He was a regular visitor to the Museum of Natural History
and its menagerie, the Jardin des Plantes, where he conducted anatomical studies in the 1820s and
where he returned frequently to sketch throughout his life.[3] "The world was not made for man,"
he speculated in a passage in his journal that suggests an awareness of current scientific thought.
"Man dominates nature and is dominated by it."[4]

Literary and artistic influences also impelled Delacroix toward the depiction of scenes of violence.
Jean de La Fontaine, one of his favorite authors, may have furnished a suggestion for pictures showing
man as the victim of wild beasts in "The Lion and the Man." In this fable, La Fontaine described a
lion's astonishment at a picture of a combat between a human being and a member of his own
species. The human painter had shown the man victorious over his prostate foe. "If lions knew how
to paint," the lion concluded, "the outcome might have been portrayed rather differently." Delacroix
clearly empathized with and perhaps identified with the lion in this fable. His own physical appearance—his short, square nose, deep-set eyes, and unruly mane of hair—was often compared to that of

a lion by his contemporaries.[5] Another crucial influence on Delacroix's animal pictures was Théodore Géricault (1791–1824). Géricault is reported to have said, "[When] I begin [to draw] a woman, it turns into a lion."[6] His work, which Delacroix knew well, is full of scenes of violence, including some sketches of lions attacking human beings and a lithograph of a lion devouring a dead horse. Delacroix probably had this print in mind when, in 1824, he first expressed a desire to make some lithographs of a tiger on a corpse.[7] He did not, however, immediately pursue this idea. His earliest depictions of animals, such as the *Two Tigers* (1831) and an etching of a *Reclining Tiger* (1832), appear superficially devoid of violence or conflict (figure 1.2). They are more in the vein of Antoine Louis Barye (1796–1875), Delacroix's companion during sketching excursions to the Jardin des Plantes. Barye specialized in small paintings and sculptures of animals to the extent that he became known as an *animalier*.[8] Unlike Delacroix, who chose to include only lions and tigers in his animal pictures, Barye portrayed the full repertory of species to be found in the Museum of Natural History and its menagerie, delighting in such subjects as a *Jaguar Devouring an Agouti,* an exotic combination which, while biologically accurate, was essentially devoid of specific iconographic meaning. Neither jaguars nor agoutis have strong traditional associations; in contrast, the lions and tigers preferred by Delacroix were iconographically loaded.

While the *Two Tigers* (also known as the *Young Tiger Playing with His Mother*) shows the great cats in an uncharacteristically idyllic mood, the *Reclining Tiger* is more sinister. In a contemporary review, this animal was described as "the Sardanapalus of the carnivores . . . exhausted by carnage, resposing on the ruins, with a smile flickering across his bloody jaws, the smile of a Goth or a Hun who has just destroyed a civilized city."[9] The reference here is to Delacroix's 1827 painting of *The Death of Sardanapalus* (figure 1.1). Having lost his kingdom, the Assyrian ruler Sardanapalus determined to commit suicide. Although in most versions of the tale, he was accompanied in death only by his favorite concubine, Delacroix chose to depict a veritable bloodbath. Sardanapalus is shown reclining on a massive bed, while all around him slaves slaughter horses and odalisques. The monarch's pose, in its angularity and intense brooding concentration, is clearly related to the *Reclining Tiger*.[10] A well-known drawing for *The Death of Sardanapalus,* which like the painting itself is in the Louvre in Paris, appears on the same sheet with the snarling head of a wolf and the roughly penciled profile of a tiger. This suggests that Delacroix did indeed equate the bloodthirsty ruler with the savage beast.[11] A striking literary parallel exists in Balzac's *The Girl with the Golden Eyes,* first published in 1834.

Fig.1.2.   *Eugène Delacroix.* Reclining   Tiger.
*Etching. Yale University Art Gallery, gift
of Allen Evarts Foster.*

This novella, in which "voluptuousness leads to ferocity" and the hero and heroine are repeatedly compared to tigers, culminates in a scene of bloody violence in a bedroom. The second edition was dedicated by the author to Delacroix.[12]

The tiger suffered from a particularly bad reputation in the nineteenth century. The great eighteenth-century naturalist Buffon had described the lion as noble, majestic, and intrepid; these characteristics were reflected in the animal's physical proportions, his splendid mane, and the physiognomy of his face. The tiger, in contrast, was condemned as too long in the body and too short in the legs. He was criticized for having no mane, and it was said that his tongue, "the color of blood," always hung outside his mouth. To correspond with his appearance, his character was supposed to be wicked and insatiably cruel.[13] An 1827 guide to the Paris menagerie, roughly based, like all such guides, on Buffon's *Natural History,* described the tiger as "a brutal tyrant who would like to depopulate the universe in order to reign alone in the midst of his victims."[14] The noble facial characteristics of the lion and the evil expression of the tiger were further confirmed by the Swiss physiognomist, Johann Casper Lavater, for whom the tiger furnished the emblem of "Satan triumphing over the fall of a saint."[15] Delacroix may have been aware of this comparison for he included marginal sketches of tigers on the proofs of one of his illustrations for Goethe's *Faust* (1828), showing the demon Mephistopheles introducing himself to Martha.[16]

Such comparisons between man and beast enjoyed great popularity in France during the Romantic period. Victor Hugo, in *Les Misérables,* claimed the animals are "nothing but the emblems of our vices and virtues wandering before our eyes." Balzac, in his Human Comedy, deliberately set out to relate the "Natural History" of the human race.[17] In the jargon of the day, animals came to stand for different social types, the lion for the dandy, the tiger for the evil seducer, and the gazelle for the innocent victim of these two great predators.[18] Delacroix never so far as is known portrayed a gazelle,[19] but Barye's sculpture of a dead gazelle moved sympathetic viewers to tears when exhibited at the annual Salon: "that charming gazelle . . . so sweet when she was alive, perhaps so unfortunate! . . . Perhaps she died for love!"[20] Barye may have been inspired by "The Gazelle," a popular poem by Charles Hubert Millevoye, in which a maiden deserted by her lover discovers a dying

Fig.1.3.   Jean Baptiste Clésinger. Woman Bitten by a Serpent. *Plaster. Avignon, Musée Calvet.*

Fig.1.4.   *Eugène Delacroix.* Woman Bitten by a
Crocodile. *Drawing. Paris, Musée du
Louvre, Cabinet des dessins.*

gazelle that the young man has wounded while hunting.[21] The equation of hunting or predation with sexual conquest provided the basis for the humor in "The Lions' Supper," a satire by the minor writer and critic Hippolyte Lucas, describing the pursuit of a gazelle (ingenue) by a lion (dandy):

> The hungry lion continues his chase. . . . He follows the footsteps of a fugitive gazelle; he shakes his mane around her and roars in an amorous fashion. The gazelle listens to the animal's speech. She is touched by his flowery language. She promises to enter the den of the lion, who then gives her a little sign, by means of which she can gain admittance from the doorkeeper, and as soon as he leaves her, he sets off to pursue one of her sisters in the same manner. When the supper hour arrives, the gazelles comes running from one side, the ravishing lions from the other. I leave you to imagine the carnage that takes place.[22]

The sadistic association of sensual pleasure with physical pain was clearly a contributing factor in Delacroix's animal paintings, and in other near contemporary works of art. A monumental example of the genre that predates most of Delacroix's treatments of the theme is Auguste Clésinger's *Woman Bitten by a Serpent* (figure 1.3). Delacroix was introduced to Clésinger by George Sand in the spring of 1847, the same year that the *Woman Bitten by a Serpent* created a sensation in the annual Salon. Clésinger was shortly to become engaged to the writer's daughter Solange. Delacroix does not appear to have had a very high opinion of the sculptor and dismissed the *Woman Bitten by a Serpent* as "a daguerreotype in sculpture."[23] Although its technical polish was not calculated to appeal to an artist who admired expressive exaggeration in sculpture as well as in painting, the subject has strong affinities with Delacroix's later representations of animals preying upon human beings, especially the *Woman Bitten by a Crocodile* (figure 1.4) and the *Indian Woman Bitten by a Tiger* (figure 1.5). Like so many of Delacroix's own compositions (*The Death of Sardanapalus* and *Medea*, for example), Clé-

Fig.1.5.   Eugène Delacroix. Woman Bitten by a
Tiger. *Oil on canvas. Stuttgart, Staats-
galerie.*

singer's sculpture was ultimately derived from a classical source, a tale related by the historian Pliny:

> The serpent that fell in love with an Aetolian woman used to visit her at night and slip under
> some part of her body next the skin and coil about her without doing her any harm at all, either
> intentional or accidental: but always at daybreak it was decent enough to glide away. And this it
> did constantly until the kinsmen of the woman removed her to a house at some distance. The
> serpent did not come to her for three or four nights, but all the time, we may suppose, it was
> going about in search of her and missing its goal. At last, when it had somehow found her with
> difficulty, it embraced her, not with that former gentleness it had used, but rather more roughly,
> its coils binding her hands to her body, and with the end of its tail it lashed the calves of her legs,
> displaying a light and tender anger that had in it more indulgence than punishment.[24]

Clésinger's figure, writhing voluptuously in the serpent's coils, also came to be known by the
suggestive title, *A Dream of Love*. Théophile Gautier, who was an influential art critic as well as a

major Romantic poet, speculated that the *Woman Bitten by a Serpent* "has received one of the golden arrows from the quiver of Eros full in the breast . . . and she writhes from the invisible injury."[25] Other critics acknowledged the erotic content of the sculpture even more explicitly: "The *Woman Bitten by a Serpent* is baptised by everyone in the name of voluptuousness. Moreover, do not the words 'pain' and 'pleasure' represent different degrees of intensity of the same emotion?"[26]

The pain, rather than the pleasure, is more in evidence in Delacroix's images of women attacked by animals, which are even more brutal than Clésinger's. While Clésinger's serpent coiled around the Aetolian woman "without doing her any harm at all," Delacroix's female victims are severely injured, if not killed, by their animal antagonists. One of the earliest of these compositions (figure 1.4) is a drawing in the Louvre that shows a woman in a pose recalling a classical river nymph, reclining on the bank of a body of water. A large crocodile, which takes up much of the page, bites her in the right hand. A second crocodile is somewhat more sketchily indicated. The two crocodiles are derived from engravings after Peter Paul Rubens's *Hippopotamus Hunt* and *Rivers of Africa and Asia*. In a journal entry for 25 January 1847 Delacroix admired the crocodile in the *Hippopotamus Hunt* as a "masterpiece of execution," remarking, however, that "its action could have been more interesting."[27] Although Delacroix's admiration for Rubens has often been noted, this particular instance of direct borrowing has never before been pointed out. Even more surprising than the use of the Rubens crocodiles, however, is the visual source for the crocodile's victim: Gustave Courbet's 1853 painting, *The Bathers*. In his journal, Delacroix expressed his dislike of this large Realist painting which showed two contemporary peasant women beside a stream. He complained that the gesture of the seated woman was meaningless—"expressed nothing"—and dismissed her as so ugly that "a crocodile wouldn't want to eat her."[28] The combination of this figure with the Rubens's crocodile in his rough sketch surely may be interpreted as a sort of personal joke, at once lending meaning to the woman's gesture and giving the crocodile a "more interesting" action. The combination of the two figures may also have been suggested by an exhibit in the Museum of Natural History where the skeleton of a crocodile from Calcutta was mounted alongside the bracelets of an Indian woman discovered in its stomach.[29] Further inspiration may have come from accounts of human sacrifices to crocodiles in contemporary travel literature. Adolphe Delegorgue, in his exactly contemporary *Journey into Southern Africa* (1847), described such practices among the Hindus "whom superstition causes to offer annually to the river god a girl, the most beautiful of all the young beauties, dressed as for her wedding day. This god, the disgusting crocodile, accustomed to feeding on corpses, of which he cleanses the river, accepts the offering and disappears with her, and both crocodile and Hindus are satisfied."[30] Seen in this context, Delacroix's *Woman Bitten by a Crocodile* assumes the dimensions of a mythical heroine, an Angelica or an Andromeda, whom no Roger, no Perseus comes to deliver. Although the drawing is usually dated ca. 1847, it might more plausibly be dated 1853 on the basis of its clear relationship to Courbet's *Bathers*.

Closely related in conception to the *Woman Bitten by a Crocodile,* and probably derived from it, is a small painting of an *Indian Woman Bitten by a Tiger* (figure 1.5). The resemblances between the two compositions are extensive enough to suggest a direct relationship. In each case a body of water occupies the immediate foreground, in each case the right side of the picture, and in each case the animal attacks from the right. Both the literary accounts and the exhibit in the Museum of Natural History suggest that the *Woman Bitten by a Crocodile* should be associated with India; and the *Indian Woman Bitten by a Tiger* was specifically situated in an Indian setting, although such settings are unusual in Delacroix's work. Although there are many contemporary references to the vast numbers of people killed by tigers in India, attacks on women are very rarely mentioned. In contemporary literary descriptions, the typical victim of a tiger attack was a male traveler on horseback.[31]

The general idea of a woman attacked by a tiger may have been inspired by a well-publicized accident that occurred in England early in 1850, when a female lion tamer named Ellen Bright was killed by a tiger during a performance.[32] Wild animal acts were extremely popular in nineteenth-century Europe, and tended to be an accurate reflection of changing attitudes toward man's place in nature. In the late 1820s and 1830s, the animal tamer Henri Martin presented audiences with a series of tableaux in which he appeared reclining on the flank of the lioness Charlotte, or playing with the tiger Atyr. Martin's act provided the immediate inspiration for "A Passion in the Desert," a tale by Balzac describing the attachment between a French soldier in the African legion and a wild pantheress.[33] By the 1850s, animal acts offered spectacles of greater violence and danger, as lion tamers made more frequent use of the whip, exciting their charges into a frenzy of teeth and claws. Ellen Bright, the "Queen of the Lions," fell victim to this new craze. Accounts of her death, complete with illustrations showing the actual attack, were obviously received with great interest (figure 1.6).

While these crude wood-engraved images may have had some effect on Delacroix's conception,

Fig. 1.6.   *Anonymous.* Ellen Bright Attacked by a Tiger. *Wood-engraving from* L'Illustration, *vol. 15 (1850). General Research Division, The New York Public Library, Astor, Lenox, and Tilden Foundation. Photograph by Robert Rubic.*

Fig.1.7. Battle of Greeks and Amazons. *Frieze from the Temple of Apollo at Bassae-Philageia. Courtesy of The Trustees of the British Museum.*

his direct visual source was a classical one, the frieze of the Temple of Apollo at Bassae-Philageia in the Greek Peloponnesus (figure 1.7). These fifth-century sculptures, which are now in the British Museum, had been discovered and published by Charles Robert Cockerell, a friend of Delacroix and Géricault.[34] In its original context, the figure copied by Delacroix was an Amazon actively engaged in combat with a Greek warrior. Although the marble is in a poor state of preservation, making it difficult to determine the exact relationship between the two figures, the Amazon, who appears to be wounded, pulls toward the left while her Greek adversary, leaning to the right, struggles to restrain her. Delacroix completely eliminated the tension between the two figures, transforming the powerful, struggling Amazon into a collapsing, helpless victim. The art historian George Mras, in a footnote to *Eugène Delacroix's Theory of Art* (1966), described this figure as "oddly sensual and languorous," expressive of "terror almost lost in desire."[35] The quotation "terror almost lost in desire" is from *Laocoon,* where Lessing discussed how "disagreeable things may give pleasure in the imitation. . . . Examples are wild beasts and dead bodies. Wild beasts excite terror even when they are not ugly; and this terror, not their ugliness, may be made to produce sensations of pleasure through imitation." Since Mras was a male viewer, he probably did not need Lessing to alert him to the erotic implications of Delacroix's *Indian Woman Bitten by a Tiger.* These implications are made quite explicit by the fact that the tiger is shown biting the woman in the breast. Alexandre Dumas, in one of his travel books, assured readers that when a lion kills a man, it is invariably the genitals that he eats first; if he kills a woman, it is the breasts.[36]

Women were not always depicted as helpless victims, however; they could also be predators in their own right, as dangerous and as deadly as the male. In the Romantic bestiary of social types, the female counterparts of the lion-dandy and the tiger-seducer were the lioness and the pantheress. A long iconographic tradition associated the pantheress with lust. Panthers were originally believed to be exclusively female, and to mate indiscriminately with animals of other species. As late as 1860, the big game hunter Bombonnel could positively assert that female panthers outnumber males ten to one because the old males seek out the young cubs and systematically kill them.[37] In the middle years of the nineteenth century, pantheress was a cant term for prostitute. In one of the same dictionaries of popular jargon that identified the lion with the dandy, the pantheress was described as

an objet de luxe . . . one can tame her very easily if one provides her with healthy, abundant and elaborate food, a very pretty cage in the neighborhood of Notre Dame de Lorette [a part of Paris known for its prostitutes], some cashmere shawls, not a few jewels, a large number of silk dresses and an income of five hundred to a thousand francs per month.[38]

The term remained current at least as late as 1854, when Gustave Doré included a pair of elegantly dressed pantheresses in his Ménagerie parisienne.

The lioness, in contrast, was the sort of "modern woman" exemplified by George Sand. Rich, stylish, clever, and at least a trifle androgynous, she was fond of riding horseback and smoking cigarettes. Although her manners and morals might not bear the strictest scrutiny, it was her boldness, her almost savage independence that characterized her for her admirers. It was in fact Sand herself who recognized the central figure in Delacroix's painting of Medea as a lioness. The subject is in its way as shocking as The Death of Sardanapalus, but in this case the murderous protagonist is a woman, not a man. In Greek mythology, Medea was the barbarian princess who guided Jason to the Golden Fleece. When Jason later abandoned her in favor of Creusa, she avenged herself by murdering their two sons. This moment in the story has rarely been visually represented, but it is the very one that Delacroix chose to portray. Looking back over her shoulder at her pursuers, Medea holds a dagger poised above the two terrified children who writhe at her feet. Although she has not already stabbed either of the little boys, it is apparent that she is about to do so. For Sand, this painting was "a magnificent thing, superb, devastating."[39] Elsewhere, she described Medea "sobbing or roaring like a wounded lioness."[40] Clearly she recognized the relationship of Delacroix's painting to standard representations of lionesses.

In traditional iconography, the lioness—that is, the female of the species Felix leo and not the stylish woman of popular jargon—was usually portrayed defending her young. Her fierce maternal instinct was confirmed by naturalists, for example, in this description from 1823:

The female [lion], smaller in all her dimensions [than the male], has no mane. Her features are less pronounced, or rather softened, suggesting a softer temperament. Her strength lies in her maternal love. Once she has young, she no longer recognizes danger; she attacks indiscriminately men and beasts, whatever their number may be.[41]

When a lioness in the menagerie of the Jardin des Plantes gave birth to three cubs in 1798, the event was commemorated in paintings, engravings, and popular prints. In some cases the cubs were shown being defended from a visible human or animal adversary; in others the lioness looks back anxiously over her shoulder at an invisible enemy beyond the picture frame. In such instances, the idea that she is defending her young is conveyed by the caption. It is the act of looking back over the shoulder that is particularly significant, for it is reproduced in the pose of Delacroix's Medea, while the squirming lion cubs correspond to Medea's struggling offspring (figure 1.8). The image gains in potency and poignancy from the fact that rather than protecting her young, Medea is on the point of slaughtering them. A format normally associated with maternal solicitude among the wild beasts has been adapted to emphasize the unnatural behavior of a human mother. As one of Delacroix's contemporaries observed: "We know very well that man, so superior in intelligence to the animals, often through his vices sinks below them; we are not unaware that one has seen and continues to see every day men more ferocious than the tigers and the hyenas to which they give chase."[42] Delacroix was clearly aware of this convention, for he portrayed a lioness defending her cubs from a tiger in a drawing that was reproduced in the Magasin Pittoresque in 1855 (figure 1.9). The lioness is shown looking back over her shoulder in the best traditional fashion, and was almost

Fig.1.8.   Eugène Delacroix. Medea. Oil on canvas. Lille, Musée des Beaux-Arts.

Fig.1.9. *After Eugène Delacroix.* Lioness and Cubs Attacked by a Tiger. *Wood-engraving from* Magasin Pittoresque, *vol. 22 (1853). General Research Division, The New York Public Library, Astor, Lenox and Tilden Foundation. Photograph by Robert Rubic.*

certainly modeled after one of the early nineteenth-century representations of the lioness and cubs in the Jardin des Plantes. The tiger, which is seen foreshortened from above, is probably derived from Delacroix's study of Japanese prints.

Delacroix appears to have been familiar with Japanese prints at an early date and incorporated images from Hokusai's *Manga* into his animal pictures beginning in the 1830s.[43] The printed description that accompanied the wood-engraving of Delacroix's drawing in the *Magasin Pittoresque* stressed the courage of the lioness in defense of her young, but suggested that her strength might prove inadequate to meet the onslaught of the tiger:

> A tiger surprises a lioness nursing her cubs, and the growling of the two animals and the glance that they exchange indicate the fight which is about to take place. Its outcome is not so certain as one might expect from the somewhat exaggerated reputation of the lion.[44]

Men as well as women could be portrayed as the victims of wild beasts. As mentioned above, the typical male victim of a tiger attack was a rider on horseback. Delacroix no doubt drew on this tradition for his painting of an *Arab Rider Attacked by a Tiger* in the Louvre, also known as the Louvre *Tiger Hunt*. A related composition, a drawing usually described as an *Arab Rider Attacked by a Panther* (or an *Arab Rider Attacking a Panther*) in the Fogg Art Museum at Harvard, has sometimes been proposed as a preliminary study for this painting. Presumably the animal is identified as a panther because of its small size in relation to the horse and rider. While the Fogg drawing may well have served as a study for the Louvre painting, it is first and foremost a free copy of the horse and rider at the left of Soutman's engraving of Rubens's *Hippopotamus Hunt,* the same engraving that suggested the pose for one of the reptiles in Delacroix's *Woman Bitten by a Crocodile*.

In literary accounts, the male victim, while sometimes an innocent traveler seized from his mount (usually in a rocky defile), was more frequently a hunter, struck down while actively pursuing his prey. A well-established tradition compared a fondness for hunting to the amorous pursuits of a Casanova or a Don Juan. Stendhal described love as "a need for activity aroused by different objects and constantly testing one's talents," adding that there is "nothing so interesting as passion; there everything is unexpected, and the agent is also the victim."[45] The poet Théodore de Banville employed the image of a "lioness in search of a huntsman" with erotic connotations in *Les Cariatides* (1842).[46] On one occasion Delacroix himself compared the emotions he experienced shooting birds in the Forest of Boixe with the feelings of a man who has just discovered that his mistress loves him.[47] The ironic position of the hunter who suddenly finds himself being hunted certainly appealed to him, and he almost invariably showed his huntsmen being overcome by their animal adversaries. No doubt he appreciated the fact that the abbey in which his family's hunting lodge was located coincidentally bore the name of Valmont, the male protagonist of Pierre Choderlos de Laclos's scandalous epistolary novel *Dangerous Liaisons*.

It is in this context that Delacroix's lithograph of a *Lioness on the Corpse of an Arab* (figure 1.10) should be understood. While de Banville's "lioness in search of a huntsman" may or may not have been a factor in the artist's decision to portray this particular predator, the sexual dimorphism of *Felis leo* was certainy a consideration. It is not always easy to distinguish between a male tiger and a female tigress, but even the most unsophisticated viewer can immediately tell the difference between a lion and a lioness. This difficulty in distinguishing between male and female animals does not extend to literary accounts, where physical appearance is less a factor and they may easily be identified verbally as "he" or "she." It is only in visual representations such as Delacroix's that a question arises. The predator who digs her claws into the chest of the Arab in Delacroix's lithograph lacks the distinctive mane of the male of her species and is very emphatically a female. This confrontation of female predator and male human recalls the lion tamer Henri Martin and his affectionate lioness Charlotte, the tender relationship between the soldier and the pantheress in "A Passion in the Desert," the popular accounts where sex and eating are equated for humorous effect. There is nothing humorous about this lithograph, however; it might best be compared to this roughly contemporary literary account of an attack by a man-eating tigress:

Fig.1.10. Eugène Delacroix. Lioness on the
Corpse of an Arab. *Etching. Amherst,
Mead Art Museum, gift of Edward C.
Crossett, Class of 1905.*

All at once [the tigress] leaped forward with a single bound and at the same instant the traveler
was writhing, expiring in a fatal embrace. The tigress, her eyes half-closed and growling softly,
in an expression of carnivorous rapture, sucked the blood from the wound which she had made
in his throat.[48]

The source for this astonishing description, which appears to prefigure the women vampires,
succubi, and *femmes fatales* of the *fin de siècle*, is an otherwise generally straightforward narrative, "The
Tiger Hunter (Extracts from my Indian Journal)," published anonymously in the *Revue britannique* in
1843. Similarly Delacroix's *Lioness on the Corpse of an Arab,* while it purports to be a straightforward
representation of a hunting accident, is fraught with sexual overtones (figure 1.10). The dead Arab
sprawls voluptuously, his pose recalling that frequently employed for odalisques. Rarely has a male
figure been shown in a position of such helpless abandon. The lioness's claws leave deep furrows in
his flesh; her expression, as she looks up at the viewer, might well be described as one of "carnivorous
rapture." Similar imagery occurs, at a much later date, in Algernon Charles Swinburne's poem, "At
a Month's End" (1878), which begins:

> Who snares and tames with fear and danger
> A bright beast of a fiery kin,

Only to mar, only to change her
Sleek supple soul and splendid skin?

and concludes:

So to my soul in surer fashion
Your savage stamp and savour hangs,
The print and perfume of old passion
The wild beast mark of panther's fangs.[49]

Clearly a part of the same iconographic tradition, this poem suggests that the identification of predatory animals with sexual aggression was not limited to France and that it persisted until relatively late in the century.

Few nineteenth-century viewers of either gender would have missed the point of these works of art. The association of men and women with particular animals was a commonplace, and the comparison of sex to predation and eating was endlessly repeated in literature on all levels, ranging from sensational accounts of lion hunting and animal acts in the popular periodicals through the masterpieces of contemporary fiction. Even the serious natural histories of the day were not unaffected. The shocked reaction to Manet's *Olympia* in 1865 was partially precipitated by the inclusion of a cat in the composition as well as by the figure's unabashed, contemporary nudity. Although *Olympia* continues to challenge modern viewers, few men or women of today without some background in iconography are likely to grasp the lewd connotations of the cat.[50] A potent image in its day, it now requires serious scholarly study to reveal its original significance as a symbol of illicit and irresponsible love.

In contrast, though few people today think of men as lions and tigers or women as lionesses and pantheresses, and the clearcut nineteenth-century stereotypes of these animals, both as social types and as biological species, have to a large extent been lost—we no longer think of lions as "noble" or tigers as "cruel," and we know that in fact the lioness is a more able hunter than her mate—Delacroix's depictions of animals attacking human beings still impress a majority of male viewers as sexually provocative. This is remarkable testimony both to their expressive power and perhaps also to the timelessness of the male obsession with sex and violence. Delacroix, like most Romantic artists, preferred to employ vague allusions rather than concrete symbols in his work.[51] Such allusions, he believed, were universally accessible independent of their social context, conveying the emotions of the artist directly to the spectator.[52] No doubt he would be pleased and perhaps a little amused at the response that his animal pictures continue to arouse in the closing years of the twentieth century.

Notes

1. Although I do not pretend to have conducted a scientific study of the differences between male and female responses to these works, I have shown photographs of the paintings involved to a variety of colleagues. The striking difference in the verbal responses and associations of men and women provided the immediate inspiration for this paper.

2. On the history of science in the first half of the nineteenth century, see Arthur O. Lovejoy, *The Great Chain of Being* (New York, 1960); Yevette Conroy, *L'Introduction du Darwinisme en France au XIXᵉ siècle* (Paris, 1974); and Toby Appel, *The Cuvier-Geoffroy Debate and the Structure of Nineteenth Century Science* (Unpublished dissertation, Princeton University, 1975).

3. The best discussion of Delacroix's visits to the Jardin des Plantes and in particular of his early anatomical studies is Eve Twose Kliman, *Eugène Delacroix: A Study of Selected Paintings, Watercolours, Pastels, Prints and Drawings of the Feline* (Unpublished dissertation, University of Toronto, 1978). This was also the topic of a paper delivered by Kliman at the 1979 College Art Association Meeting.

A further discussion of the material is to be found in her article "Delacroix's Lions and Tigers: A Link Between Man and Nature," *Art Bulletin*, 64 (1982), pp. 446–66.

4. Eugène Delacroix, *Journal* (André Joubin, ed.), 2 (Paris, 1932), p. 273 (September 21, 1854). Hereafter cited as *Journal*. All translations from the French are my own.

5. "La force, la dédaigneuse tranquilité, le calme du lion se lisent sur cette tête osseuse, vigoureusement modélée, dont le nez est carré et droit, dont les yeux enfoncés et profonds sont pleins de nuit, tandis que sur le front, plutôt large qu'élevé, éclate la lumière. La chevelure, lourde, épaisse et presque sauvage—brune, longue, relevé sur le front—est celle des hommes de 1830." Théodore de Banville, *La Lanterne Magique, Camées parisiens, La Comédie Française* (Paris, 1883), p. 211. Other authors also likened the artist's appearance to that of a lion. Joubin, in his notes to Delacroix's *Correspondance* 6 (Paris, 1938), p. ii, wrote that during his last years "he hid like an old wounded lion." Théophile Silvestre, in *Histoire des artistes vivants* (Paris, 1856), p. 67, described how in Delacroix's old age, his "love

of solitude became more savage from day to day; he shut himself up in a den (un antre) in order not to be disturbed." Delacroix referred to La Fontaine's fable "The Lion and the Man" in his article, "Sur les critiques en matière d'arts," *Revue de Paris*, 2 (1829).

6. "Je commence une femme, disait-il, et cela devient *un lion.*" Cited in Pierre Couthion, *Géricault raconté par lui-même et par ses amis* (Paris, 1947), p. 117.

7. *Journal*, 1 p. 76. (April 12, 1824).

8. See Lee Johnson, "Delacroix, Barye and the 'Tower Menagerie': An English Influence on French Romantic Animal Pictures," *Burlington Magazine*, 106 (1964), pp. 416–19; George Heard Hamilton, "The Origin of Barye's Tiger Hunt," *Art Bulletin*, 18 (1936), pp. 248–57; Stuart Pivar, *The Barye Bronzes* (Woodbridge, Suffolk, 1974); and Charles Otto Zieseniss, *Les Aquarelles de Barye, Etude critique et catalogue raisonné* (Paris, 1954). Other exotic subjects by Barye include a *Python Killing a Gnu* and an *Eagle and Ibex.*

9. A. L., "Etude de tigre," *L'Artiste*, 1st series, 4 (1832), p. 305.

10. For a discussion of this painting, see Jack Spector, *Delacroix: The Death of Sardanapalus* (New York, 1973).

11. Louvre, Cabinet des Dessins RF 6860. See Kliman, "Delacroix's Lions and Tigers," p. 454 for a discussion of this drawing.

12. On Delacroix and Balzac's "La Fille aux Yeux d'Or," see Georges Hirschfell, *Balzac und Delacroix: Streiflichter auf den Roman, "La Fille aux Yeux d'Or"*, (Basel, 1946); and Olivier Bonnard, *La Peinture dans la création balzacienne* (Geneva, 1969).

13. Georges Louis Leclerc, Comte de Buffon, *Oeuvres complètes* (Paris, 1863), 4, pp. 173–75. Delacroix refers familiarly to Buffon's works several times in his journal. It is not clear, however, that he agreed with Buffon's negative assessment of the tiger. In some notes for an article in the *Revue de Paris* (1829), he stated, "The question of Beauty may be reduced to this: which do you prefer, a lion or a tiger?" *Journal*, 3, p. 344.

14. *Ménagerie du Jardin des Plantes* (Paris, 1827), p. 28. It is worth noting that there was no tiger in the menagerie of the Jardin des Plantes in 1827. Most negative judgments of the tiger were not based on firsthand knowledge of the living animal.

15. Cited in Coleman O. Parsons, "Blake's 'Tyger' and Eighteenth-Century Animal Pictures," *Art Quarterly*, 31 (1968), p. 305. See also George Levitine, "The Influence of Lavater and Girodet's 'Expression des Sentiments de l'Ame,'" *Art Bulletin*, 36 (1954), pp. 33–44. Delacroix included Lavater's name in a list of references in a sketchbook in the Louvre, RF 6736, fol. 61v.

16. On Delacroix's illustrations for Faust, see Ursula Sinnreich, "Delacroix' Faust Illustrationen," in *Eugène Delacroix: Themen und Variationen: Arbeiten auf Papier* (Frankfurt am Main, Städelisches Kunstinstitut, 1987), pp. 56–99. The precise relationship of these marginal drawings to the illustrations is unclear, but in some cases, such as this one, there appears to be a thematic connection. These marginal scribblings do not, of course, appear in the published state of the lithographs.

17. On Balzac's animal imagery, see Fernand Baldensperger, *Orientations étrangères chez Honoré de Balzac* (Paris, 1927); Gilbert Malcolm Fess, *The Correspondence of Physical and Material Factors with Character in Balzac* (Philadelphia, 1924); and Dorothy Wirtz, "Animalism in Balzac's Curé de Tours and Pierrette," *Romance Notes* (1969), pp. 61–67. Balzac was one of the contributors to the popular and highly influential anthology, *Scènes de la vie privée et publique des animaux* (Paris, 1842).

18. According to V.G., "Types de notre époque," *Revue britannique*, 4th series, 5 (1837), p. 164, the identification of certain social types with certain animals originated in England, and their importation into France was a manifestation of the anglomania of the period. "Lion," for example, was apparently pronounced in the English fashion "Lie-on," and not "Lee-on," as in French. One of the most complete listings of animal types is Louis Huart, *Muséum parisien: histoire physiologique, pittoresque, philosophique et grotesque de toutes les bêtes curieuses de Paris et de la banlieue, pour faire suite à toutes les éditions de M. de Buffon* (Paris, 1841). By the time Alfred Delvau published his *Dictionnaire de la langue verte: argots parisiens comparés* in 1866, many of these terms were regarded as obsolete.

19. Although it appears to be true that Delacroix never depicted a gazelle, a sketch of a lion in the Louvre (RF 9472) is inscribed in the artist's hand "regardant des gazelles" ("looking at gazelles"). According to the lion hunter Jules Gérard, "If the human race had not degenerated, one might compare the gazelle to the woman and the lion to the man; but there remain few women worthy of that comparison, and moreover, the handsomest man of our century would appear ugly beside the king of beasts." *La Chasse au Lion* (Paris, 1855), p. 155.

20. _____, "Barye," *L'Artiste*, 5 (1833), p. 289.

21. See A. Lytton Sells, *Animal Poetry in French and English Literature and the Greek Tradition* (Bloomington, Ind., 1955), p. 157. The complete text of Millevoye's poem "La Gazelle" may be found in C. H. Millevoye, *Oeuvres de Millevoye* (Paris, 1833), pp. 131–32.

22. Hippolyte Lucas, "Le Souper des Lions," *L'Artiste*, 7 (1841), p. 136.

23. *Journal* (7 May 1847). The phrase "Daguerreotype in sculpture" is derived from Gustave Planche's review "Le Salon de 1847— La Sculpture," *Revue des Deux Mondes*, 18 (1847), p. 542. Clésinger was so enraged by Planche's criticism that he challenged him to a duel. For a discussion of the *Woman Bitten by a Serpent,* see Peter Fusco and H. W. Janson, *The Romantics to Rodin* (Los Angeles County Museum, 1980), pp. 174–76.

24. Plutarch, *De Sollertia Animalium*, 972. Cited from Harold Cherniss and William C. Helmbold, *Plutarch's Moralia* (Cambridge, Mass., 1957).

25. Théophile Gautier, "La Femme piquée d'un serpent," *L'Artiste*, 4th series, 10 (1847), p. 122.

26. L. R. d'Arnem in *La Démocratie pacifique* (7 April 1847), n.p. *La Démocratie pacifique* was a periodical dedicated to the theories of Charles Fourier, a utopian socialist whose writings on free love and social progress enjoyed great popularity immediately prior to the Revolution of 1848.

27. *Journal* (25 January 1847).

28. *Journal* (15 April 1853). The painting in question is clearly Courbet's *Bathers,* now in the Musée Fabre, Montpellier, and not the *Demoiselles de Village* as stated by René Piot in his note to this journal entry in *Journal de Eugène Delacroix* (Paris, 1893), 2, p. 159n. This is evident from Delacroix's vivid description of the two figures. The *Demoiselles de Village,* now in the Metropolitan Museum of Art, New York, was exhibited in the Salon of 1852 and not in the Salon of 1853. The *Bathers* was exhibited in 1853.

29. Louis Rousseau and Céran Lemonnier, *Promenades au Jardin des Plantes* (Paris, 1837), p. 96: "Above the cabinets are four crocodile skeletons and two gavial skeletons. Beside one of the crocodiles . . . sent from Calcutta by M. Wallach, are suspended the bracelets of an Indian woman which were found in its stomach."

30. Adolphe Delegorgue, *Voyage dans l'Afrique Australe,* 1 (Paris, 1847), p. 126. Although there is no evidence that Delacroix knew this particular source, he was fond of reading travel literature. In "Des variations du beau," he cited passages from Major Dixon Denham, *Voyages et découvertes dans le nord et dans les parties centrales de l'Afrique . . .* , 1 (Paris, 1826), p. 53. "Des variations du beau" was first published in the *Revue des Deux Mondes,* 15 July 1857.

31. See, for example, Georges Cuvier, *Le Règne animal distribué d'après son organisation pour servir de base à l'histoire naturelle des animaux et de l'introduction à l'anatomie comparée,* 1 (Paris, 1816), p. 191: "The strength and swiftness [of the tiger] are so great that . . . sometimes he is able to seize a rider from his horse's back and carry him off into the woods without being intercepted." The source of this incident, which is repeated by other authors, is not direct observation, but rather an account by the classical author Pomponius Mela in *De Situ Orbis,* Book III, Chapter V, here quoted from the Paris 1827 edition, p. 84: "[The tiger] is an extraordinarily fierce animal, and so swift that nothing is more common than for him to seize a rider [from his horse's back]."

32. Henry Thétard, in *Les Dompteurs, ou la Ménagerie des origines à nos jours* (Paris, 1928), p. 133, inexplicably situates Ellen Bright's death in 1870, though it is perfectly clear from contemporary accounts that it took place in 1850. A wood-engraving of Bright being attacked by the tiger that killed her, published in *L'Illustration,* 15 (1850), p. 53, resembles Delacroix's *Indian Woman Bitten by a Tiger.* Michel Florisoone, in "Moratin, Inspirer of Géricault and Delacroix," *Burlington Magazine,* 99 (1957), p. 308, suggested that the

Indian Woman Bitten by a Tiger was inspired by a study by Goya for the *Disparates* series showing a *Woman Carried Off by a Horse.* I fail to find this comparison very convincing.

33. The connections between Martin's wild animal act and Balzac's tale, "A Passion in the Desert," is made absolutely explicit by the author. In the prologue, two characters leaving Martin's menagerie are discussing whether animals are capable of feelings. The narrator then proceeds to relate the story of the soldier and the pantheress, which he claims was told to him by a veteran of Napoleon's campaign in Egypt. "Une Passion dans le Désert" was first published in the *Revue de Paris,* 21 (1830). Delacroix was a regular contributor to this periodical.

34. The sculptures from the Bassae frieze, discovered by Cockerell in 1812, were purchased by the British Museum in 1814 and arrived in London in 1815. They were published in *A Description of Ancient Marbles in the British Museum with Engravings,* Part 4 (London, 1820). The group in question appears in Plate XII. It is not inconceivable that Delacroix might have seen the sculptures themselves when he was in England in 1825. On the acquaintance of Delacroix with Cockerell, see Lee Johnson, "Géricault and Delacroix Seen by Cockerell," *Burlington Magazine,* 113 (1971), pp. 547–56.

35. George Mras, *Eugène Delacroix's Theory of Art* (Princeton, 1966), p. 28n. The quotation is from Gotthold Ephraim Lessing, *Laocoon* (E. Frothingham, tr.) (Boston, 1889), p. 155. First published in 1766.

36. Alexandre Dumas, *Impressions de Voyage: Le Véloce, ou Tanger, Alger et Tunis,* 2 (Paris, 1898), p. 51. First published in 1849.

37. Bombonnel, *Le Tueur des Panthères: ses chasses écrites par lui-même* (Paris, 1860), p. 17. The tradition that the panther is always female (the noun, in fact, is feminine in French) was repeated as late as 1770 in De Petity, *Manuel des artistes et des amateurs, ou dictionnaire historique et mythologique,* 2 (Paris, 1770), pp. 424–25.

38. Huart, *Muséum parisien,* p. 20.

39. George Sand, *Correspondance,* 4 (Paris, 1968), pp. 407–8.

40. The reference occurs in George Sand, *Consuelo* (Paris, 1959), p. 82. *Consuelo* was first published in 1844. Delacroix used biological jargon in a letter to Sand describing "une magnifique lorette de la grande espèce" (a magnificent "greater lorette"), *Correspondance,* 2, p. 203 (2 November 1844). A lorette was an inhabitant of the *quartier* Notre Dame de Lorette (*i.e.,* a prostitute). See above, note 38. "Consuelo" was Delacroix's nickname for his mistress, Madame de Forget.

41. *Nouvelle description de ce qu'il y de remarquable à la ménagerie et au cabinet d'histoire naturelle* (Paris, 1823), p. 8.

42. Paul Cap, *Le Muséum d'histoire naturelle* (Paris, 1854), p. 195.

43. See Nancy Finlay, "Japanese Influence on a Lithograph by Delacroix," *New Mexico Studies in the Fine Arts,* 4 (1979), pp. 5–7.

The lithograph in question there is the *Standing Lion,* which is usually dated 1833.

44. *Magasin Pittoresque,* 23 (1855), pp. 116–17. Combats between lions and tigers fascinated Delacroix's contemporaries, although in nature such confrontations would rarely if ever take place, since in general the ranges of the two species do not overlap. The printed description in the *Magasin Pittoresque* may have been written by Delacroix himself, and reflects his generally positive assessment of the prowess of the much-maligned tiger. See above, note 13.

45. Stendhal, *De l'amour,* 2 (Paris, 1927), pp. 162 and 180. First published in 1822.

46. Théodore de Banville, *Oeuvres de Théodore de Banville: Les Cariatides* (Paris, 1889), p. 5. Similar love-death imagery pervades de Banville's poem.

47. Eugène Delacroix, *Correspondance générale* (André Joubin, ed.), 1 (Paris, 1932), Vol. 1, p. 19.

48. M.M.M., "Le chasseur de tigres (Extracts from my Indian Diary)," *Revue britannique,* 18 (1843), p. 394.

49. Symbolist artists seem to have had a predilection for panthers. A black panther figures in Gustave Moreau's representation of *Salomé Dancing before Herod;* the feline portion of the sphinx in Fernand Khnopf's painting, *The Caresses of the Sphinx* (1896), is spotted. See Philippe Julian, *Dreamers of Decadence: Symbolist Painters of the 1890s* (New York, 1971); Philippe Julian, *The Symbolists* (Oxford, 1973); and Edward Lucie-Smith, *Symbolist Art* (London and New York, 1972).

50. The literature on Manet's *Olympia* is vast and continues to grow. Major studies include Theodore Reff, *Manet: Olympia* (New York, 1976); Beatrice Farwell, *Manet and the Nude: A Study of Iconography in the Second Empire* (New York, 1981); and the relevent section in *Manet, 1832–1883* (New York: Metropolitan Museum of Art, 1983). A good summary of contemporary criticism of the painting is to be found in George Heard Hamilton, *Manet and His Critics* (New York, 1969). An interesting discussion of the significance of the cat is to be found in Anne Coffin Hanson, *Manet and the Modern Tradition* (New Haven and London, 1977).

51. "A difference in coloring between the Romantic and the Classic is that the Romantic prefers vague symbols to precise symbols, and the Classicist prefers precise symbols to vague symbols. . . . The Romantic tends to spiritualize material nature, while the Classicist tends to materialize spiritual nature." Jouffroy, *Cours d'Esthétique* (Paris, 1843), pp. 136–37. This distinction, which seems to me a valid one, deserves further study.

52. According to Delacroix, "I've told myself a hundred times that painting, that is, material painting is . . . the bridge between the spirit of the painter and that of the spectator." *Journal,* 1, p. 391 (18 July 1850). See Mras, *Delacroix's Theory of Art,* p. 168, for a discussion of this subject.

2

The Female Gaze: Women's Interpretations of the Life and Work of Properzia De' Rossi, Renaissance Sculptor

NATALIE HARRIS BLUESTONE

The Tale Begins: Giorgio Vasari and Properzia

PROPERZIA DE' ROSSI (1490–1530) IS THE FIRST FEMALE SCULPTOR ABOUT WHOSE EXISTENCE WE can speak with any degree of certainty. Until recently only Renaissance scholars had paid much attention to her life or art. With the current interest in women artists throughout the centuries, feminist art historians have now begun to take an interest in her minute carvings and her sculpture for the facade of the Church of San Petronio in Bologna, Italy. However, few have actually examined this work, and her story, which is indeed a dramatic one, has not yet reached the broader public who search for female heroes of the past.

There have, however, been a number of women writers in the last two centuries who found Properzia's life and work significant. Their treatment of her is both more extended and more revealing of their own preoccupations than the brief admiration, condescension, or sheer astonishment accorded her by those male art historians who have bothered to mention her. The women writers I shall discuss have each used Properzia to further an agenda of their own. They chose to discuss her because she was female; that is, all of them had a special interest in her because of their own gender. However, there is no central insight, no core of agreement that these interpreters share. What is true of women artists—that they have more in common with their counterparts of the same nationality and the same historical period than they do with each other (no matter how hard some would try to argue for a common female sensibility)—is also true of these female critics.[1] Nevertheless the gender of the women writers remains important, but in each situation gender, as we shall see, plays a different role.

Properzia's gender was important, too, in the account given of her by Giorgio Vasari (1511–74,) the original source of our information about the sculptor. Vasari chronicled the lives of the artists of Italy from Cimabue in the thirteenth century to those practicing in his own time, in his long colorful work, *Le Vite de Piu Eccellenti Pittori Scultori ed Architettori*.[2] This painter, art critic, and biographer was the first to write about Properzia and to praise her accomplishments. His work, despite its inaccuracies and exaggerations, provides a great source of information about the flowering of Renaissance art. It also makes entertaining reading for anyone interested in the aesthetic ideas, psychology, and personal eccentricities of men of his time.

Indeed the "eccellenti artisti" were almost exclusively men, but Vasari was particularly eager to include the very few women artists whose work he knew about in his narrative. He begins his account of Properzia with the observation that whenever women at any time have devoted themselves to the study of any art or the exercise of any talent,"they have always succeeded most excellently" (p. 73).[3] He then gives a long catalog of women warriors, poets, philosophers, scientists, etc., of the past. And he ends his section on Properzia with a quote from Ariosto's *Orlando Furioso* extolling women who have come out well in every art which they've undertaken (p. 81).

Since this extravagant homage becomes an issue in later interpretations of Properzia, it is important here to explore Vasari's general attitudes to women.[4] He has been called "a uxorious little man," condescendingly described as having sent his *cara consorte* passionate poems to tell her how he missed her presence.[5] He also seems to have been a devoted son. Although a man who loves his wife and mother can hardly be said to hate all women, Vasari nevertheless clearly shared the misogynist attitudes of his contemporaries. He generally considered wives to be an encumbrance that prevented artists from moving to new centers for their work. When he set about acquiring one of his own—a fate he had long avoided—he was advised by a colleague not to "buy a cat in a sack."[6] He needed someone to look after his elderly mother and his new house, however. And when he finally found a candidate he bargained aggressively over the dowry. He also took off for Rome immediately after the wedding, leaving his wife Cosina behind in Arezzo. It is true that he painted her in the stereotypical pose of Muse. However, he also, supposedly in jest, painted a wife with a rake in one hand—representing the fact that she had raked all she could from her father's house—and in the other hand a lighted torch—showing that wherever she goes she brings the fire that destroys and consumes.[7] Although intended as a joke, it does suggest that Vasari's own attitudes to women and marriage were mixed.

Like men from Socrates on he also seems to have struggled with the idea that women are actually the true creators because they bear children. Plato tried to counter this view; Socrates asks in the *Symposium* who would not prefer brain children to "ordinary human ones?"[8] Vasari, however, expresses the opposing attitude, clearly regretting his childless marriage and seemingly blaming himself. He wrote to a newly married friend that he wished him children, "whereas he, Giorgio, could only cover walls, panels, canvas, and paper with figures."[9] He ends his remarks about Sofonisba Anguissola, one of the few Italian women painters of his time, with what may seem to us the strange conclusion that "women know how to make living men so well, what wonder is it that those who wish to paint them can do it well also." Despite this logical leap, Vasari actually seems to have considered Properzia very much a wonder. He tells us that her fellow citizens thought her to be "one of the greatest miracles of nature" (p. 78).

The details of Properzia's life as we have them from Vasari are briefly these: she was born in Bologna, was remarkably beautiful, sang and played on musical instruments, was skilled in household matters, and gained enviable distinction in many sciences. She began by carving peach stones and achieved remarkable results, particularly in one stone described by Vasari as depicting the entire Passion of Christ including his crucifiers and the apostles. Vasari describes her small carvings as subtle and well carved, with elegant figures, admirably composed.

Properzia then, through the agency of her husband (of whom he tells us nothing), arranged for a chance to participate in the work to be executed in marble for the three doors of the main facade of San Petronio. The superintendents required her first to show them some work in marble, and she consequently sculpted a head which was widely approved in the city and secured her the desired commission.

For the facade Properzia produced a bas-relief representing the Old Testament story of Joseph's temptation by the wife of his overseer, Potiphar, the chief of Pharoah's guards (figure 2.1). Vasari says clearly that she executed this work because she was at the time enamored of a handsome young man who did not return her love. By depicting this biblical woman Properzia gained great satisfaction from expressing in part (*isfogato in parte*) her own ardent passion. The gesture of Potiphar's wife in holding on to the cloak of the escaping Joseph is one of "wonderful feminine grace" (p. 77).

Vasari says at first that Properzia did not execute any other works because of the envy of Amico Aspertini, a fellow sculptor who discouraged her and spoke ill of her to the superintendents. Although others begged her to continue her work, Aspertini maligned her to the extent that she was paid very badly for her labors. Vasari then adds that she did two other angels of beautiful proportions for San

Fig.2.1. *Properzia de' Rossi.* The Chastity of Joseph *(or* The Temptation of Joseph by the Wife of Potiphar). *Marble relief. Bologna, Museo di San Petronio.*

Fig.2.2. *Properzia de' Rossi.* Eleven Peach Stones Embedded in a Silver Filigree Crucifix. *Carved stones, Bologna, Museo Civico.*

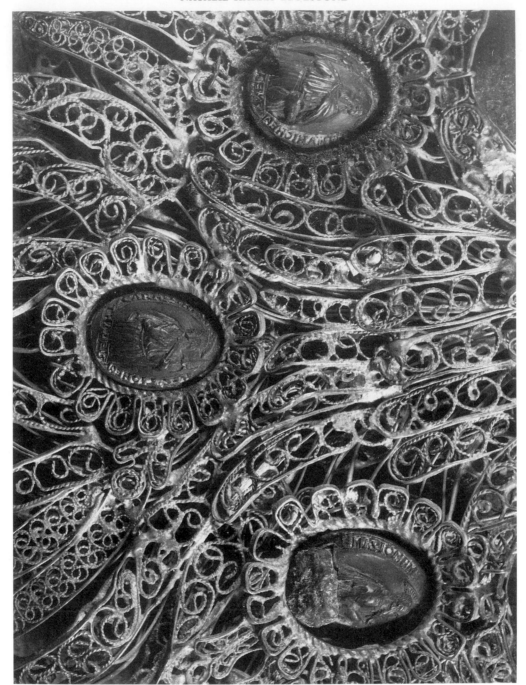

Fig.2.3.   Properzia de' Rossi. Three Carved
Peach Stones *(detail of fig. 2.2).* Bologna, *Museo Civico.*

Petronio, but these he says were done "against her will" (p. 77). She ultimately turned to copperplate
engraving at which she also succeeded. Vasari adds that Properzia did extremely well at everything
but love.

Pope Clement VII, while in Bologna to crown the emperor, heard of the fame of this "noble and
elevated genius," and expressed a wish to meet her. Unfortunately the ill-fated woman had died and
been buried that very week in the Hospital of Death. Vasari concludes by telling his readers that he

himself owns some very well-executed drawings by Properzia and also a portrait of her given him by some painters, intimate friends of hers (p. 78). To this brief but fascinating story subsequent scholars have added other details, sometimes controverting Vasari with facts gleaned from documents, court records, and examinations of the archives of the workshop, the Fabbrica, of San Petronio.[10] After a period of questioning whether Properzia was not perhaps from Modena, it was established that her father was indeed Bolognese, and that she was probably born in or around 1495. The peach stone with the Passion of Christ was reportedly still extant in 1864 but has now disappeared.[11] Properzia probably did other minute carvings on fruit stones. What has survived are eleven peach stones carved with, on one side, the figures of saints, on the other, those of the apostles, their names and references to their particular virtue carved on each stone. The stones are now embedded in a filigree crucifix, an elaborate setting with a two-headed eagle and an imperial crown, now at the Museo Civico Medievale in Bologna (figure 2.2). The quality of the carving of each stone is an impressive achievement (figures. 2.3 and 2.4).

Another work attributed to Properzia, now in Florence at the Museo d'Argenti at the Pitti Galleries, is a cherry stone carved with what has been described as a Gloria of Saints "executed with astonishing exactitude" on which "there have been counted no fewer than sixty heads of extreme minuteness."[12] Since the pit measures about one-quarter inch in diameter, it is difficult for the average viewer to make accurate judgments about it. My photograph of the stone taken with an electronic camera with a high-powered lens reveals the astounding fact that there are actually far more than sixty heads on the pit! It also shows that the tiny stone appears to be in a style different from the less rounded carving of the peach stone saints (figure 2.5). The stones set in the cross at the center of the filigree crucifix are smaller than peach stones, and one indeed may be a cherry pit. If we assume as I do that the smaller stones, less than 1 cm. long, are also by Properzia, we can compare one of them to the cherry stone with multiple heads. An examination, for example, of the stone carved "Dorotea, Premia Calcavit" and a nineteenth-century engraving of that stone, shows that the style is markedly different. These considerations lead me to side more with those who attribute the work to a seventeenth-century male carver who also did minute carvings on fruit stones. However, under the circumstances—the details are literally microscopic—the usual complexities and uncertainties of attribution are greatly increased. Indeed it is difficult to imagine how anyone could mount a convincing argument on stylistic grounds that the work is indeed Properzia's.

We do know that she studied with the celebrated engraver Marc-Antonio Raimondi. We know, too, that she executed arabesques, marble ornaments, sculptured lions, griffins, birds, censers, vases, eagles, heads, and scroll work on the flat spaces of the arch over the high altar in the church of the Madonna del Barracano.[13]

According to documents in the workshop office, Properzia was paid for two pictures (quadri), presumably bas-reliefs. One relief is surely that scene of Joseph and Potiphar's wife now entitled *The Chastity of Joseph,* which is referred to repeatedly by the women writers to be discussed. The other is currently said to be the relief now placed next to it in the Museum of San Petronio. Well into the twentieth century this relief, also in marble, was assumed to be Solomon receiving gifts from the Queen of Sheba. Recently, as I shall show later, this identification has become problematic. Properzia was also paid for other work, angels and sybils, done under the direction of Tribolo, and she most probably executed some figures designed by him.

We also know from court records that Properzia was named in two law suits. Her neighbor Francesco da Milano accused her and her lover Antonio Galeazzo Malvasia of having caused the trunk of a tree and twenty-four feet of vine to be thrown into his garden. On another occasion she and a fellow artist, Domenico Francia, were charged with assault and battery by the painter Miola who exhibited the scratches she made on his face as evidence against her. That same Amico Aspertini mentioned by Vasari as her jealous enemy was a witness in this case. Properzia died of the plague in February 1530.

These then are the sketchy details, some well authenticated, others less so, of Properzia's life and

Fig.2.4. Properzia de' Rossi. Saint Apolonia (detail of fig. 2.2). Carved Peach Stone, Bologna, Museo Civico.

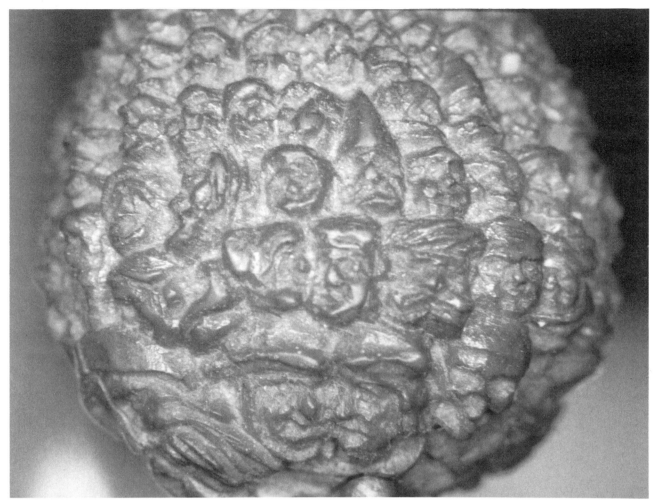

Fig.2.5.   Attributed to Properzia de' Rossi.
Carved Cherry Stone with More than
Sixty Heads of Saints. *Florence, Museo*
degli Argenti.

work. They make a colorful story, full of inconsistencies and questions. The women who write about Properzia pick up different themes and elaborate on different aspects, fleshing out the basic facts and earlier conjectures or perhaps outright inventions, and weave tales that I maintain are largely projections. That is, their accounts have much in common with the associations and explanations offered for the ink blots of Rorschach cards and the stories told about scenes in projective tests. Only in this light can we explain the wide divergence of views on such issues as the credibility of Vasari's tale of unrequited love, the proper interpretation of the court records, the degree of difficulty of Properzia's situation as a sixteenth-century woman artist, and even the value of her work. Precisely because it is impossible to verify Vasari's account or even to ascertain which of the surviving works are authentic, Properzia's story has provided a particularly fertile opportunity for critics and scholars to reveal their own class, national, and gender biases.

Philosophical Considerations: Art, Epistemology, and Interpretations

It is important to clarify at the outset that a basic opposition to certain current views of interpretation underlies the following analysis of women critics. This opposition consists of a denial of the view that criticism is *always* a form of fabrication. My assumption is rather that some analyses of a work are clearly better, more accurate, and of greater value than others. I do not suggest that a critic can produce interpretations of works completely divorced from the assumptions and accepted aesthetic standards of her time. Like artists, critics and historians of course operate from a particular temporal vantage point. Nevertheless, the search for objectivity is a necessary and worthwhile one, and the constant examination of such presuppositions as those exhibited by the writers I shall discuss, should be an ongoing enterprise. A belief in the possibility of reaching a true consensus should guide our efforts. We can grant that too much emphasis has been placed on determining which works are great to the detriment of efforts outside the mainstream. Still judgments of "better" and "worse" remain necessary to artistic as well as interpretive efforts. Some works *are* great, some criticism valid and insightful, and truth, as was said in the Renaissance, is indeed the daughter of time.

A lengthy epistemological justification of the necessity and usefulness of a concept of truth would be misplaced here. However, I do wish to point out that by saying the writings of female commentators reveal their own concerns, I am not saying that one is no more right than the other. Even in the interpretation of Rorschach tests, certain responses indicate signs of psychotic aberration precisely because there is no way that the reasoning offered for what is reportedly "seen" is convincing. One may see an image as either a duck or a rabbit, but if an observer sees it as a woman killing a man, we judge that there is nothing IN IT that accounts for the response. He/she is outside the community of human intentionality and meaning. Without some shared human theory of truth—whether you espouse a realist correspondence to fact, or accept a coherence theory in which the aim is to arrange all our perceptions into a cohesive whole—I do not see how we can engage in any kind of discourse or create any kind of beauty. Beauty is not in the eye of the individual beholder; individual preference does not determine it, though of course beauty or artistic greatness, like truth, requires the judgment of a human perceiver. If my family were to insist that my drawings are as good or beautiful as Rembrandt's, they would be mistaken.

Feminist theorists have been eager to avoid hierarchies and have produced a beneficial critique of male-dominated art history as preoccupied with scorecards and rating systems. No doubt such systems resulted in the overlooking of much worthwhile artistic activity. In stressing the importance of historical context they have done a great service. But in the eagerness to avoid "essentialism" it is perhaps too easy to lose sight of the impossibility of making sense without assuming some universal standards of investigation and interpretation.[14]

My examination of the varying treatments of Properzia is intended as an ongoing search for truth rather than a relativist attempt to prove there can be no "correct" interpretations. Even the Rorschach examination was designed with a range of possible acceptable interpretations. Just as an understanding of the reasons offered by a subject can provide reliable information about that interpreter, so I contend that there are important facts to be revealed about the way personal and historical assumptions about gender have shaped women's views of Properzia.

My analysis of these views is intended to shed additional light on the important questions raised by feminist art historians in the last decades. That is, do women as a group look at visual objects differently than men? Is there in fact a "male gaze," presumably different from a "female gaze"? Men, we are told, get voyeuristic, "scopophilic" pleasure in looking at certain images of women. When in these cases women seem to be seeing the same qualities as men, is this because they are disturbingly "male identified," adopting the standards of the dominant group? By following the artistic conventions of her time does a woman artist merely take over the male view of what she is representing? Or is there a subversive element involved in even the most conventional of women's presentations? Or is it impossible to tell?

It has been said that there are two choices open to the woman spectator. In viewing much of the world's art a female viewer must either take the place of the male, or accept the position of male-created "seductive passivity" gaining only the masochistic pleasure of her powerlessness.[15] In creating her own work and viewing it, was the female artist of the past inevitably caught in such a trap? These questions underlie the analysis which follows of six women critics.

The Women Speak: Six Authors in Search of a Character

The first woman interpreter of the life and work of Properzia was the Bolognese countess Carolina Bonafede who devotes a chapter to her compatriot in her *Cenni biografici e ritratti d'insigni donne bolognese (Biographical Allusions and Portraits of Illustrious Women of Bologna)* published in 1845.[16] The aristocrat Bonafede was a passionate Italian nationalist who clearly represented the interest of her class in maintaining the status quo. Her ornate style, replete with endless rhetorical flourishes, reflects the attitudes and conventions of an upper-class woman of her time. And yet her account contains a glimmer of what might be called "gender solidarity" that cannot be ignored. The fact that Bonafede chose to write an entire book about notable women, a topic perhaps commonplace now but of less interest to most nineteenth-century readers, is traceable to her search for what we now call "role models."

Bonafede addresses her book to the *gentili giovanette bolognese* and hopes these young ladies will draw a moral from the example of their illustrious female ancestors. She admonishes these young Italian women whom heaven has given "superior ability and understanding" to acquire a classical education and an acquaintance with literature. She reminds them that it is not only for their renowned piety, nor that singular prudence and common sense in managing family life, that women have merited a place in history. "Our sex," she informs them, "has distinguished itself in arms and even in politics" (Preface).

But what is the example of a woman like Properzia whom she calls a "genius of sculpture" meant to inspire these young women to do? It is not an ambition for great deeds that she wishes to foster in them. Their role rather should be to encourage their men to respect the laws of the land. They must use their *dolce possanza* (gentle strength or manipulative weakness?) primarily to spur the acomplishments of their brothers, husbands, and sons.[17] In other words, the countess does not, as one might assume offer Properzia's achievements as an inspiration to her female audience to attempt great artistic feats themselves. She expects only that the sculptor's success will fill them with civic and gender pride. But most of all Bonafede, using dubious reasoning, concludes that the sculptor's example should lead women to study hard and, above all, to encourage their men folk.

It is particularly ironic that Bonafede includes Properzia as an inspiration for good citizenship. The countess surely knew, even from the sketchy biographical details available, that Properzia led a life far from that of the conventional good wife and mother. In fact Bonafede must have been aware that Properzia did not even uphold the laws; she evidently knew of the lawsuits against the sculptor.

Bonafede was aware of the researches of scholars in the archives of the workshop at San Petronio and attempted to integrate the documentary evidence into her writing. A woman of her class would undoubtedly have been encouraged to do everything in an amateur fashion, to dabble in history and literature, but hardly to undertake serious historical study. In this light she surely deserves some credit for undertaking her study.

Bonafede herself is aware of her own limitations. Her tone in speaking of illustrious women differs from that excessive adulation, with its undertone of incredulous wonder, employed by Vasari and Boccaccio before him. Bonafede laments the inadequacies of the education of young girls when she was growing up. She is not only providing models for young women, she is also talking about herself. And with a glimmer—admittedly very faint—of dawning feminist awareness she asserts that women's education is still greatly lacking in the 1840s (Preface). In the midst of all her rhetoric there remains a doubleness of consciousness because of her gender.

In this context Bonafede's reaction to the idea that Properzia made her bas-relief as an expression of the sculptor's sorrow at being abandoned by her lover, is very revealing. Most critics have taken a decisive position on the credibility of the story. As we shall see women in particular have reacted to it strongly. Their judgments have ranged from finding it believably tragic to considering it sexist, demeaning, and false. Bonafede, despite her pervasive deference to Vasari, says the following:

> It is repugnant to believe that gifted as this woman was, with such good sense, even if she was tyrannized by this misbegotten lover, would have put herself in the place of a wanton, shameless female, and would have flouted her failure in triumph, when a gentlewoman should and would have wanted to hide this failure, not only from others *but even from herself* . . . we can consider this notion as one of those tales which in every age envy has not failed to invent against this wretched sex *(questo misero sesso).* (My italics, p. 21, n.1.)

Discounting the rhetorical and genteel language, it is clear that Bonafede wishes to make two points. Nice girls don't behave that way, and if they do, they certainly shouldn't. Repression, not sublimation, is the order of the day. A woman she calls a "genius of sculpture" ought not to make her love life public, particularly ought not to flaunt her rejection by a man. In fact, anyone who says she did so is just inventing it out of jealousy and intending to malign the gender to which Bonafede belongs. In short, the countess sees Vasari's story as a slight, and in her "poor us" vein, she resents it. Her reaction certainly contains a hint of the anger at male envy that only surfaces in full force more than a hundred years later in the work of feminist critics. But at the same time her response reveals that burden put on women for generations to grin and bear it, to keep their private affairs and their shames hidden from the world.

At roughly the same time that Bonafede was writing, a Mrs. Jonathan Foster in Great Britain was working on a translation not only of Vasari's account of Properzia but of all eight volumes of Vasari's work. In 1850, two hundred years after the publication of Vasari's "best seller," Mrs. Foster undertook the labor of making the first translation of Vasari into English. She translated and published not only the complete text, but also selected notes from numerous previous scholars. Furthermore, she offered some comments of her own. Although translators are in general unsung heroes, it is particularly unfortunate that we know so little about this woman.[18] It has been said that "in few instances have author and translator become more closely identified." However, following the custom in Britain until very recently, this woman, who "had the courage and enthusiasm to attempt such a task, and having attempted, accomplished it with so much thoroughness, sincerity and felicity," is known to us only by her husband's name.[19]

In translating the section on Properzia, Foster underplays the story of the unrequited love affair. She inserts an unwarranted qualification in Vasari's unequivocal statement that the sculptor made the relief "periciocche, that is, because, *"in quel tempo la misera donna era innamoratissima d'un bel giovane."* In translating this she adds the tentative *"it is indeed reported that* the unhappy woman was in love with a very handsome young man" (my italics).[20] She also neglects to translate any of the notes from the earlier Italian editions pertaining to the presumed identity of the youth, though she otherwise draws heavily on such annotations.

Foster, who usually confines her notes to clarifying textual points, also allows herself a comment here about male-female relations. Earlier editors have expressed outrage at Vasari's extravagant praise of the deeds of ancient women. And she is outraged at their outrage. In speaking of the poet Erinna, Vasari had repeated an ancient claim that her verses had equaled those of Homer. Foster resents the objections of an angry critic who wrote, "if ever such a judgment was pronounced in ancient Greece," it was "the greatest . . . literary wrong ever committed." She complains that the critic was undoubtedly jealous of the honours so justly paid to ladies by the excellent Messer Giorgio."[21] She goes on in this vein and deals sarcastically with all those who quite justifiably in my view were unwilling to credit this dubious claim that Erinna's work surpassed the *Iliad*. Like Bonafede, she clearly believes that men are jealous of women's accomplishments.

Earlier in the century, before Foster translated Vasari, the English poet Felicia Hemans was inspired by a painting by the French neo-classicist Louis Ducis (1773–1847) to write a poem called "Properzia de' Rossi" (figure 2.6). Hemans, the author of the well-known "Casabianca" poem that begins, "The

Fig.2.6. *Louis Ducis*. Sculpture *or* Properzia de'
Rossi. *Oil on canvas. Limoges, Musée
Municipal de L'eveche, Dépôt de Musee
National Adrien Dubouché.*

boy stood on the burning deck" was separated from her husband and left to support five children on her own through her poetry. Although her poems leave much to be desired, she seems to have been admired by Scott and Wordsworth. She certainly deserves admiration if for no other reason than the fact that from 1812 until she died in 1835 she published a book of poetry every year and succeeded in supporting her family by her art.[22]

According to Hemans's sister, who edited the poet's collected works, Ducis's painting shows Properzia offering a last work to a Roman knight. The work depicted in the painting we are told is a relief of the mythical Greek figure Ariadne. In actuality, there is no reason to believe that Properzia ever executed such a work; the relief depicted was totally invented by the painter. The editor describes the knight in the painting as the object of Properzia's affections who regards the work with indifference. Writing after her sister's death, the editor adds that Properzia died "in consequence of an unrequited attachment," an unwarranted but significant extrapolation of the Vasari story.[23]

The feminist writer Germaine Greer, whom I shall deal with at greater length presently, seems to consider the Hemans poem as just an extension of the tendency of the vulgar to construe Properzia's bas-relief as a "hopelessly indiscreet self-portrait."[24] And she seems to deride Hemans for giving the story of a real woman "the status of myth."[25] Why Hemans should be blamed for doing what poets have often done, i.e., building an imaginary world based on a scene from a painting, is not clear. Hemans no doubt recognized the painting for what it was, an allegorical treatment of an historical figure. She may have known from a wider tradition, if not directly from reading Vasari, that Properzia was said to have put her own experience of rejection in love into her work. The poet then takes the sculptor's situation as a jumping off point to express her, Hemans's, own sorrows. This would be an unjustified practice for a biographer or a critic, but is certainly legitimate for a creative artist.

In the poem Hemans intertwines the myth of Ariadne, the story of Properzia's unrequited love, and the poet's own situation. There are many versions of the Ariadne myth, all of which agree that she was abandoned by Theseus on the island of Dia (Naxos); there are varying accounts of her final fate. What is most striking about the poem is how nearly Hemans comes to forgetting that she is writing about a woman whose fame derives from her sculpture. She clearly identifies with Properzia and expresses her, Felicia's, own feelings of loneliness and longing. Even to a reader who knew nothing of Felicia Browne's biography, who was unaware that she married Alfred Hemans, an Irish naval captain, who suddenly deserted her and went to live in Italy, never to see her again,[26] the poet's identification with these abandoned women would be clear.

The poem speaks of Properzia's "song" and describes the artist's work as stemming from a power born within her "with its rushing train of glorious images." Hemans even describes the sculptor's final work as growing "line by line." The Properzia of the poem, speaking of the invented bas-relief, says, "I give my own life's history to thy brow, forsaken Ariadne" (p. 168). So, too, does Hemans give her own life history to Properzia. She expresses her own attitudes toward work and fame through the persona of the Italian woman. Fame is worthless because such renown still "wins not for my name Th' abiding place it asks" (p. 170). Heman's Properzia seeks a triumph for her last work as a compensation for having loved vainly. She wishes her work to be "something immortal" in the hopes that the lover who rejected her "may yet, feeling sad mastery there, perchance regret thine [her spirit's] unrequited gift" (p. 168).

Hemans no doubt speaks of herself when she writes that the artist might have given birth to "creations of far nobler thought," but she has been denied "a heart whereon to lean," "an eye to be my star," "a voice to bring/Hope" (p. 169). Her theme is that fame is as nothing compared to the love of a good man. To weep on the breast of her beloved would be happiness, but, alas, to Hemans's Properzia, "earth's gift is fame." Her only hope in presenting the bas-relief is that it and the name she leaves behind on her country's air will "one day in thy heart revive sad thoughts of me" (p. 171).

In the poem the sculptor addresses the figure of Ariadne as "the mould wherein I pour . . . fervent thoughts" (p. 169). Thus the story of Properzia becomes the vehicle for the fantasies of the poet, the mold wherein she pours her own wishes and desires. The role of gender in this situation is complex.

A male poet might still have written convincingly about an abandoned female artist. He might even have seen in her situation the age-old predicament of the artist in general, echoing the cry from Petrarch on that he would sacrifice all worldly renown and creative gifts for one "brief moment" with Laura. Many years later Freud maintained that what artists really seek is sexual union, that art and other accomplishments are only substitute gratifications. Therefore, even if the sculptor in the Ducis painting had been a deserted male offering a last work to a noble lady, the theme of the poem might have been similar.

Hemans, however, clearly intends to dramatize the belief articulated later by Byron that "Man's love is from his life a thing apart / But when a woman loves she loves with all her heart." Feminists might see this as Hemans's identification with the oppressor, an unfortunate assimilation of male-imposed beliefs. We might consider it deplorable that the poet values for herself, and consequently depicts Properzia as valuing, male affection over artistic success. Nonetheless in this case it is because of her gender that Hemans expresses so poignantly the worthlessness of worldly acclaim, the anguish in the cry "But I have been / Too much alone."

Another woman writer who was struck by the melodrama of Properzia's story sees the "sculptress," as she calls her, as representative of the difficulties of the professional woman, rather than of women in general. In Laura Ragg's *The Women Artists of Bologna,* written more than seventy years after Hemans's poem, the British historian concluded that "a profession may often be an excellent substitute for a husband."[27] But the labor we delight in, she writes, often causes great physical pain. About Properzia she speculates "sorrow and disappointment may beget and in turn be nourished by bodily disease." Unfortunately the artist had no access to the change of air and scene "so readily prescribed and taken" in Ragg's day—that is by the upper-class Victorian Englishwoman.[28] Therefore she languished and died in the hospital for the indigent.

Ragg herself came to live in Bologna in the first decade of the twentieth century only because of her husband's work, a predicament not unknown to women scholars even today. Forced by circumstances to choose a topic outside her field she occupied herself examining historical documents and produced her book. Her account of Properzia is lively, almost chatty. She embellishes the available facts with details of the musical life of Bologna in Properzia's time, and offers peripheral historical information about the institution where Properzia died. Ragg read what had been published previously and made use of the documentary evidence. She states regretfully that she did not have the opportunity to personally examine the records of the Fabricca which might have given her more definite information about the works that Properzia executed. Despite the informality of her tone, then, she had standards of scholarship beyond the ambitions of Bonafede and tried to fulfill them.

Later women scholars are dismissive of Ragg's efforts, possibly because to a modern feminist she seems so singularly unenlightened. The assumption of some theorists that women's "voices" are more supportive, that females are more likely to see intellectual investigation as a cooperative pursuit, certainly does not apply to the women writers I am discussing here. They are every bit as critical of the work of their female predecessors, generally as dismissive or even snide and contemptuous as their male counterparts.[29] Ragg's suggestion that Properzia was just one of many multitalented Renaissance women who, through a "mere accident," what she chooses to call a "feminine caprice," turned from amateur to professional, is, of course, irritating to contemporary feminists. Nevertheless Ragg deserves much credit. She provided a popular account of Properzia for readers who would otherwise not have heard of the Renaissance sculptor, and her coherent overview of the crucial documents has not yet been substantially supplanted.

Ragg recounts the latest evidence pertaining to Properzia's origins, correctly rejecting Bonafede's surmise that because the sculptor was called "Madonna Properzia" by Vasari that Rossi may have been her maiden name. In the 1850s M. Gualandi discovered documents of the years 1514, 1516, and 1518, which mention *"Domina Propertia, filia q. Ieronymi de Rubeis Bononiae civis."* No doubt pleased to include Properzia as a true daughter of Bologna she did not add that Properzia's purported father,

Girolamo, son of a Bolognese notary, came back to the city about a year before her birth after spending eighteen years of his life in the galleys to which he had been condemned for manslaughter.

Ragg also comments on the few other documents that we must count on to fill out the meager evidence we have of Properzia's life. In 1520 and 1521 there are records of an action brought against the sculptor by a velvet merchant, Francesco da Milano, for damage done to his garden which adjoined her own. He describes her as the "mistress of Antonio Galeazzo di Napoleone Malvasia." Ragg translates "concubina" in the charge as "mistress," a term rather too genteel in this context. Antonio denies this connection and declares that he lives at a distance from Properzia. The enterprising Ragg points out that Antonio could not have been telling the truth, a fact that she ascertained by walking the streets of Bologna. She, however, offers no explanation for his denial.[30]

As I have mentioned the records also show that an action was brought against Properzia and Domenico Francia, a painter, by another painter Vicenzo Miola. The two had come to his house and abused and attacked him, Properzia scratching his face. Ragg sees the fact that one of the witnesses against the accused was Amico Aspertini as corroborating Vasari's story that Aspertini had it in for Properzia. In this incident Ragg completely identifies with Properzia. She also inserts in her narrative a condescending digression on the lack of inhibitions of Mediterranean people, particularly Renaissance Italians, describing "the little bit of low comedy" which ends the public quarrels that this Victorian woman finds amusing. She calls the record of the trial "a pleasing sidelight . . . on the manners and customs of sixteenth century Bohemia" (p. 181). She does not seem to disapprove at all of "the feline fury of the woman."

In fact, Ragg defends Properzia wholeheartedly. She writes: "One is tempted to hope that the ugly and malicious Amico came in for a share of Properzia's summary revenge, since from all accounts the words of Shakespeare's Beatrice might have been applied to him: 'Scratching could not make it worse and 'twere such a face as yours.'"

But Ragg's vicarious venom is no expression of feminist outrage. It is nothing of the sort—consciously at any rate. Many years after Bonafede's cry about the victimization of our wretched sex, Ragg explicitly rejects the possibility of male chauvinism. Although she went to university after the publication of Mill's *On the Subjection of Women,* at a time when feminist ideas were influencing many educated women, Ragg denies vociferously that Aspertini's malice could possibly have anything to do with Properzia's gender. Unlike Countess Bonafede, Ragg makes a great effort to show that Aspertini had no grudge against Properzia beyond the fact that "she was an artist of rare talent" (p. 181).

Here and elsewhere Ragg bends over backwards to show that discrimination was not an issue for Properzia. To suppose that Aspertini disapproved of female competition and was indignant that a woman should have a share in the work of San Petronio "is to endow the sixteenth century with one of the most curious and ugly features of recent times" (p. 182).

Since no direct historical evidence exists to explain why Aspertini resented Properzia, the incident is a clear-cut test of the projected attitudes of our female observers. Ragg's unwillingness to recognize even the possibility of difficulties for Properzia because of her gender do involve her in other pronouncements which historical evidence can refute. She quotes with approval the statement of a Bishop Creighton that the notion of rivalry between the sexes "was as foreign to the Italian Renaissance as that of rivalry between the classes." She seconds his idea that "all were at liberty to do their best" (p. 182).

It is hard to see how any twentieth-century researcher, regardless of gender, could make such a claim. It is true that the great scholar Burckhardt thought that the Renaissance brought equality to women, and that it is only in the past twenty years that this view has been systematically refuted.[31] Still, one wonders how a woman who knew what the conditions were like in the all-male artists' workshops, who knew how few Renaissance women artists there were, who had every reason to be aware of continuing discrimination in art and academic circles in her native Britain, could yet believe that art was a career completely open to talent. And yet so she seems to have convinced herself.

She chooses to believe that none of the difficulties in Properzia's career are directly attributable to her being a woman. In her discussion of Properzia's alleged unrequited love affair Ragg once again attempts to avoid any recognition of the discrepancy of power between men and women. With scholarly caution she notes that Anton Galeazzo's denial of connection to Properzia is "subtly worded . . . not retrospective and may mean anything or nothing" (p. 180). All that can be concluded she says is that at some time between 1524–26 their relations were severed. And since Anton Galeazzo took his bachelor's degree in 1524 the alliance was ended "doubtless by the natural development of the career of a well educated young man of good family" (p. 180). She admits that the popular conception of the relationship between Properzia and Antonio may be a "crude misrepresentation" of a flirtation that was a pastime for the man and the "whole existence" of the woman (p. 179). This formulation is surely inappropriate when you consider that Properzia's existence clearly included "nontraditional" work, done with much skill. Ragg also suggests that it may have been one of those platonic friendships "which in the case of the young and handsome of artistic and ardent temperament, usually end in the misery of one or the other." That is, the woman is no more likely to be the victim than the man. Her conviction does not seem to be at all shaken by her realization that Properzia's death in the charitable institution, the Spedale della Morte, could only have resulted from "poverty or absolute friendlessness."

She sees nothing offensive in Vasari's suggestion that the bas-relief of Joseph and Potiphar's wife has an autobiographical element. She criticizes Bonafede, who, as Ragg puts it, found the story "unimaginably inconsistent with womanly reticence and proper pride" (p. 178). To Ragg it seems perfectly consistent with our knowledge of Properzia and her time. She makes an admirable attempt to place her interpretation of Vasari in historical context. Undoubtedly, her view of a Renaissance Italy lacking in both public and private morality, a society where suppression of emotion was suspect, is somewhat condescending and simpleminded. However, she is surely right that Vasari's contemporaries took a different attitude to the expression of emotion than did Ragg's British contemporaries. All in all, Ragg finds Vasari's story perfectly reasonable, an illustration of his belief in the desirability of expressing emotions "an opinion still in some measure prevalent among Latin peoples" (p. 178). For Ragg, Properzia's incorporating herself and her lover into a work has no special gender significance.

But here again there is a certain doubleness of vision, which in Ragg's case amounts to bad faith. In a book about the accomplishments of serious women artists, she at the same time glorifies amateur rather than professional activity for women. Properzia she describes as having that keen, full-rounded sense of beauty that makes the professional dilettante and is apt to make the imperfect professional (p. 170). She believes the true direction of the sculptor's genius was discovered only through female capriousness; yet she expresses no regret or sense of loss to the world for any female genius left undeveloped. She is clearly in conflict about which kind of activity is better for women. Of the sense of beauty of the dilettante she writes, "Such a sense was the special dower of the women of the renaissance. They played, they sang, they danced, they dabbled in the classics, they wrote letters and made verses, and were altogether charming companions, excellent critics, graceful amateurs" (p. 170). Spoken like a true Edwardian gentleman![32]

Ragg actually comes close to suggesting that Properzia's professional labors killed her. Lacking a husband, a woman's profession "may become an idol on whose shrine all the affections of a life are laid" (p. 183). But in nine cases out of ten such labor will produce illness. Ragg clearly accepts the Victorian view so damaging for decades that intellectual or serious artistic activity would endanger women's health. She allows that most women might recover from the strain but in some there may be no reserve of physical energy for reorientation. "Sorrow and disappointment may beget, and in turn be nourished by, bodily disease" (p. 183).

Ragg not only saw the scanty details of Properzia's biography in the light of her own concerns. She also interpreted the surviving visual images according to her own expectations. Although Vasari mentions only the one bas-relief, by Ragg's time scholars in search of the additional "picture" for

Fig.2.7. *Attributed to Properzia de' Rossi.* The Wife of Potiphar Accuses Joseph. *Marble Relief. Bologna, Museo di San Petronio.*

which Properzia was paid had found a likely candidate. This attribution, which I maintain is still questionable, is now titled *The Wife of Potiphar Accuses Joseph* (figure 2.7). Originally, however, it was thought to depict the visit of the Queen of Sheba to King Solomon. And so Ragg herself sees it. She speaks of a figure kneeling at the feet of King Solomon, offering a garment of needlework. The Queen and her maidens stand respectfully aloof. Perhaps. Ragg does not question whether the figure is indeed a queen, nor look very closely at her expression. Instead, like most observers, she

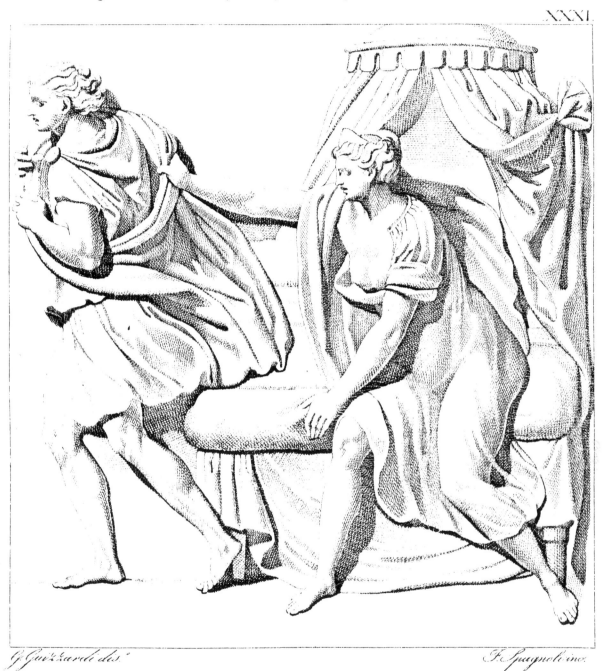

Fig. 2.8. *Guiseppe Guizzardi*. The Chastity of Joseph. *Engraving from* Le Sculpture delle Porte della Basilica di San Petronio in Bologna: Con una Memoria e Documenti inediti dal Virgilio Davia *(Bologna: della Volpe, 1834).*

tends to see what she is told is there.

In the authenticated relief Properzia lays a detaining hand on Joseph's flying cloak. Ragg sees in it natural, vigorous movement and action, graceful gestures, unbroken harmony of line, all "without violence or contortion" (p. 175). In an early nineteenth-century engraving of the work, a rendering which was intended as a faithful reproduction, the male artist has, I believe, created a scene of greater desperation (figure 2.8). Properzia in this male version is hanging on for dear life, an impression that the sharpness of line of the medium probably emphasizes. For Ragg, however, Properzia's relief is admirable precisely because unlike other Renaissance artists, whom she consideres too individualistic, "the sculptress" has been studying classical models.

Seventy years later the feminist thinker Germaine Greer finds this use of classical models far from admirable. It is instead part of Properzia's general mediocrity, a mediocrity which stems from the oppressive conditions that made artistic achievement all but impossible for women. Greer's book details a long and miserable chronicle of women's failures to overcome the obstacles that kept them from creating great paintings.[33] Women had little or no opportunity for artistic training unless their fathers, husbands, or other male relatives were painters. And even then, when they showed talent, they sacrificed their own abilities to supporting others. Greer does not blame women's failures on these external conditions alone. She also criticizes the internalized factors in their personalities that made it impossible for women to break away from what they saw around them, to make new visions or trust themselves, all of which are necessary for genius. Properzia she sees as a prime example of such an unliberated woman.

Greer pities the sculptor. She calls her "poor Properzia," and describes the bas-relief that Vasari found so beautiful as an "interesting, chastely *classicheggiante* relief of Potiphar's wife snatching at the skirts of fleeing Joseph." Again one wonders how carefully the observer really looked at the work, for the exposed breasts with their erect nipples might not strike everyone, particularly if they had been done by a male, as particularly chaste. Greer finds there is little originality and limited merit in the relief.

Part of the reason that "she achieved very little" is that like all women she was a victim of extravagant praise by men. This condescension has done great harm and kept women from testing themselves and developing through criticism. Greer, like many other feminists, sees Vasari as one of the prime perpetrators. She accuses Vasari not only of exaggeration as in his eulogy of ancient women. The real crime is that by patronizing and flattering women males assert their superiority. Vasari adopted a double standard in writing about female artists, was more interested in them as prodigies of nature than in assessing their contributions. She is surely right that excessive undeserved praise has a detrimental effect. But she also adds that Vasari is guilty of an "egregious credulity" in writing about women which he would scorn to adopt for any other topic (p. 2). Greer surely exaggerates herself here. In fact Vasari tells outrageous tales as if he believed them about many male artists. And some of his incredible claims have even turned out to be true.[34]

Greer thinks Vasari's praise for Properzia's minutely carved fruit stones is unwarranted. In general she finds all miniaturization aesthetically less valuable, though she admits (seemingly without much conviction) that her judgment may be the result of the masculine standards of excellence that were a part of her education. It is her belief that in viewing either huge or minute objects one automatically translates them into another scale, and then judges them aesthetically (p. 109). This I believe is an erroneous atomistic view of aesthetic perception. It would take us too far afield to dispute her assumption at length. However, I would maintain that one can judge works as they are, comparing one miniature to another, delighting in the artist's skill while tending to other aspects as well. There need be no "translating" process involved at all.[35]

Greer sees smallness as primarily appreciated by the "spontaneous judgment of the uneducated."[36] Many a semiliterate museum attendant she tells us will pluck a visitor by the sleeve to call attention to some prodigy of littleness, to what she calls Properzia's "Crucifixion sculpted on a cherry stone"

(p. 208). No such crucifixion ever existed; as others have pointed out, Greer's scholarship leaves much to be desired. But the question remains whether Properzia in fact did minute carving out of frustration because she was driven away from carrying out her commissions for the basilica of San Petronio. From Vasari onward it has been assumed that Properzia began with minute carvings and proceeded to larger works. But Greer maintains the opposite without providing any evidence. While her uneducated custodian sees something wonderful in the carved stones, Greer says the feminist will find it yet another instance of victimization.

She also sees discrimination in the fact that Properzia had to submit test pieces although she had already carried out work for another church. Greer notes but gives no credit to Vasari for stating that the sculptor was destroyed by male persecution. She is more interested in attacking him as in his own way one of the persecutors. It is not clear if she includes Vasari himself, who originated the story, when she writes that the bas-relief "is vulgarly construed to be a hopelessly indiscreet self-portrait" (p. 208). This theme of the demeaning character of such use of biographical information reaches fever pitch in the essay of the late twentieth-century art historian whom we shall now consider.

Vera Fortunati Pietrantonio, a well known art historian at the University of Bologna and an ardent feminist, wrote a long article in the early 1980s intended to reinstate Properzia as a strong "feminine presence" in the artistic life of sixteenth-century Bologna. In her scholarly account she carefully traces the references to and judgments of Properzia in the writings of previous Italian art historians, and acknowledges the influence of the collection of women artists' work by Harris and Nochlin. Fortunati makes clear at the outset that her interest in Properzia "has undoubtedly been stimulated by the problematic questions brought about by the feminist movement."[37] She reiterates Harris's observation that the fact that sculpture was not women's work was commonly used by sixteenth-century writers to demonstrate a point. Since there were no female sculptors, sculpture must be more difficult and therefore superior to painting (p. 168). In this feminist context, Fortunati of course deplores Ragg's account. She describes it as generally of poor quality, *cattiva letteratura,* and finds almost nothing of a nonromanticized nature in her piece.

In general Fortunati finds a dogged denigration of Properzia by previous art historians, a pervasive "masculine hostility" toward what they all persist in calling "the sculptress" (p. 171). She has to admit that this hostility or condescension she finds pervasive has exceptions, exceptions I would consider very significant. For example, the noted nineteenth-century sculptor Canova was very impressed with the surviving work. He is reported to have said "among the great misfortunes that the Belle Arti have suffered in Italy one must place the early death of Properzia" (p. 171).[38] She even grants that some of the hostility and neglect may be due to the confused state of attributions of the work on the doorways of San Petronio. But in general she deplores male critics' stress on the eclectic nature of Properzia's efforts. Fortunati manages to maintain her annoyance even though she herself cannot deny the influences of Michelangelo, Tribolo, Lombardi, and others on the previously misidentified works that she now wishes to attribute to Properzia.

She turns the full force of her wrath on the "mito vasariano," that myth promulgated by Vasari that Properzia vented her own feelings of rejection by her lover in her representation of the plight of Potiphar's wife. Vasari is the vilest villain in all this. His sin seems to consist mostly of choosing to write primarily about the private life of a woman who "has broken every tie with her traditional role"—the description is Fortunati's, of course (p. 168). (It is necessary to identify which words are Fortunati's because her article, admittedly more scholarly than the others we have discussed, is also disturbingly filled with short phrases in quotes. Some of these she identifies, some she does not. Some words are perhaps surrounded by quotes for emphasis, other expressions seem to appear in quotation marks to indicate and indict the irony involved, but one cannot always be sure.)

This tendency of male writers to look to the biography rather than the work has disturbed other feminists.[39] Fortunati particularly objects to the fact that in Vasari's account, as she puts it, "the professional life of Properzia is legendarily framed by . . . two masculine figures, husband and lover

. . . the husband as the intermediary with the workers at San Petronio . . . and the lover as the inspiring cause" of the picture (p. 169).[40]

Alas, later when Fortunati reviews the information from the archives herself, she is forced to support the hypothesis that Properzia's lover Antonio Malvasia, of whom we have already heard much, was actually the man who facilitated Properzia's entrance into the workshop. Fortunati does not seem to notice any difficulty in her own tracing of Properzia's career to a man. Her dilemma is like that of the woman who decides to use her maiden name as a protest when she marries, thus choosing to be identified by her father's name rather than her husband's. That is, the critic's attempt at "demystification" to use the fashionable term she herself employs, does not really succeed in liberating Properzia.

Most of all Fortunati, like Greer a few years earlier, resents the melodramatic tale of lost love purportedly expressed in the relief. Fortunati is surely right that the picture's subject fits well into the cycle of tales of Joseph designed for the doors of San Petronio. (Vasari, of course, does not claim that it does not.) Male writers have also found the tale objectionable. Like Greer, they have seen acceptance of the story as succumbing to the opinion of the vulgar from which they wished to dissociate themselves. And like Bonafede they have refused to believe that a "woman of genius" would want to make such a public confession. But Fortunati's interpretation of the relief is entirely different from that of any previous critics.

This contemporary feminist sees the *Chastity of Joseph* as a "transcription into a feminine mode" of the Old Testament tale ("*[L]a 'transcrizione' in 'femminile,'*" p. 173). Properzia, she says, was attempting to use her technical mastery of the artistic language of the time to reach an approach in the feminine,—using the gender term borrowed from grammar—to the biblical tale. Nobly classical, the female figure as Fortunati sees it is the major protagonist. Potiphar's wife "emerges aggressively from the pictorial story because of the stronger 'attention' with which her 'body' is developed as a field for expressive motives which are specifically 'feminine' in their states of mind" (p. 173; the internal quotes are Fortunati's). Insofar as one can penetrate her prose, the claim seems to be that it is apparent from the depiction of the female body that it arises from personal experience. Properzia has avoided the androgyny of the female archetype of her time. Fortunati writes:

> The transparent shift shows without rhetorical amplification but with instinctive naturalness the sexuality of the person; the ample décolleté uncovers with nonchalant spontaneity as in a reflection in a mirror for domestic use, the little breast regarded without rhetorical complacency but with instantaneous immediacy. The androgynous quality is kept for the muscular Michelangelesque arms with which the woman tempts Joseph, as if to proclaim without reserve the will to feminine self-determination of her own affective, sentimental and sexual life. (p. 174).

Thus Properzia becomes a proto-feminist and her work becomes a protest against male domination. And the story of unrequited love according to Fortunati was probably invented only to relegate the sculptor to that state of "subordination to male power" against which she rebelled. Where Greer saw chaste pseudo-classicism Fortunati finds the will to self-determination.

This is not the place to evaluate at length the other attributions to Properzia that Fortunati makes, contributions which she hints might have been obscured because of Vasari's shifting our focus to the demeaning love story. Suffice it to say that no additional archival evidence has turned up to allow a precise determination of which other carvings she may have executed. I would agree that some of the other sybils—and we know from the records that she was paid for several sybils—are very likely to be Properzia's work as Fortunati claims. The first and third sybils from the bottom of the small columns on the right of the righthand door of San Petronio do seem to me to be her work; more questionable perhaps is the fifth figure because of the different treatment of the hair. The fourth sybil from the bottom I would claim is so close stylistically and in feeling to the figure of Potiphar's wife that Fortunati is surely correct on this attribution. The important issue here, however, is what I claim is an inaccuracy in her (and the curatorial) attribution of the other relief in the Museum of San

Petronio to Properzia.[41] Ragg and others as we have seen also believed this crowded relief to be the other work for which Properzia was paid.

This relief, which as we have noted was previously identified as *The Visit of the Queen of Sheba to King Solomon,* Fortunati and her Florentine colleague Maria Grazia Ciardi Dupré believe represents an entirely different subject. They consider it to be another relief by Properzia continuing the iconographic program of the story of Joseph. Ciardi Dupré, another female art historian, finds the relief definitely to be by an artist from Emilia rather than by Aspertini. She thinks it is the work of Properzia because of its stylistic similarity to the *Chastity* relief, and, among other reasons, because its space is "cut up as in a cameo."[42] I believe that in fact Ciardi Dupré and Fortunati's eagerness to find more work by the sculptor has led them to make a serious misjudgment in this case.

The theory that the work was Properzia's was actually propounded one hundred fifty years earlier by A. Saffi, who also saw stylistic similarities between the two reliefs (p. 174). But at that time, as we have seen, it was believed that the female figure, not dominant in this work, was an Oriental queen sharing the stage with a seated king, who I would claim is far more forcefully developed. Following Fortunati's own logic this might lead her to suggest that it was carved by a man. But instead, clinging to her hypothesis, she describes the relief as the result of "a less innovative attitude" on Properzia's part due to the tight control by the male sculptors in the workshop (p. 174). Nevertheless she thinks the costumes and hairdresses of the women are given special attention, as she claims they are in the female saints, as opposed to the male apostles, carved on the peach stones. Determined to have it both ways, Fortunati speculates that it is almost as if the work were a "forced return to order" after the daring exploit of *The Chastity of Joseph* (p. 174).

My own examination of the relief now retitled *The Wife of Potiphar Accuses Joseph* finds stylistic differences so pronounced that I believe the attribution to Properzia is surely wrong. Small details indicate a marked discrepancy (figure 2.7). For example, the toes on the figures are long, thin, and angular with indented moons on the nails, a treatment which differs markedly from that of the toes in the authenticated relief. The hands, too, are different. Potiphar's wife has completely different fingers in this work; they are long and tapered with a pronouncedly longer middle finger, and a thumb which is not spatulate as it is in the other relief. The cloak, too, with a heavy folded-over collar is different from Joseph's garment in the other work. It is hard to believe that the graceless carving of the leaves on the chair could have been done by the woman we know carved intricate leaves and flowers in the Baraccano church. The treatment of the hair is also much less delicate. Even Ciardi Dupré's comment on the cameolike quality of the work does not hold up. The work as a whole is not cameolike. And the heads inset in the round, which can be seen as cameos, are more like the cameo-type heads in another relief titled *The Construction of the Ark* than they are like anything else that we know Properzia to have done. Particularly telling I think is the fact that on close examination the wife of Potiphar in this second relief has very long hair all the way down her back. We might allow for the following unlikely possibility. The same sculptor could surprisingly have portrayed the Egyptian woman who is trying to seduce Joseph as having put her hair up in the bedchamber, but then appearing in her husband's official quarters afterward with her hair down. But this is not very convincing. The short, beautifully waved coiffure carved by Properzia differs not only in length but also markedly in style of execution from that of the woman's hair in the second relief. If the same sculptor had executed both works, would she have made the wife's locks appear so different at the time—presumably shortly afterward—of the accusation? Furthermore, and perhaps most decisive of all, is the fact that the proportion of head to body in the figures is different in the two reliefs.[43]

Even if the cramped, top heavy, less effective composition could be explained by Properzia's return to conventional expectations, I do not see how the technical anomalies could be accounted for. In making this attribution it seems that Fortunati has weakened a case that might otherwise have some validity. She has first claimed that Properzia depicted a strong woman with a forceful arm as a protest. Then we are asked to accept that in a cycle, which presents a scene that occurred shortly afterward, Properzia sculpted an uninteresting, stylized figure, with a dull conventional face and a stylized gesture which is hard to interpret. (I, of course, am not alone in finding the gesture confusing, since scholars have long identified the theme as having nothing to do with the Joseph story.) If I am correct, why then have these two highly trained late twentieth-century women chosen to see the lesser relief as the work of the Renaissance sculptor? Divining motives is a suspect enterprise at best. But it is tempting to believe that they, more than their male counterparts, might want to discover additional work by this elusive woman who extended the boundaries of female opportunity and about whom we know so tantalizingly little.

An Ongoing Story: My Own Interpretations

In the face of the widely divergent views of the female critics we have examined and the claim that interpretation can often tell more about the observer than about what is observed, is it possible for any viewer to describe a work objectively? One can only try to present evidence and ask the viewer to check the reasoning with the evidence of her/his own senses. My own view is that despite the dangers of "reading into" the efforts of past artists, particularly those who left us no expressions of their conscious intentions nor material that might shed light on unconscious preoccupations, art objects can still provide valuable information. The problem is in determining, as with a scientific hypothesis, how such information could be falsified. If we did not believe that *The Chastity of Joseph* was done by a woman, then Vasari's story of an autobiographical self-expressive element would clearly be false. On the other hand, knowing that the sculptor was female provides the critic with more justification for saying, as I do, that the particularly strong arm of the woman is reminiscent of the arm of a female sculptor. This suggests that the artist identified with the woman represented. Even if the artist were unknown, the fact that the figure of Potiphar's wife is more effectively developed would allow us to say that the artist, regardless of gender, identified with the woman.

As evidence of this I would offer the painting of *Joseph and Potiphar's Wife* painted by Properzia's compatriot, Guido Reni, exactly one hundred years later (figure 2.9). As a fellow Bolognese Reni may well have been familiar with Properzia's relief. The composition, particularly when left and right are reversed, is strikingly similar. The sympathy in this work is again clearly with the woman. In fact, the expression of longing written on her face is more moving than in the Properzia relief. The art historians Rozsika Parker and Griselda Pollock believe that the women in Reni's paintings are not shown to the viewer for the psychological impact of the event.[44] However, their observation seems to me wrong in this case. The painting, though done by a male, is less erotic, more poignant, and every bit as expressive. Even given the differences in medium and artistic vocabulary of the period, the desire of the woman and her sorrow at rejection is psychologically convincing and a crucial element in the painting.

No doubt elaborate theories could be built if it were suddenly suggested that this painting were the work of a woman. Since it is not, we can say only that in this painting the artist identifies with, that is, puts himself in the place of, the woman. The comment made about Properzia's relief, that Joseph is merely a "street boy" also applies here to Reni's Joseph. If the fact that more attention was given to the woman's costume and hairdo were to lead to any conclusions about the gender of the artist as Fortunati claims in attributing *The Wife of Potiphar Accuses Joseph* to Properzia, this as well as many other works would surely be judged to be by a woman.

We know that viewers describe and interpret paintings differently if they believe the work was done by a woman than if they think it was the work of a man.[45] This process is similar to the phenomena observed in a study conducted at Tufts University in which adults applied one set of adjectives to an infant when it was identified as male and a different set when that same infant was identified as female. Some of the same process of projection, of seeing what you expect or want to

Fig.2.9. *Guido Reni.* Joseph and Potiphar's Wife. *Oil on canvas. Fitzwilliam Museum, Cambridge, on long-term loan to Holkham Hall, Norfolk.*

see, I have tried to show is operative in the interpretations of Properzia of the six female viewers I have discussed. In all of them their gender has been a factor in their evaluations. Though all female, their views have nevertheless on many issues been diametrically opposed. They have disagreed in evaluating the veracity and mendacity of Vasari, in interpreting the details of Properzia's biography, and in identifying and judging the sculptor's work. It comes as no surprise, then, that my own views also reflect my own concerns, some of them also gender-based.

I find Properzia's marble relief as beautiful as Vasari did, far more worthy than many male scholars have admitted.[46] I do not believe that my admiration of the erotic portrayal of the woman is in any way demeaning to me nor does it require that I accept powerlessness as some feminists have claimed about female nudity (or seminudity) in art. In this case my pleasure is aesthetic rather than masochistic, and would be so regardless of the gender of the sculptor. In fact, the work's portrayal of the active sexual desire of a woman strikes me as particularly meritorious in a world where men have so often thought of women as passive partners.[47] But considering that there is so little of her work, and that the carving on fruit stones is necessarily limited in its scope, I am well aware that it is the astounding fact of her being the first and only Renaissance female sculptor known to us, that sustains my interest. As for the details of Properzia's biography, I put some stake in the fact that Vasari, unlike our commentators, was actually in Bologna at the time and knew Properzia's coworkers. Biased against women as he may have been, his report of Properzia having a lover at one time is borne out by the documentary evidence. We also know that she died friendless and impoverished, which does not speak well of her partner's devotion.

My interest in philosophical aesthetics leads me to a judgment about Vasari, which is far different from that of my "sisters." Hemans and Ragg find tragic truth in Vasari's claim of an autobiographical element in Properzia's work. Bonafede, Greer, and Fortunati see only error and/or willful condescension and malice, whereas I see philosophical insight. Vasari's view that Properzia gained satisfaction from giving vent to her strong emotions through the creation of an art object is important in the history of aesthetic theory. His assertion is one of the first (perhaps even the very first) formulations of a theory of art as sublimation. More than three hundred years before Freud, Vasari advanced the idea that artists sometimes make use of their personal experiences in their work as an effective means of discharging strong emotion.[48] Therefore, no matter what other motivations he may have had, as friends of truth as much as friends of women, we all owe him and Properzia a debt.[49]

Notes

1. Linda Nochlin made this point in her important essay "Why Have There Been No Great Women Artists?" reprinted most recently in her *Women, Art, and Power* (New York: Harper and Row, 1988), p. 149. Her discussion generated much controversy, with many insisting on some common feature in women's art and searching for a female sensibility. For a discussion of diverse views on the issue, see the admirable survey by T. Gouma-Peterson and P. Mathews, "The Feminist Critique of Art History," *The Art Bulletin* LXIX, no. 3 (September 1987) pp. 327, 334–37. The authors themselves seem to believe that "a whole lot of recent research in psychology, literature, art, music, sociology, and education indicates that women perceive reality differently than men" p. 334. However, they do not explain exactly what they mean by a "different perception of reality."

2. The first edition was published in 1650 and a second version in 1568. A definitive annotated edition of Vasari's text by Gaetano Milanesi appeared in 1858. Page numbers in my text are from a reprinting of the Milanesi edition, *Le Opere di Giorgio Vasari*, tomo V (Florence: G. C. Sansone, 1906). Translations of Vasari are my own unless otherwise indicated.

3. Mrs. J. Foster, the first translator of Vasari into English, seemingly balked at translating this hyperbole literally and wrote instead that women "*for the most part* have acquitted themselves well"

(my italics), for "siano sempre *riuscite eccellentissime.*" She thus tones down the meaning and adds a qualification which does not appear in the Vasari text. *Lives of the Most Eminent Painters, Sculptors, and Architects* translated by Mrs. Jonathan Foster (London: Bell and Daldy, 1868), vol. III, p. 236. For more about this female translator, see below, p. 48.

4. This is not the place to discuss the original source of Vasari's list of great women. However, the usual attribution to Pliny via Boccacio's *De Claribus Mulieribus* is an oversimplification that merits further inquiry.

5. Alfred Werner, in his introduction to *Lives of the Artists* (New York: Farrar, Straus and Giroux, 1971), p. v.

6. T. S. R. Boase, *Vasari, The Man and the Book* (Princeton: Princeton University Press, 1979), p. 40.

7. Ibid., p. 42.

8. *Symposium*, 209. In *The Dialogues of Plato*, trans. B. Jowett (New York: Random House, 1937), p. 333.

9. Boase, *Vasari the Man*, p. 301.

10. The bulk of our information comes from the nineteenth-century researches of Virgilio Davia reported in *Le Sculture delle Porte della Basilica di S. Petronio* (Bologna, 1834) and from Marsilio Gualandi, *Memorie Originali Italiane Riguardanti le Belle Arti* (Bologna, 1840–45) and *Memorie intorno a Properzia de' Rossi Scultrice Bolognese*

originally published in "*L'Osservatorio,*" no. 33, 34, 35 (Bologna, 1851).

11. Milanesi, *Le Vite,* p. 75, n. 1.

12. Ibid.

13. Charles C. Perkins, *Italian Sculptors* (London: Longmans, Green, 1868), pp. 240–41. Of what is now there to see I hazard a guess that in the lower left corner in one of the flowers there is the head of a woman. Could this be an early signature head, Properzia leaving her own fanciful image amidst the decoration? Due to the perpetual darkness of the church—and the Church Guide does not even mention any contribution by Properzia—I freely admit that this may be wishful thinking on my part.

14. In my opinion the art historian Linda Nochlin has not resolved this difficulty. In *Women, Art, and Power* she assures us that she is not assuming some hidden Truth behind her own "reading" of a given work. However, she cannot avoid the fact that some objective standard is needed to validate her claims of "misreadings" by others and to justify the correctness of her own observations. The spatial metaphor of truth hovering behind a "text" may not be useful. But some universally applicable principle for ascertaining the truth of a judgment remains necessary.

15. Nochlin attributes the articulation of these choices to Laura Mulvey in an argument taken over from her film criticism. *Women, Art, and Power,* pp. 30, 36n.37. Nochlin cites the often reprinted article "Visual Pleasure and Narrative Cinema," *Screen* 16, no. 3 (Autumn 1975), but though the language and views are characteristic of Mulvey, they do not in fact appear in the article cited.

16. Numbers in my text refer to this work. Translations are mine.

17. I am indebted to the late Piero Paci for his suggestion of this nuance which he believed would have been a code understood by young Italian women even in his youth. I am grateful to Dr. Paci for generally encouraging me in this project, and deeply regret that due to his untimely death he did not see its completion.

18. She is understandably misidentified in several volumes at the Fogg Fine Arts Library of Harvard University, confused with another Mrs. Foster who wrote a handbook on Italian literature, and who is, of course, also known by her husband's name. This practice, even for those who find it generally harmless, must often have resulted in similar confusion, making it difficult to unearth biographical information about women.

19. The comments are those of E. H. and E. W. Blashfield and A. A. Hopkins in the Preface of their annotated edition of *Lives of Seventy of the Most Eminent Painters, Sculptors and Architects* (New York: Scribner's, 1896), p. 6. Having thus paid homage to the English lady, they go on to speak of her failings. Nevertheless it is her "direct and simple" translation that they chose to use as their basic text.

20. Foster, *Lives of the Most Eminent Painters,* p. 240.

21. Ibid., p. 237.

22. *Oxford Companion to English Literature,* ed. M. Drabble and J. Stringer (Oxford: Oxford University Press, 1987), p. 257.

23. *The Works of Mrs. Hemans* (Philadelphia: Lea and Blanchard, 1840), vol. 5, p. 167. Page numbers in the text refer to this edition.

24. *The Obstacle Race* (London: Pan Ltd., 1981), p. 210.

25. Ibid., p. 348, n.8.

26. *The International Dictionary of Women's Biography,* ed. Jennifer S. Uglow (New York: Continuum, 1982).

27. *The Women Artists of Bologna* (London, 1907), pp. 182–83. Page numbers in my text refer to this work.

28. To Ragg's credit she notes that this useful remedy "was not available to a woman of Properzia's class and time." Ibid., p. 183. Griselda Pollack assumes for some reason that Properzia was an aristocrat, and argues that her class might have been an advantage since she was outside the ordinary training system. See *Old Mistresses: Women, Art and Ideology* (New York: Pantheon, 1981), p. 17.

29. See, e.g., Fortunati's rude dismissal of Ragg below, p. 57. Germaine Greer credits Ragg only with summing up information, while Greer is often undervalued by other feminists. Parker and Pollock in *Old Mistresses* fail to emphasize that Greer published many of the same conclusions about the difficulties for women artists before they did. Other feminists also vociferously disdain Greer for

continuing to use the concept of the artist as "genius." They believe that any such recognition of a superior individual necessarily underestimates the importance of "context," as, e.g., it is discussed in Part Two of the present volume.

30. She explains exactly where the houses were, showing Malvasia's house to be only three minutes walk away. Ragg, *Women Artists,* p. 179.

31. For an excellent analysis of the inequality of Renaissance women, see Joan Kelly-Gadol's "Did Women Have a Renaissance?" in *Becoming Visible,* eds. Bridenthal and Koonz (Boston: Houghton Mifflin, 1977), pp. 137–64.

32. This idea of the desirability of gifted women performing as amateurs rather than working as serious professionals goes at least as far back as Plato. Although the philosopher queens of *The Republic* were intended to perform the same onerous "professional" duties as male guardians, by the time Plato wrote the more reality-based *Laws,* his prescriptions for women had changed. He no longer found it quite as desirable for them to perform as experts. And since then many male theorists to the present day have emphasized the desirability of women remaining gifted amateurs.

33. *The Obstacle Race.* Page numbers in my text refer to this work.

34. See Werner's Introduction in *Lives,* p. viii.

35. My contention is that any such "translation" to another size is both unnecessary and undesirable. An analysis of the critical appreciation of medieval ivories, Holbein minatures, etc., suggests that, in fact, observers have historically been able to consider each object in its own terms. Appreciating small works, as well as enormous ones such as Eastern Island stone sculptures or very large Chinese terra-cotta figures, involves taking them as they are. Phenomenologically, judging such objects need not involve any act of changing their scale.

36. Pliny reports with admiration the *microtechnia* of Theodorus, Myrmekides, and Kallikrates. He gives the well-known example of an ancient work in marble of a four-horse chariot and charioteer that could be covered by the wings of a fly. The author of the modern commentary on Pliny's text, Eugenie Sellers, thinks the chariot may be apochryphal but compares it to an existing example of the art of the goldsmith, a tiny chariot led by a Nike, with Erotes at each side, which is part of an ear pendant. These seems to have been admired more widely than Greer would admit. See *The Elder Pliny's Chapters on the History of the Art,* trans. by K. Jex-Blake (Chicago: Argonaut, 1968), pp. xxxvi, 43, and 215–16, n. 8.

37. "*Per una storia della presenza femminile nella vita artistica del cinquecento bolognese: Properzia De Rossi 'schultrice,'*" in *Il Carrobbio,* 7, 1981, p. 168. Page numbers in my text refer to this article.

38. She quotes this from M. Minghetti, *Le donne italiane nelle belle arti al sec X e XVI,* p. 311.

39. See Harris and Nochlin, *Women Artists,* and Havice, below p. 73.

40. Cf. the critique by Julie Levinson of conventional Hollywood "women's weepie" films whose heroines were defined and fulfilled solely through their relationships with husbands, lovers, and children and inevitably disappointed by them. See below, p. 140.

41. This attribution is assumed by M. Fanti, director of the Fabricca and included in his *La Basilica di San Petronio in Bologna,* vol. II (Bologna, 1948).

42. "La scultura di Amico Aspertini" in *Paragone* (Florence, 1965).

43. I am indebted to Professor Fred Licht for this suggestion. Professor Licht, an authority on Italian sculpture and author of a major work on Antonio Canova, agrees that the two reliefs are not by the same hand.

44. *Old Mistresses* (New York: Pantheon, 1981), p. 26.

45. See, for example, the study conducted at the Greenville, South Carolina County Art Museum, K. Freeman, "Gender Stereotypes in the Aesthetic Eye," *Radcliffe Quarterly,* 74, no. 2 (June 1988), p. 5.

46. Charles Perkins found both reliefs, which he believed to be by Properzia, "cold and uninteresting." *Italian Sculptors,* p. 241.

47. Along with the myth of the vastly stronger urges to promis-

cuity in males than in females that pervaded Victorian times and has persisted in sociobiological theories in our own day, there has sometimes subsisted a conflicting myth of women's insatiability. For an exploration of this duality in men's views of women, see Natalie Harris Bluestone, *Women and the Ideal Society: Plato's Republic and Modern Myths of Gender* (Amherst: University of Massachusetts Press, 1987), pp. 184–85. It may be the latter view of women as dangerous seducers that was in the minds of the male writers of the Old Testament. It is interesting to note in this connection that the Hebrew word used to describe Potiphar as the chief of Pharoah's guards, who were eunuchs, often led readers to assume that the officer was himself sexually neuter. Poor Mrs. Potiphar! See, for example, R. Seguineau and O. Odelain, *Dictionary of Proper Names and Places in the Bible,* p. 308.

48. Even the staunchest feminists are quite willing to see Artemesia Gentileschi's biography as a factor in her portrayal of themes of violence against men. Both Greer in *The Obstacle Race* and more recently and in great depth Mary Garrard in *Artemesia Gentileschi: The Image of the Female Hero in Italian Baroque Art* (Princeton: Princeton University Press, 1989) make use of the grim details of Artemesia's rape and other suffering at the hands of men to interpret her work.

49. I would like to express here my personal debt to all those who helped me in preparing this essay. This includes the many librarians in Florence, Bologna, Cambridge, Brookline, and Lyndonville, Vermont who aided me in my research. I also wish to thank my friends Hugh and Judy Amory, Judy Kantrowitz, Meg and Fred Licht and Annette Pringle for their encouragement, suggestions, and help with translations. I wish to acknowledge The National Endowment for the Humanities for a Travel Grant. And as always I am deeply grateful to my children, Hanya and Sasha, and my husband, George, for their patience and continuing support.

Part Two
Women as Patrons: Toward an Expanded Concept of Agency

3

Women and the Production of Art in the Middle Ages: The Significance of Context

CHRISTINE HAVICE

THE SCHOLAR OF MEDIEVAL ART NORMALLY WORKS WITHOUT DATA WHICH REVEAL THE PERsonality, or even the identity, of the maker of the physical object. Accidents of survival are partly responsible—much medieval art has been destroyed or lost—but more significantly, medieval art was created in a context that can be characterized less by the action of a single individual than by the intervention and collaboration of two, three, or more agents, some acting on behalf of even larger groups, such as families or institutions. More often we have sufficient evidence to identify the sponsor(s) for whom a work was made, and recent art historical scholarship has begun to sketch in the outlines of patronage and patron-artist relationships during this lengthy and not at all homogeneous period of more than one thousand years. What emerges is a nexus of relationships and interactions that do not readily suggest themselves in our current usage of the terms "artist" and "patron." Furthermore, certain works of medieval art began as the visions or interpretations of authors, some of whom, working in a predominantly visual culture where literacy was little evident and largely unnecessary, saw to the translation of their words into images. While not artists in the strict sense, nor patrons in the fashion which emerged from the Renaissance, these authors must be imagined leaning, literally or figuratively, over the shoulder of the illuminators who created the original physical equivalents to their visions and words.

This expanded concept of agency in the creation of medieval works of art grows out of an increasing need on the part of current scholars to describe better the complex interreactions and decisions that condition those works. Research over almost two decades has sought both to identify women and men—not necessarily functioning as artists—who were involved in artistic production, as well as to understand the nature of the roles they played. To find the women in particular, we have had to examine widely dispersed sources and material evidence, frequently difficult to interpret and lacking the systematic synthesis that begins to characterize later periods. Medieval historians, in all disciplines, have had to base their efforts of recovery on indirect evidence, which can take the form of hagiography, traditional accounts, or literature and which reflect ideals even more clearly than they do actual practice or fact. As we focus here on medieval women who shaped works of art, we will make use of traditional secular and legendary accounts that offer important readings or versions of art practice and that throw into relief ideas not regularly encountered in other types of documents. Thus we broaden the range and types of evidence brought to bear on the question of women's role in the production of art at the same time as we broaden the terms by which we define women's participation.

Put another way, modern labels for the actors in the art world and contemporary terms for conceptualizing the process of production and reception are inadequate. To understand the art, and ultimately the people and culture within which it was generated and had meaning, the historian must add some flexibility to the traditional terms. This has become especially clear to me as an art historian looking for the evidence for women's participation in the medieval art world, but certainly the general method applies to all humans. What I propose to do here is to review selectively objects and scholarship by which to reconceptualize and better describe human agency, and women's role in particular, in the production of art during the Middle Ages. Within each of the categories "artists," "sponsors/commissioners," and "authors/visionaries," I propose to show, through the works of art, how we have used the terms to describe a range of differing interventions in the art-making process. In all cases, the fuller understanding of the nature of the intervention requires that we investigate the peculiar circumstances surrounding each work's creation—in short, its context—more carefully and with fewer preconceptions.

Artists

The quest to identify medieval women who physically made the objects we term art can be dated from Dorothy Miner's celebrated 1972 lecture, "Anastaise and Her Sisters."[1] Miner opened her lecture with a remark by Christine de Pizan in *The Book of the City of Ladies* (1404–5) on the contemporary painter, Anastaise,

> . . . who is so learned and skilled in painting manuscript borders and miniature backgrounds that one cannot find an artisan in all the city of Paris—where the best in the world are found—who can surpass her, nor who can paint flowers and details as delicately as she does, nor whose work is more highly esteemed, no matter how rich or precious the book is. People cannot stop talking about her. And I know this from experience, for she has executed several things for me which stand out among the ornamental borders of the great masters.[2]

The writer employs terms that reflect identifiable late medieval workshop practice: different tasks in the production of manuscripts were carried out by different specialists—the scribe copied the text, one artist executed the various sized initials, another filled in backgrounds of scenes and/or borders of pages, and the main artist painted figures and major objects represented in each figural composition. Miner and other scholars have debated how to interpret the above reference to Anastaise and to which portions of an illuminated book her "work" may be extended to include,[3] but even allowing for a certain inflation of reputation that we might expect in Christine's work on women of achievement, the evidence for the activity and reputation of a woman artist is indisputable. Moreover, Anastaise does not stand alone as an illuminator: Miner, referring to studies of tax and guild records pertaining to book production from the late thirteenth century onward,[4] noted the "substantial position" occupied by women artists. To this general picture, Annemarie Weyl Carr[5] adds further information on "Anastaise's sisters" by carefully reviewing signatures on manuscripts from convents and double monasteries—male and female houses governed side-by-side by a single superior—dating as early as the eighth century. Carr points out the early existence of female scriptoria or copying centers, of colophon signatures in the feminine, and of hagiographical texts that describe women illuminating and otherwise involved in book production. Some works from as early as the tenth century survive: the Gerona Beatus of ca. 975 CE, for example, bears the names of two illuminators, Emeterius the presbyter and Ende "pintrix," who seem to have worked together in the scriptorium of the double monastery of San Salvatore at Tabara (figure 3.1).[6] Carr painstakingly adds to the developing list a number of twelfth-century and later manuscripts in which many female illuminators may be identified: to Miner's famous example of the young painter Claricia, who represented herself swinging as the tail to an initial "Q" in a twelfth-century psalter from Augsburg,[7] Carr adds the self-portrait of the nun Guda in a tenth-century Homiliary (sermon book)[8] and lists a number of other manuscripts

Fig. 3.1. *The scriptorium and tower of S. Salvatore at Tabara (Spain), from the Beatus Commentary on the Apocalypse, Tabara. Madrid, Archivo Historico National, cod. 1097 B, fol. 168r, ca. 970.*

copied, and presumably also illuminated by women religious.[9] The evidence for the involvement of women in the production of the great Merovingian Gelasian Sacramentary and related works is not absolutely conclusive, but some scholars have suggested that these works were produced in convent workshops such as that at Chelles[10] founded by Charlemagne's sister Gisela. Carr points to several women's names in manuscripts of this group,[11] as well as to references to women illuminators in early medieval saints' lives.[12] As had Ende at Tabara, many of these women worked alongside monks in the scriptoria of double monasteries, which flourished through the twelfth century.

Now Guda, Ende, and others were nuns, "professional artists" in the sense that most of their energies went toward perfecting and practicing their skills. Anastaise, a laywoman, was evidently similarly dedicated, in return for which work she received pay. Claricia, the young laywoman learning to illuminate initials as part of her education in an Augsburg convent, may have gone on to practice that genteel art as an accomplished lady, as Carr points out,[13] but she probably was not a "professional" in any sense that we would today recognize. Thus, our deceptively straightforward category "artist" must be understood with some flexibility, conditioned by a fuller understanding of the various contexts in which medieval works of art were created and some appreciation for the ways in which these contexts varied from those more familiar in modern times (although the notion of some skill in painting as an index to a young woman's gentility had not altogether died out before our own century).

A further nuance to the term "artist" arises from an examination of needlework. This was the medium in which, until the end of the Middle Ages, women certainly made the greatest—although almost invariably anonymous—contributions.[14] The activity of women needleworkers across social classes and through time requires no elaboration, although the greater impermanence of their materi-

*Fig.3.2.   Death of Harold, detail, Bayeux Tapes-
try. Bayeux, Cathedral, ca. 1080s.*

als, the ubiquity of their labor and production, as well as the generally utilitarian nature of their products, have led art historians of more traditional mind to ignore or devalue both work and worker until recently.

Of the surviving pieces of medieval embroidery and tapestry, one of the best-known is that now in the Cathedral at Bayeux, the late eleventh-century embroidery traditionally known as "Queen Matilda's tapestry" (figure 3.2). Twentieth-century scholarship has modified the legendary attribution to William the Conqueror's consort and her ladies and now sees the "tapestry" as exemplifying both the technique of the embroidery known as "English work" *(opus Anglicanum),* for which medieval Englishwomen were celebrated throughout Western Europe, and the guiding and executing hands of Anglo-Saxon creators, evident in various iconongraphic and formal choices.[15] David Bernstein's recent study of the epic needlework story suggests most convincingly that the designer of the piece— including major compositions and many (apparently) minor motives—must have been a male cleric, most likely associated with the monastery of St. Augustine in Canterbury and working for William's brother, Odo, bishop of Bayeux, Earl of Kent and Viceregent of England.[16] The iconography and detail of the embroidery reveal a subtle, theologically and typologically intricate subplot in the selection and presentation of historical events. Bernstein takes this to indicate that the anonymous designer's sympathies lay with the Saxons.[17] Yet there can be no doubt that the actual handiwork, the embroidery, was done by women.[18] Bernstein fails to explain who these needleworkers were, where they came from, or how and where the tasks of designing and then embroidering were organized and carried out, although he does demonstrate that the designer—"master artist" in his words—must have had access to manuscripts in the libraries of both St. Augustine's and Christ Church.[19] Beyond these basic considerations, it remains unclear where the designer's role stopped and that of the executants began. There are details in the borders and stylistic, technical, and even color choices which must have been left to those involved in the embroidering itself. Nonetheless, in this famous example, we encounter the medieval woman artist in yet another relation to the work: (presumably paid) executants working rather closely to the specifications of a designer. This would correspond to practices that have continued into our own time in the studio organization of successful artists such as Henry Moore, for whom assistants and technicians carried out his sketches and designs.

However, it should also be noted that, with the most celebrated women for whose stitchery we have documentation, there is little indication that the artists worked with designs not of their own making. Carr reminds us of the renowned embroiderer Mabel, whom Henry III of England honored, of the Prioress Joanna of Lothen (Germany), who with her nuns made tapestries recounting the history of their convent, and of other professional women involved in creation of tapestries and embroidered pieces such as Agnes of Avion, who created a series of tapestries for Yolande of Soissons.[20] As well, there are recorded instances in which noblewomen, as Aelgiva, wife of Edward the Confessor of England, or Gisela, Queen to Stephen I of Hungary and sister of Henry II of Germany, worked—and sometimes signed—elaborate and precious ecclesiastical hangings and vestments.[21] In these cases we may assume the artist to have undertaken the tasks of generating the image (within, of course, the limits of current iconographic and formal convention, and probably in consultation with a church official or theologian and other needleworkers) and then executing it, also likely with some collaboration. Thus, the context of the conception, design, and execution of figured textile works must have been highly variable, within which the precise nature of the woman artist's participation must needs be carefully examined, free of the preconceptions and limitations that contemporary art world dynamics provide.

Legendary Artists

A special glimpse of women producing art is offered by legendary accounts circulating in the Middle Ages. There are two sets of these that are particularly instructive: one taken from Pliny the

Fig.3.3. *Thamar paints an image of the Virgin,*
from Boccaccio, De claris mulieribus.
Paris, Bibliotheque nationale, ms. fr. 12
420, fol. 86r, xvth century.

Elder's *Historia naturalis* and other Antique sources, the other wholly of medieval and later invention.

From the former I have selected three brief notices of women artists[22]—the Greeks Thamar (Gr: Timarete) and Irene, and the "Roman" Marcia—which enjoyed considerable popularity in the West toward the end of the Middle Ages and the early Renaissance. Boccaccio is presumably responsible for the widespread familiarity with those accounts, for they are included in his treatise *Concerning Famous Women (De claris mulieribus,* 1355–ca. 1359).[23] Numerous illustrated copies of this text were created, especially in the fifteenth century; they furnish us with images as well as texts representing (apparently) medieval women artists working in a range of media, including painting (figure 3.3), sculpture, weaving, and other textile arts. Apart from the fact that Boccaccio's is a free elaboration on an ancient text, the accounts and the images raise the question of the numbers of women in the cohort of late medieval artists. The facts, alas, do not bear out the promise implicit in the representations. The absolute numbers gleaned from tax rolls and guild rosters in the later Middle Ages do list both women sculptors and *enlumineresses,* but those numbers are relatively small. Miner[24] cites an unpublished study by Douglas Farquhar on the percentage of women in the guild of illuminators at Bruges, which he estimated to have increased from about 12 percent to about 25 percent through the middle of the fifteenth century, while Ann Sutherland Harris more recently published rather more modest figures for women painters in late medieval Italy,[25] even as she adduces substantial numbers of women at work in the "less skilled trades," such as textiles[26] and cooking and baking.[27]

The function of these legends, to dress both literally and figuratively conceptions of the past in modern form, becomes more readily apparent if we compare Boccaccio's account of the careers of Thamar[28] and Marcia[29] with that by Christine de Pizan, who mentions these ancient artists in a discussion just prior to the praise of her contemporary, the painter Anastaise.[30] Of Thamar, Boccaccio makes considerable effort to identify her father precisely, then states that Thamar scorned womanly duties and practiced her father's art, which, Boccaccio concludes, is even more praiseworthy in view of the spinning and weaving activities in which most women engage. By contrast, Christine devotes some time to establishing Thamar's dates through a discussion of the notion of the Olympiad, then praises Thamar's subtlety of mind as she abandoned more habitual womanly duties, for which subtlety Thamar continues to be celebrated "even today." Following Boccaccio and Pliny, Christine describes a marvelous painting of the goddess Diana that demonstrated Thamar's skill and specifically approves Thamar's craft and excellence. In the medieval pictorial tradition (figure 3.3 again), we see Thamar, an elegantly clad lady, painting an image of the Virgin rather than Diana and working in a minutely detailed medieval *atelier,* complete with male assistant who grinds her colors. These last details derive from none of the texts (this particular miniature comes from an illustrated Boccaccio) and may be due either to medieval convention or observed practice. We are left in the realm of conjecture, but clearly the image offers yet another, and independent, version of the text, and one not entirely at variance from contemporary practice.

In the case of the story of Marcia,[31] Boccaccio's interest in the artist reveals itself in the two substantial passages on her virginity which bracket his descriptions of her achievement with brush and chisel. Boccaccio returns to the subject of Marcia's "unique moral sensitivity" by asserting that, to avoid representing the male nude, the more common subject of ancient art, Marcia limited her subjects to women. Christine, by contrast, refers to Marcia's virginity in a single introductory epithet and instead concludes (omitting most of the hyperbole in Boccaccio) with praise of the artist's creation of her self-portrait, which moment becomes Marcia's identifying attribute in medieval painting.[32] The contrasting treatment of the female artist that we find in Boccaccio and Christine prepares us for Vasari and a host of subsequent learned authors, who consider first the personal and social assets of the woman artist, only secondarily her art. As Christine before us, feminist historians have sought to balance and refocus the discourse.

Perhaps the best-known legend of a medieval woman artist associates itself with the name of Sabina von Steinbach, alleged to have completed two sculptures (figure 3.4) for the south portal of Strasbourg Cathedral upon the death of her sculptor father, Erwin (d. 1318). The latter's work at

Fig.3.4. Ecclesia *and* Synagogue, *Strasbourg Cathedral, south transept portals, ca. 1225+.*

the cathedral is well documented. The legend of Sabina stems from a misreading and mistranslation of an inscription on the portal, which identifies one "Sabina" as the donor who made it possible for the sculptures to be cut from "petra dura" or hard (read "expensive") stone.[33] "Steinbach" is not a literal translation of "petra dura" and probably stems from some desire to elaborate the romantic legend that had grown up around the name of the (documented) Erwin. In fact, the style of the pseudo-Sabian figures, *Ecclesia* and *Synagogue,* indicates a manufacture of ca. 1225, some fifty years before the recorded activity of Erwin and long before his death, which in the legend provides the occasion for Sabina's intervention.[34] The truth that inheres in this legend, however, consists in its example of a Western medieval tradition: the woman artist who learns her craft from an artist-father (or some other male relative, such as husband, brother, or uncle). In these circumstances, the woman was unofficially but effectively an apprentice; given the structure of medieval society, only women of the artisan class would have had access to such training. Should the male artist die, on occasion the daughter/wife/sister/niece would inherit and run his workshop: Guild records from the late Middle Ages repeatedly describe wives as business partners and specifically allow for them to inherit and take over their deceased husbands' craft or trade.

Such opportunities for women in artisans' workshops characterize the later Middle Ages, when more of the task of art production shifted from monastic and clerical control to the professional laity. However, by the beginning of the Renaissance and thereafter, while the phenomenon of artist-daughters and artist-wives is well documented,[35] guild regulations increasingly disallowed the practice of female inheritance and management of male workshops.[36] At the same time, the twin processes of specialization and the aspiration to higher status for the visual artist gradually subdivided hierarchically the various tasks associated with production (whether that be of a painting or a saddle) among different hands, at the same time moving the specialized workshops away from the domestic setting— where women had moved from kitchen to worktable as needed—to separate, "professional" quarters, almost exclusively male.[37]

Thus, with changes in context, which varies considerably over time and from one part of Western Europe to another, these legends partially explain real situations and partly reflect ideals, not only of the past but also of a contemporary and rapidly changing society.

Sponsors and Commissioners

In Antiquity, the written sources provide us with many names of artists as well as some notion of the media in which they worked, the subjects which they handled, and important works for which they were especially noted. We have already noted medieval authors such as Boccaccio and Christine de Pizan who reworked such sources to celebrate their "famous women." In some cases we can associate the artists named in the ancient sources with surviving works of art, or with works now lost but well known through later attests. However, should we begin with a surviving work of visual art and attempt to identify historical individuals responsible for its production, from Roman times onward we are far more likely to discover a patron or recipient, rather than the executant artist. By "patron" we generally mean the individual for whom the work was made.[38] More specifically, the patron was often a commissioner, an individual who sought out and paid an artist. Sometimes the artist had already been retained or sponsored at court for such purposes or worked at the behest of an institution within a clerical or monastic setting, but in the later Middle Ages the artist was more often a layperson working independently or within an independent workshop, "for hire" and producing a work of art to the specifications of whomever initiated the transaction. As always during the medieval period, the final work of art followed certain general conventions, depending upon intended context and function and upon the nature of the image itself (its iconography or "message"). However, in a number of cases, the conventionality of the work may be altered or qualified according to the commissioner's stipulations, as we shall explore briefly.

Very early in the Middle Ages, some works can be explicitly or traditionally associated with particular individuals, male or female. For example, from the sixth century we have the reading desk of St. Radegonde, former consort of King Chlotar I, who (Radegonde) retired to the Abbey of Ste.-Croix at Poitiers and received at her request a relic of the True Cross from the Byzantine Emperor Justin II.[39] We also have the sarcophaghus of the abbess Theodochilde in the crypt of St. Paul in the Abbey of Notre-Dame in Jouarre[40] and that of the Lombard princess Theodota, from the Abbey of Sta. Maria della Pusterla and now in Pavia.[41] Since the late 1950s, sixth-century tombs of a Merovingian princess and queen have been excavated in Cologne and St. Denis (Paris) respectively, revealing extensive personal ornaments and grave goods.[42] In all these cases, however, it is difficult to define the context by which the art objects came into the possession of these aristocratic women: some may have been specifically made to order, but other works, on the basis of style or external evidence, seem to have been gifts from distant areas,[43] while some were probably acquired ready-made, or, in the case of the burials, were associated with the women only in the grave.[44]

On the other hand, certain objects and classes of objects were certainly commissioned by highly placed women and men, more than have actually survived. For example, we know as early as the fourth century CE that imperial women ordered paintings and other objects of Christian art: a letter reputedly from Eusebius to Constantia, sister of the Emperor Constantine, reproaches her for deputing him to fulfill her request for an image of Christ, apparently a painting.[45] Even though the authenticity of this document has been called into question (it may reflect eighth-century apologetics rather than fourth),[46] it describes a phenomenon evidently familiar in these centuries, as suggested by the daughter of Constantine I, Constanza, who paid for the building and decoration of a mausoleum, once attached to the Basilica of Sant-Agnese and now simply known as Santa Costanza, for herself and her husband. In the early sixth century, a famous example of an aristocratic woman commissioner is provided by the Constantinopolitan Juliana Anicia, recorded by inscription as the "patron" of the now destroyed Church of Hagia Polyeuktos, ca. 524–527.[47] The best-known product of Juliana Anicia's support of the arts is the magnificent herbal now in Vienna, a copy of Dioscorides's *De materia medica,* which contains an image celebrating her as sponsor of this manuscript and of works in other media, specifically architecture.[48] In the miniature, Juliana Anicia is accompanied by the personifications of Magnanimity and Prudence and receives homage from a figure identified as the "Gratitude of the Arts," while the encircling inscription and a series of grisaille putti also allude to her patronage of works in architecture. The specificity of the details which promote this reading of her qualities, goes beyond standard conventions of donor images—which, as this one, are concerned to indicate rank and status of the donor—and suggests that, as in the dedicatory inscription of H. Polyeuktos, Juliana Anicia directly intervened in determining the content, as well, perhaps, as the style. As this is both "an original creation" and, apparently, the "oldest dedication miniature in existence,"[49] it bears our attention.

The attempt to associate later Carolingian manuscripts produced in convent scriptoria with female commissioners does not, as we have seen in looking for records of women artists from this same period, prove especially rewarding. However, in the Germanic lands of the late tenth and particularly the eleventh centuries, we encounter numerous objects with which royal and aristocratic women were clearly involved as sponsors or commissioners. Even if we leave to one side a whole series of conventionalized portraits of women as royal or imperial partners in the act of donation or of receiving works—in manuscripts, on bookcovers, altar frontals, and various objects in ivory[50]—we still have a considerable range of works in which, by inscription or image or both, a female commissioner may be identified.

In the convent of the Holy Trinity in Essen, the abbesses Matilda (973–1011) and Theophano (1039–56) saw to the building of the church.[51] Matilda, granddaughter of the Emperor Otto I and sister to Otto, Duke of Bavaria and Swabia, had herself represented with her brother in enamel on one of two large processional crosses she gave to the convent.[52] Evidently another processional cross in the same convent was a gift to the community from the later Theophano.[53] Elsewhere, in 1006,

Gisela, wife of St. Stephen of Hungary and sister of the Emperor Henry II, had a large bejeweled and enameled crucifix made in Regensburg to be placed upon the tomb of her mother, Gisela, in the Abbey of Niedermünster.[54]

Two celebrated manuscripts of the early eleventh century also bear the imprint of powerful abbesses: Hitda of Meschede (978–1040) had herself represented in the act of offering her vividly illustrated Gospels to St. Walburgis,[55] who had herself been abbess of the double monastery at Heidenheim and companion to St. Boniface in his missionary activity to the Germans in the eighth century. This choice of dedication miniature is far from conventional and must reflect Hitda's desire to associate herself, through this presentation, with the powerful early abbess and saint.[56] An even more idiosyncratic intervention of an abbess, in this case the second Uota of Niedermünster (1002–25), may be observed in her Evangeliary in Munich.[57] One scholar has characterized Uota as having been "a woman of considerable intellectual abilities and exacting taste,"[58] and, if we are correct in ascribing to her intervention the particular forms of the miniatures of the Evangeliary, which latter is lavishly gilded and heavily inscribed, we may characterize this work as an early example of a religious commissioner who controls both content and form of the images accompanying a text. In Uota's case, the images are complex assemblages of both allegorical and traditional forms, the allegorical figures introducing contemporary theological comment, which is made specific by the lengthy texts worked into and around them.[59] That Regensburg was a center of early eleventh-century thought as well as artistic and literary activity seems to have furnished the context in which an ambitious, costly, and intricately constructed visual and textual statement such as Uota's codex could be designed and carried out.

In the High Middle Ages, we most frequently encounter women of the nobility as commissioners, or, at the least, underwriters (sponsors) of works in a range of media. For example, we know that Eleanor of Aquitaine (ca. 1122–1204) provided a place in her courts for poets working in the *trouvère* tradition, the founding of which is associated with her grandfather William IX. Moreover, Eleanor corresponded with many of her illustrious contemporaries, including the visionary mystic Hildegard of Bingen, of whom we shall have more to say shortly. The queen ordered the construction, according to tradition, of the Church of St. Pierre de Mons near her ancestral chateau in Belin.[60] With greater certainty can we credit her with the sponsorship of a marriage vase, given to Louis VII on the occasion of their marriage in 1137 and now in the Louvre.[61] At the royal abbey of Fontevrault, to which Eleanor retired in her later years, not only did she provide for the construction of the famous nuns' kitchen, which her daughter Joanna then endowed,[62] but the effigy on her tomb there, evidently made to her specifications, represents the recumbant queen in the act of reading from an open book (presumably a prayer book or psalter). This choice stresses Eleanor's literacy and intellectual accomplishment, as well as the more conventional feminine attribute of piety.[63] The multidimensional character of Eleanor's interest in and support for cultural expression is a paradigm for much of what we find when we look specifically for women who commissioned, or who sponsored the creators of, visual works.

Eleanor's granddaughter, Blanche of Castille, mother of the later St. Louis (IX) of France, left us documentation of her financial sponsorship of the decoration of the north transept of Chartres Cathedral in the form of her coats of arms—the lilies of France from her marriage to Louis VII and the castles of her native Castille—which are fitted into the spandrels below the rose window centering upon St. Anne and her daughter, Mary.[64] The iconography of the window, and of the sculptural program of the portals below, emphasizes the genealogy both of Christ, which culminates in the figures of his grandmother and mother, and, by extension, of the lineage of the sponsoring royal household, in the persons of Blanche and her son. Further, Blanche was an important commissioner and purchaser of illuminated manuscripts, first as consort to Louis VII (1223–26), then as Queen Mother until her death in 1252. Among her other acts of art patronage, she founded the Abbey of Notre-Dame-la-Royale at Maubuisson, consecrated in 1244, to which she subsequently presented numerous objects as furnishings to the church.[65]

In an important study of manuscript production in Paris during the time of St. Louis and Blanche, Robert Branner noted a significant number of works that can be specifically associated with the Queen mother.[66] The precise nature of Blanche's intervention in the modification of the conventional iconography has yet to be determined, but Branner notes that she was keenly interested in theology as well as art, a fact that he marshalls to help explain the distinctive iconography in the great moralized Bibles *(bibles moralisées)* of Toledo and Oxford.[67] Contemporary appreciation for this aspect of Blanche's interest in books and their illumination seems to be reflected in a famous miniature on the last folio of the Toledo moralized Bible, now in the Morgan Library (figure 3.5), where a queen and a king, usually identified as Blanche and Louis, are seated above a dictating monk and a busy scribe.[68] Louis is enthroned with orb and sceptre and turns to Blanche, who in return gestures with animation. Comparably, and we should understand as a result of the interaction above, the monk below the queen gestures toward the scribe, who bends to his task. We know that Blanche ordered manuscripts and that among these were some in which her son learned to read.[69] In addition, several miniatures exist that emphasize her role in the education of the future monarch and saint. Thus her role as teacher to the young king through the commissioning of books seems to be emphasized in this contemporary visual source.[70]

This significant, if often overlooked, role of women as users and commissioners of books was scrutinized carefully for the first time in 1982 by Susan Groag Bell, who highlighted the impetus that women as readers gave to the translation of religious texts into the vernacular tongues and the roles as transmitters of culture, across countries and through time, which women book owners played as they moved with dowries and family goods, taught their children, and made bequests to (largely women) family members of their precious books.[71] In particular, the Book of Hours, a private devotional book of prayers and readings to be used through the day, was associated with women, by use and by purchase or commission. Scholars can still identify, by the feminine nouns, pronouns, and adjectives in certain prayers, those Books of Hours which were written specifically for women. Some of the most celebrated illuminated manuscripts from the later Middle Ages were either made for or associated with women, such as those of Jeanne d'Evreux, Catherine of Cleves, Isabelle of Bavaria, Isabella Stuart of Brittany, Marguerite de Foix of Brittany, Anne of Brittany and Queen of France, Yolande de Lalaing, and many others.[72] The image of an elegant woman reading her devotions in the Hours now associated with Mary of Burgundy (1457–82) provides a paradigm as well as certain exceptional features (figure 3.6). The stylishly dressed reader protects her book with a green velvet cover and sits at her window casement with all the attributes of her station: a small lapdog, jeweled brooch, veil, cut flowers, and an embroidered purse.[73] The prayer to which she has turned in her book is the opening prayer to the Virgin in Books of Hours, "Obsecro te . . .," which frequently bears a miniature of the donor of the manuscript kneeling before the Virgin, whose praises constitute the unifying theme of the book. In this case, however, Mary has apparently seen fit to vary the type significantly by displacing the scene of adoring donor to the Gothic chevet onto which her window opens. The Virgin and Child appear before an elaborate altar, surrounded by angels with candles, and worshipped by Mary again, prayerbook tucked under her arm, with her retinue of ladies behind her at the left. This unusual minature occurs at a textually rather unimportant position in the book, at the prayer on the Seven Joys of the Virgin. We know that in other aspects of her life and patronage, Mary of Burgundy demonstrated special devotion to the Virgin—she was patron of the church of Notre Dame in Bruges. In her will (dictated on her deathbed), she several times named the Virgin as her special protectress[74] and she stipulated that a large statue of the Virgin be placed near her tomb. This association of the Virgin Mary and Mary of Burgundy seems to have been developed by others at the Burgundian court during the latter's lifetime and after her death, in order to stress her genealogy as the basis for the political and territorial claims of her offspring,[75] not entirely different from the association of Blanche of Castille with the genealogical and thus dynastic implications of the north transept program at Chartres. In Mary of Burgundy's Book of Hours, both the "image within an image" and its position in the text seem to reflect an idiosyncratic

Fig.3.5. Blanche of Castille and St. Louis (?), Bible moralissée. New York, N. Pierpont Morgan Library, M. 640, fol. 8r, ca. 1230s.

Fig.3.6.   Mary of Burgundy at prayer, Hours of Mary of Burgundy. Vienna, Oesterreichische Nationalbibliothek, cod. 1857, fol. 14v, ca. 1477.

choice that demonstrates the commissioner's strong will and interest an innovation, in this case a sort of *trompe-l'oeil* that prefigures the impending dramatic change in artistic values of the early Renaissance.

Two final examples of women commissioners of art will demonstrate the ways in which they could shape details of iconography to suit the particular circumstances of their lives, thus to correspond more precisely to their individual contexts. The Hours of Mary of Guelders, of 1415, bears a miniature (figure 3.7) of another elegant, aristocratic woman reading a book offered to her by an angel within a walled garden.[76] Despite the apparent fashion plate contemporary costume, the miniature is clearly intended as an allusion to the Annunciation, for a second angel approaches with a banderole inscribed "O milde Maria," a German echo of the "Ave Maria gratia plena" with which the angel greeted the Virgin Annunciate. Above we see God the Father who releases the dove of the Holy Spirit to descend upon this Mary. Such allusion to the Annunciation to the Virgin is confirmed by the walled garden, a *hortus conclusus* that refers both to the virginity of Christ's mother and to the garden of delights which will be Paradise, attained through Christ's sacrifice and the faith of the Christian believer. Panofsky connected these iconographic details to this manuscript's sponsor, Marie d'Harcourt, Duchess of Guelders, who remained childless in her marriage to Renaud IV. Panofsky saw in this miniature an unusual rendering of a traditional motif: the fifteenth-century duchess's childlessness is likened to the Virgin's unblemished state by the symbolic blue color of the robe, and her wish for a son and heir refers to the Virgin's own destination as mother to a son.[77] Among female commissioners of Books of Hours, invocation of the Virgin's aid to remedy childlessness was apparently not uncommon—Harthan cites Marguerite of Foix and Anne of Brittany as expressing similar longings in their prayerbooks[78]—but uniquely here, Mary of Guelders has directed the artist to alter the standard iconography in favor of her particular petition by audaciously painting her portrait for that of the Virgin.

A final example of the intervention of a female commissioner occurs in the Lincoln Typikon, a late Byzantine charter of donation and regulation for the convent dedicated to the Virgin of Good Hope in Constantinople.[79] The text, which was written in two chronologically distinct sections, is accompanied by a series of miniatures, also subdivided. The first miniatures contain the representations the *ktetorissa* or founder, Theodora, and her husband John Komnenos Doukas Synadenos, followed by the images of their sons and daughters and their consorts, all dressed in ceremonial garb to indicate their respective positions in the complex administration of the late Byzantine court.[80] Among the couples of adult children and spouses, it appears that "(t)here is a recognizable order of precedence according to the husbands' court-rank or lack of it," while their children (Theodora's grandchildren) appear to be ordered according to parentage. The opening miniature of the foundress and husband is followed on fol. 7r by another portrait of Theodora, now identified by her monastic name of "Theodoule" and dressed in monastic garb, with her husband, now "Ioakeim," and their small daughter, Euphrosyne, who is named in the cartulary as heiress to the convent. This second miniature testifies to their taking of monastic vows. Thus Theodora/Theodoule, as founder of the monastery and matriarch of the family,[81] visually sets forth the prominence and achievement of her family in a stunning series of detailed ceremonial portraits. Of special interest to us is the last series of three miniatures, which exhibit "a return to more strictly religious preoccupations,"[82] and which Cutler has shown to be later additions by the daughter Euphrosyne, who represents herself (now grown) led by her mother into the presence of the Virgin and Child. These latter receive the joint gift of the convent from mother and daughter (figure 3.8). This dedicatory pair of images is followed and concluded by the representation of the entire congregation of nuns, distinguished as to their convent status, who witness the presentation (figure 3.9).[83] Cutler carefully analyzes the several portrait modes used by the artist in these miniatures and concludes that the image of Theodora/Theodoule in the dedication pair is posthumous, with its masklike pallor, stylized form, and upturned eyes, to contrast with the lively, varied handling of the faces of Euphrosyne and the nuns of the convent. This distinction between the representation of living and dead can be identified in later

Fig. 3.7. *Mary of Guelders in a walled garden (An-*
nunciation). Berlin-Dahlem, Staatsbiblio-
thek, Stiftung Preussischer Kultgurbesitz,
ms. germ. quart. 42, fol. 19v, 1415.

Fig.3.8. *The* ktetorissa *Theodora/Theodoule and her daughter Euphrosyne present their convent, dedicated to the Virgin of Good Hope, to the Virgin and Child, from the Lincoln College Typikon. Oxford, Lincoln College, Ms. gr. 35, fol. 11r, ca. 1340s.*

Fig. 3.9   The congregation of the Monastery of the
Virgin of Good Hope, Constantinople,
from the Lincoln College Typikon. Oxford, Lincoln College, Ms. gr. 35, fol. 12,
ca. 1340s.

Byzantine art with some regularity and is not an innovation here; what is clear is that Theodora/ Theodoule and Euphrosyne successively intervened in the pictoral dynastic portrait laid out in Typikon to emphasize the eminence of first their blood laid out in the Typikon to emphasize the eminence of first their blood families, and then their family in spirit in the convent, which was founded by the mother for transmission to her daughter.[84] The large group portrait of the members of the convent, unusual in Byzantine art, must be credited to Euphrosyne's wish to demonstrate the continuity of her mother's investment and ideals through another generation.[85]

As sponsors of works of art, then, we can adduce numerous instances in which women intervened to emphasize or recast features of the final product, even as we must also suspect that many, perhaps even most by the later Middle Ages, simply acted as purchasers of ready-mades. Aristocratic and royal women seem to have acted to underscore concerns of genealogy or succession, whether in the world or in the convent, or to emphasize qualities of devotion and learnedness. A few cases of conventual sponsorship stressed spiritual filiation or theological erudition. In sum, women who sponsored or commissioned works of art, like their male counterparts, did so within definable conventions. While their absolute numers are smaller than those of their male counterparts, these women "patrons" shaped medieval art in ways that require us to acknowledge their contributions.

Authors and Visionaries

Two of the most celebrated women of the Middle Ages, Hildegarde of Bingen and Christine de Pizan, also occupy a place among those who shaped works in the visual arts. Both were writers and have been extensively studied, both in the most recent period of feminist interest and previously,[86] as authors and examples of women of achievement during periods when the rest of their sex remains relatively anonymous and unrecognized. Both might generally be classed among the commissioners and sponsors, but their roles in shaping the works of art go far beyond any we have thus far considered. As authors of works that required the provision of visual counterparts to their words, Christine de Pizan and Hildegard of Bingen each established the iconography of the images and, as logic dictates, must have participated in at least a supervisory manner in the actual process of the creation of those images at an initial stage.

It is as a mystic and visionary that Hildegard of Bingen (1098–1179) interests us primarily here, but we should also recall that she was an important author of both spiritual and medical texts, a correspondent to luminaries of her own time, an advisor and preacher, an administrator, a composer, and a playwright. Christine de Pizan (1365–ca. 1430) has been variously characterized as feminist or "proto-feminist" but was foremost a survivor by her courtly accuity and an activist by the products of her pen. We know both women today through their written works. Because those works were widely copied and frequently illuminated (ranging from simple decorative initials to complete figural compositions with settings), nonspecialists often first encounter these writers through reproductions of their portraits (figures 3.10 and 3.11). Actually, these portraits are highly conventionalized insofar as the individual physical traits of each subject are less important than the delineation of the activities in which each is engaged, and these activities are to some extent stereotyped by pose, gesture, and attribute. However, in our effort to broaden the definitions by which we identify women's involvement in the artistic process, a close examination of the images and texts associated with each writer is warranted.

The literature on Hildegard's visionary writing is immense and has received special impetus from late twentieth-century explorations of women's contributions to the Western tradition, as well as reawakened interest in expressions of personal spirituality. In this regard, many of the illuminations accompanying her most influential books, *Scivias* (1141–51) and *De operatione dei* (1163–73), have appeared in accessible form,[87] although the most thorough-going studies of both the writings and the miniatures accompanying them in their various copies may be found in scholarly, usually German,

Fig.3.10.   Hildegard of Bingen inspired and dictating
Scivias *to a scribe, opening miniature to*
the   Scivias.   Wiesbaden,   Landesbiblio-
thek, cod. minor 13 321, fol. 1v.

Fig.3.11. Christine de Pizan presents her book to Isabelle of Bavaria, detail. London, British Library, ms. Harley 4431, fol. 3v, xvth cent.

contexts.[88] We shall limit ourselves to examining two miniatures from Hildegard's works, as they reveal the role of the writer as transmitter of ideas and the relationship of the writer to the illuminations set forth.

In the opening of *Scivias* ("Know the Ways"), written in a sometimes abstruse language that Hildegard, probably self-taught and none too secure in Latin, devised to express her visions, the author has had herself represented in the act of receiving inspiration from heaven.[89] Five tongues of fire descend to engulf her head while Hildegard calmly sits, feet raised on a stool, marking on a wax tablet. Her male secretary, one of several who assisted her during her writing years, peers in to witness the source of the extraordinary vision as he records it, presumably at Hildegard's dictation. While the scribe seems to hold a codex into which to write, it is not clear that Hildegard herself also writes; the instrument she holds, a large stylus, may also be used for drawing. At this point, however, whether writing or sketching, the miniature proclaims Hildegard as medium of divine wisdom, while her secretary acts as requisite witness to this event.[90] This emphasis on the immediacy of her visions and on the fact that they come from outside her, uncontaminated by other elements, finds echo in a letter she wrote in 1175 to another (future) secretary, Guibert of Gembloux: "Whatever I see or learn in this vision, I retain as a memory for a long time, so that when I see or hear it, I remember it, and at the same time I see, hear, and know, and as if in an instant, I learn what I know. But what I do not see, I do not know, since I am uneducated."[91] Seeing is learning for Hildegard. This image stresses that, for her, knowing is directly transmitted, uncontaminated by any other intervening agent. Since the particular manuscript in which this miniature appears was copied and kept in Hildegard's convent on the Rupertsberg, most likely created during her lifetime, we may be justified in interpreting this miniature to reflect her specific instructions. Hildegard is the transmitter of the vision and the guarantor of the truth of its record, both in written and visual forms.

Further assertion of Hildegard's guidance in the images which accompany and body forth her visions[92] occurs in all ten of the visions contained in a manuscript of *De operatione Dei*,[93] probably copied within a generation of her death. Repeatedly the miniaturist has inserted, as in this image of the Cosmic Wheel (figure 3.12), the small, almost footnotelike, figure of Hildegard in her study, writing as she witnesses. As with the previous image prefacing the *Scivias,* this detail associates the visionary with the vision. On another level, it maintains the authority of the vision after Hildegard's death: this is how she saw and described it, and her presence in the lower corner indeed becomes the footnote that substantiates her as the source of the "quotation" above.

Accordingly, we must recognize in Hildegard, through the witness of the images in several of the manuscripts completed during or shortly after her lifetime, the artist as well as the author. On analogy with the "master designer" invoked by others as the source of the ideas of the Bayeux Tapestry, she was not responsible directly for the material production of the work of art (at least no twelfth-century sources so indicate). However, we can easily imagine her looking over the shoulders of the illuminators at St. Mattias's or critically examining their initial sketches or first completed miniatures. The unique qualities of Hildegard's cosmology and cosmogeny have been thoroughly explored from a variety of perspectives elsewhere; there is no question of her originality, and thus contemporary conventions would have been of little help in composing these images. Moreover, the miniatures which do illustrate her visions[94] follow her words closely and without deviation or error. We must hardly be surprised, then, to add her to our list of agents in the creation of medieval works of art. It is likely that the images that re-present her poetic and deeply mystical understanding of the world were the products not only of a careful reading of her sometimes difficult and highly colored words but also of her careful review and scrutiny during the process of their creation. The following generation of artists who illumined her works took pains to assure us of this continuing fidelity to her vision. It remains for us to scrutinize these same manuscripts for evidence of how this process actually occurred.

Hildegard, as author and "idea woman," stands in good company during this period and the later Middle Ages; several other words have analyzed in detail the text and images of the now lost *Hortus*

Fig.3.12   Hildegard's vision of the Cosmic Wheel,
De operatione Dei. *Lucca, Biblioteca
governativa, ms. no. 1942, ca. 1200.*

Deliciarum, composed by Herrad of Landsberg, Abbess of the convent at Hohenburg during the late twelfth century.[95] One of its most famous miniatures represents the inhabitants of the convent, with Herrade and, opposite, her own teacher, in a general Western counterpart to the Lincoln Typikon.[96] At the end of the Middle Ages, Christine de Pizan fulfills a similar role in generating new iconographies, creating a vision in writing, and seeing to its translation into the miniatures that illustrate the many copies of her works, such as the *Book of the City of Ladies* (1404/5) and *The Book of the Three Virtues* (1405) (to consider only those titles best known for setting forth Christine's views on women). Charity Cannon Willard has suggested that the newly widowed Christine may have worked first as a copyist of manuscripts before beginning to write her own works and so would have known firsthand the details of book production.[97] The conventional images of her as author generally feature her "sitting alone in [her] study surrounded by books on all kinds of subjects, devoting [her]self to literary studies."[98] They probably do not do justice to this woman's astute analysis of how a successful author, dependent upon the patronage of noble sponsors, should operate. Not only do we know that Christine worked to commission,[99] earning for herself the reputation of "the first professional writer," but she also wrote several texts independently but with a potential patron in mind, dedicating and then presenting these books to their destinator.[100] Intimately familiar with the book trade in Paris, Christine was well aware, as her remarks on Anastaise indicate, of the importance of miniatures and decorative borders as an embellishment and enhancement of the value of a book. In one of the most famous miniatures associated with this writer (figure 3.11), the very pomp of the setting within which she presents her book to Isabelle of Bavaria reminds us that she paid careful attention to the copying and illumination of her works.[101] The precise nature of this intervention has not yet been fully defined,[102] but what we know of Christine's experience as a writer and participant in the "Querelle des femmes" in the first years of the fifteenth century would lead us to expect her full and active attention to these important elements in the final presentation copy, and its own copies, of her words.

   Although not fitting comfortably into any of the foregoing categories, the women author-visionaries of the Middle Ages undoubtedly made important contributions to its art, contributions long recognized but falling outside of the traditional categories used to characterize the agents in a work's creation. The lack of an adequate conceptual descriptor for the nature of their contributions only indicates the impoverishment of contemporary appreciation for the complexity of the artistic process, or at least of the labels by which we have tried to understand that process in the past.

Conclusion

   In looking for women who were involved in the production of medieval art, scholars have demonstrated the failure of the modern construct of "artist as isolated and alienated hero." Well-known examples of medieval collaborative effort, the illuminated manuscript no less than the Gothic cathedral, have long been known. However, beyond specialists in the field, art historical and general scholarship has not responded thoughtfully: much medieval art is branded "craft" or "minor art," and little of its production or use is considered except stereotypically. The neglect of the context out of which these works were created and in which they were viewed and responded to leaves us unable to make much sense of the art, and, more significantly, unable to recognize patterns of human behavior other than a few which are superficially defined.

   Feminist scholarship in the arts since 1970 has identified and criticized some of the institutional and structural factors that have shaped and perpetuated the myth of the "artist as hero."[103] And it has exposed the sexist bias inherent in that myth, pointing out where, when applied to women, the myth does not offer the symmetrical possibility.[104] These and other scholars have repeatedly demonstrated the slim "historicity" of the discipline of art history and have called for the most careful scrutiny of context, not simply as "background" but as the matrix out of which all human expression originates and within which it is given meaning.[105] Sociologists, anthropologists, and ethnologists—and art historians who have worked in close conjunction with them—have been thoughtfully involved in the consideration of the complexities of the creative processes beyond those normally accommodated by art historical classification, and in some cases specifically the making of visual art.[106] We, in other art historical specialties, have been rather slow to notice. In 1962, George Kubler recounted that the great medieval art historian Henri Focillon passed his last years troubled by the thought that we can never truly understand the configuration which gives rise to the present, or the object, unless we stand outside of it, at which point we also lack what we need to truly understand. For Kubler, "configurational analysis" became impossible and led to adopt a more strictly formalist and materialist approach to the "history of things."[107]

"Context," as I have been calling it, may well not be susceptible to absolute definition, but its complexity should not deter us from approaching and querying it. Recently, in a critique of Panofsky's classic definition of iconology, Suzanne Preston Blier showed that in African art—and by implication, in the arts of other areas and other periods in human history—the construction of meaning in and for a work takes place beyond the activities of artist and "patron" or commissioner, residing as well in the formulations by cultural spokespersons and in the experiences of beholders or "users" after the object had been manufactured.[108] Put another way, she considers the context, on its own terms, as the *locus* of the creation of meaning, and she demonstrates that any particular meaning exists in a state of continuing change and reinterpretation.

The analysis of women's agency in the production of medieval art that I offer here analogously sketches in highly varied conditions in which or by which these women participated. Not all the conditions can be precisely described, and no single description adequately conveys the different types of female agency in the creative process: Hildegard was an artist through her visions although she did not directly put paint to parchment; the anonymous Anglo-Saxon needleworkers executed the designs of one whom contemporary scholarship terms "master artist"; and a long series of aristocratic women reshaped the details of conventional imagery to better convey their individual ideals or familial dignity. Without a broader approach to medieval art making, without greater attention to that elusive yet signally important circumstances of context, these women would be lost from view.

Notes

1. Delivered on April 23 on the occasion of the opening of the exhibition "Old Mistresses—Women Artists of the Past" at the Walters Art Gallery and published in 1974 by the Baltimore Bibliophiles to celebrate their twentieth anniversary.

2. Miner, "Anastaise," p. 8; the translation here is from *The Book of the City of Ladies,* trans. E. J. Richards (New York, 1982), p. 85.

3. Miner, "Anastaise," p. 21. She refers to the scholarly opinions of M. Meiss, *French Painting in the Time of Jean de Berry,* I (New York, 1967), p. 3 and H. Martin, *Les Miniaturistes français* (Paris, 1906), pp. 85–86. A. W. Carr, "Women Artists in the Middle Ages," *The Feminist Art Journal* (Spring 1976), p. 5, follows the more conservative interpretation of the passage from Christine in identifying Anastaise as a painter of borders and backgrounds alone.

4. Miner, "Anastaise," pp. 22, 24; F. Baron, *Bulletin archéologiques du comité des travaux historiques et scientifiques,* n.s. 4 (1968), pp. 37–121.

5. Carr, "Women Artists in the Middle Ages," pp. 5–9, 26, esp. pp. 5–8.

6. J. Williams, *Early Spanish Manuscript Illumination* (New York, 1977), frontispiece and pp. 92–99, and J. Marques Casanova, et al., *Sancti Beati Liebana in Apocalypsin Codex Gerundensis* (Oltun and Lausanne, 1962). Wherever possible for this and subsequent works of art cited, I have tried to refer the reader to reproductions in readily accessible publications.

7. Miner, "Anastaise," pp. 11–12 and figure 14; comparison with other, "fine[r]" miniatures in this German psalter led Miner to conclude that Claricia was a student in the convent, who learned painting of miniatures as an amateur under the tutelage of a "finished, experienced artist" whom Miner refers to in the masculine.

8. Carr, "Women Artists in the Middle Ages," p. 5.

9. Ibid., pp. 5–6.

10. Ibid., p. 5.

11. Ibid., p. 6.

12. Ibid., p. 6.

13. Ibid., p. 6.

14. R. Parker, *The Subversive Stitch: Embroidery and the Making of the Feminine* (London, 1984), argues that the general anonymity of the maker and the invisible, because ubiquitous, nature of the work made it over the centuries a "naturally revolutionary art" even as its practice served to inculcate and propagate certain limited definitions of femininity. Carr, "Women Artists in the Middle Ages," pp. 8–9, also included discussion of needleworking in her 1976 survey.

15. Carr, "Women Artists in the Middle Ages," p. 8; A. Sutherland Harris, "Introduction: Medieval Women Embroiderers," in A. S. Harris and L. Nochlin, *Women Artists, 1550–1950* (New York, 1976), p. 16; Parker, *The Subversive Stitch,* pp. 26–28, considers the

"tapestry" from the point of view of the persistence of its attribution to Queen Matilda and the romantic view of women and femininity attaching to that tradition.

16. David Bernstein, *The Mystery of the Bayeux Tapestry* (Chicago, 1986), pp. 28–36, 37–50, 60–88, and esp. 162–64.

17. Ibid., pp. 51–59, 82–88, and esp. Part III, pp. 166–95.

18. Curiously, Bernstein, *Bayeux Tapestry*, after demonstrating the legendary nature of the attribution to Matilda, does not treat at all of the identity of the needleworkers. Presumably, he adduces the "circumstantial evidence of English origin" (pp. 38–39), with reference to other examples of *opus Anglicanum* done by women of all classes, in order to explain the identity of the needleworkers of the "tapestry." While the author quickly elaborates (pp. 37–50) the circumstances of inspiration and realization of the work by the "master artist" (used interchangeably with "master designer"), his consideration of the mechanics of production of the actual work stops at this point. For an earlier but corrective marshalling of the evidence, see A. G. I. Christie, *English Medieval Embroidery* (Oxford, 1938), esp. Appendix I.

19. Bernstein, *Bayeux Tapestry*, pp. 60–81.

20. Carr, "Women Artists in the Middle Ages," pp. 8–9; see also the detailed summary in Harris, "Introduction: Medieval Women Embroiderers," in *Women Artists, 1550–1950*, pp. 15–17; and Parker, *Subversive Stitch*, "Fertility, Chastity, and Power," pp. 40–59.

21. U. Thieme and F. Becker, *Allgemeines Lexikon der bildenden Künstler* (Leipzig, 1908–36), I, p. 96 (Aelgiva) and XIV, p. 197 (Gisela). We will encounter Gisela further on as an important commissioner of works as well as creator. Further references to individual aristocratic women and professional women needleworkers may be found in Harris, pp. 15–17, and in Parker, *Subversive Stitch*, pp. 40–59.

22. While Pliny's text contains notices of women artists working in several media, including sculpture, I have chosen here to concentrate upon the accounts of the painters, as they seem to offer the greatest possibility for comparison to known instances of women painters, as we have seen.

23. Caps. 54, 57, and 64.

24. "Anastaise and Her Sisters," p. 24.

25. Harris, *Women Artists, 1550–1950*, p. 14, n.6.

26. Including "belt makers, silk spinners, lace makers, embroiderers, linen manufacturers" (p. 14, n.4). For a broader consideration of the various trades in which women are recorded to have participated, see the edition of Etienne Boileau's *Le livre des métiers*, ed. R. de Lespinasse and Fr. Bonnardot (Paris, 1879).

27. Cf. also the general treatments of women and work during the Middle Ages in E. Power, *Medieval Women*, ed. M. M. Postan (Cambridge, 1975) and F. Heer, *The Medieval World* (London, 1961); S. Shahar, *The Fourth Estate: A History of Women in the Middle Ages* (London, 1983), pp. 189–210; M. A. Labarge, *A Small Sound of the Trumpet* (Boston, 1986), pp. 143–218; and B. S. Anderson and J. P. Zinsser, *A History of Their Own: Women in Europe*, vol. 1, *From Prehistory to the Present* (New York, 1988), esp. chap. V, pp. 353–430.

28. Giovanni Boccaccio, *Concerning Famous Women*, cap. 54; in this and subsequent references to this text, I use the 1963 translation by G. A. Guarino (New Brunswick, N.J.).

29. Cap. 64.

30. Christine de Pizan, *The Book of the City of Ladies*, I.41.1–3; Anastaise is the subject of I.41.4.

31. The Greek form of this name is Iaia, later corrupted to Lala. She was misidentified in Boccaccio as Roman because he understood her to have been the daughter of Varro.

32. For a reproduction of one such image of Marcia, see V. W. Egbert, *The Mediaeval Artist at Work* (Princeton, 1967), figure XXXI.

33. The inscription reads "GRATIA DIVINAE PIETATIS ADESTO SAVINAE / DE PETRA DURA PER QUAM SUM FACTA FIGURA" (in H. Reinhardt, *La Cathedrale de Strasbourg* [Paris, 1972], p. 101, n.5). The earliest recorded version of this story dates from the seventeenth century, but it appears to derive from previous oral tradition.

34. Reinhardt, *La Cathedrale de Strasbourg*, p. 101.

35. Harris, "Introduction," to *Women Artists, 1550–1950* (New York, 1976), pp. 13–44. Note the catalog entries for Lavinia Teerlinc, ca. 1520–76 (by Harris, pp. 102 ff.), Caterina van Hemessen, 1528–post 1587 (by Harris, pp. 105 ff.), Lavinia Fontana, 1552–1614 (by Harris, pp. 111 ff.), and Fede Galizia, 1578–1630 (by Harris, pp. 115 ff.). By way of example, of the first six artists presented in the catalog, these four were born into families headed by artist fathers.

36. B. S. Anderson and J. P. Zinsser, *A History of Their Own: Women in Europe*, vol. 1, *From Pre-History to the Present* (New York, 1988), pp. 392–94; also M. C. Howell, *Women, Production, and Patriarchy in Late Medieval Cities* (Chicago, 1986), and M. E. Wiesner, *Working Women in Renaissance Germany* (Rutgers, 1986).

37. R. Parker and G. Pollock, *Old Mistresses: Women, Art and Ideology* (New York, 1981), pp. 14–20; J. Kelly-Gadol, "Did Women Have a Renaissance?" *Becoming Visible: Women in European History*, ed. R. Bridenthal and C. Koonz (Boston, 1977), pp. 137–64; cf. also Anderson and Zinnser, as above.

38. For the moment, I disregard the gender-specific etymology of the word "patron"—the substitution of its linguistically symmetrical "matron" here promises only confusion and carries its own charge that may complicate the definition which I will attempt to develop.

39. P. Lasko, *The Kingdom of the Franks: North-West Europe before Charlemagne* (New York, 1971), figures 59, 60, and pp. 73–77, and also G. Henderson, *Early Medieval* (Baltimore, 1972), figures 139, pp. 213–14; on Radegonde herself, the primary sources are by the nun Baudonivia, *De vita s. Radegundis Liber II*, ed. B. Krusch, *Monumenta Germaniae Historica Scriptorum rerum Merovingicarum* 2:377–95, the poet Fortunatus, *De vita sanctae Radegundis*, ed. B. Krusch (*Monumenta Germaniae Historica: Scriptorum rerum Merovingicarum* 2: 368) and St. Gregory of Tours, *Historia francorum* (*Monumenta Germaniae Historica Scriptorum rerum Merovingicarum* 1). Twentieth-century studies of Radegonde and of the text written by Baudonivia include R. Aigran, *Sainte Radegund* (Paris, 1918), L. Coudanne, "Baudonivie, moniale de Sainte-Croix et biographe de sainte Radegonde," *Études mérovingiennes: Actes de Journées de Poitiers*, 1952 (Paris, 1953), pp. 45–51, and G. Marié, "Sainte Radegonde et le milieu onastique contemporaine," *Études mérovingiennes: Actes de Journées de Poitiers*, 1952 (Paris, 1953), pp. 215–19. For treatment of Radegonde from recent feminist perspectives, see S. F. Wemple, *Women in Frankish Society* (Philadelphia, 1985), pp. 38–39, 140, 183–85; J. McNamara, "A Legacy of Miracles: Hagiography and Nunneries in Merovingian Gaul," *Women of the Medieval World*, ed. J. Kirshner and S. F. Wemple (Oxford, 1985), pp. 40, 45, 46–47; and M. Skinner, "Benedictine Life for Women in Central France, 850–1100: A Feminist Revival," *Distant Echoes: Medieval Religious Women*, vol. 1, ed. J. A. Nichols and L. T. Shank (Kalamazoo, Mich., 1984), pp. 87. An image of Radegonde, from an eleventh-century illustrated copy of the vita by Baudonivia, appears in M. W. Labarge, *A Small Sound of the Trumpet: Women in Medieval Life* (Boston, 1986), figure 2.

40. Lasko, *The Kingdom of the Franks*, figures 94, 96, and pp. 97–100. Theodochilde was the first abbess of the convent of Notre-Dame at Jouarre, which was founded by her uncle, Adon, brother of St. Ouen; Theodochilde's brother, Agilbert, bishop of Wessex, who is recorded speaking at the Synod of Whitby in 664, is also buried nearby in this crypt.

41. R. Salvini, *Medieval Sculpture* (Greenwich, Conn., 1969), figure 6 and catalog entry, p. 309, along with earlier bibliography; this sarcophagus appears to postdate Theodata's death by about fifteen years, so its relation to her as commissioner is unclear.

42. Lasko, *The Kingdom of the Franks*, pp. 46–51 and figures 41–43 on the tomb of the princess, and figures 46–52, pp. 55–58 on the Queen's tomb, which may be that of Chlotar I's first wife, Arnegonde, and certainly does not date much later than about 570 CE.

43. The reading desk of St. Radegonde appears to have East Christian (or Byzantine) characteristics, according to Lasko, p. 74.

44. For a discussion of the various styles and of the sources of the various objects in the tomb of the Merovingian queen, one of which appears to have been a man's belt, see Lasko, pp. 55–58.

45. An English translation of part of this document is contained in C. Mango, *The Art of the Byzantine Empire, 312-1453 (Sources and Documents in the History of Art Series)*, ed. H. W. Janson (Englewood Cliffs, N.J.: 1972), pp. 16–18.

46. Sr. C. Murray, "Art and the Early Church," *Journal of Theological Studies*, n.s. 28, pt. 2 (1977), pp. 326–36 in particular.

47. T. F. Matthews, *The Early Churches of Constantinople: Architecture and Liturgy* (University Park, Penn., 1971), p. 52; the inscription is contained in the *Greek Anthology*, I. 10, trans. Paten, I, 6–11, and has a commentary (scholia) on lines 5–6 noted in the *Anthologia graeca*, ed. H. Studtmüller (Leipzig, 1894), vol. 1, p. 6.

48. Vienna, Nationalbibliothek, ms. med. gr. 1, fol. 6v; reproduced in K. Weitzmann, *Late Antique and Early Christian Book Illumination* (New York, 1977), pl. 15.

49. Weitzmann, *Late Antique and Early Christian*, p. 61.

50. Just a sampling may be found in manuscripts and ivories of the late tenth and first half of the eleventh century: Otto II, his Byzantine princess wife Theophano, and their son Otto III, on a panel (J. Beckwith, *Early Medieval Art* [New York, 1964], figure 109); Henry II and Empress Kunigunde, in the Pericopes of Henry II (1002–114) (Beckwith, figure 94), Henry II and Queen Agnes, and Conrad II and the Empress Gisela, from the *Codex Aureus* of Echternach (1045–46) (Beckwith, figures 103 and 104).

51. W. Zimmerman, *Das Münster zu Essen* (1956); also Beckwith, *Early Medieval Art*, pp. 86, 234 n.11.

52. H. Schnitzler, *Rheinische Schatzkammer*, vol. I, no. 43; also Beckwith, *Early Medieval Art*, pp. 138–42, bibliography p. 240, n.42, and figures 126, and 127. The second processional cross bears a portrait in enamel of Matilda kneeling before the Virgin and Child, with partial later restorations; Beckwith, *Early Medieval Art*, p. 240, n.42.

53. Beckwith, *Early Medieval Art*, p. 240, n.42.

54. H. Schnitzler, "Zur Regensburger Goldschmiedkunst," *Wandlungen christlicher Kunst im Mittelalter, Forschungen zur Kunstgeschichte und christilichen Archäologie*, vol. 2 (Baden-Baden, 1953), 171 ff.; and Munich, *Residenz-Schatzkammer, Katalogue* (Munich, 1958), no. 8; also Beckwith, *Early Medieval Art*, p. 143 and figures 130–31.

55. Reproduced in Beckwith, *Early Medieval Art*, figure 98.

56. H. Ehl, *Die ottonische Kölner Buchmalerei (Forschungen zur Kunstgeschichte West-europas*, vol. 4 (Bonn and Leipzig, 1922); E. Schipperges, "Die Miniaturen des Hitdacodex in Darmstadt," *Jahrbuch des Kölner Geschichtevereins* vol. 79 (1937); *idem., Der Hitda-Codex, ein Werk ottonischer Kölner Buchmalerei* (Bonn, 1938); and A. Boeckler, "Kölner ottonishce Buchmalerei," *Beiträge zur Kunst des Mittelalters* (Berlin, 1950), pp. 144ff. English-language works referring to the Hitda codex include Beckwith, *Early Medieval Art*, p. 119 and figures 98, 99, and 101, and C. Nordenfalk, *Early Medieval Painting* (London, 1957), p. 210.

57. Munich, Stadtsbibliothek, Clm. lat. 13601; see Beckwith, *Early Medieval Art*, pp. 116–18. The manuscript is also provided with a sumptuous gold cover, studded with enamels, pearls, and other gems (reproduced in Beckwith, *Early Medieval Art*, figure 132). Other studies of this highly unusual work include B. Bischoff, "Literarisches und künstlerisches Leben in St. Emmeram während des frühen und hohen Mittelalters," *Studien und Mitteilungen zur Geschichte des Benediktiner-Ordens*, 51 (1933), pp. 102 ff.; A. Boeckler, "Das Erhardbild im Uta-Kodex," *Studies in Art and Literature for Belle da Costa Greene* (Princeton, 1954), pp. 219 ff.; and Nordenfalk, p. 213.

58. Beckwith, *Early Medieval Art*, p. 116.

59. Beckwith, *Early Medieval Art*, pp. 116–18. The texts seem to have been devised by one Hartwic, a theologian who had studied with the celebrated Fulbert of Chartres and was available to the cloister at Niedermünster.

60. A. Kelly, *Eleanor of Aquitaine and the Four Kings* (Cambridge, 1950), p. xi.

61. Kelly, *Eleanor of Aquitaine*, photo facing p. 20. The inscription on the base, evidently added at some point after the divorce in 1152, reads "Hoc vas Sponsa dedit Aunor Regi Ludovico, / Mitadolus avo, mihi Rex, sanctisque Surgerus." On the occasion of Eleanor's marriage to Henry II Plantagenet in 1152, the couple donated a stained glass window to Poitiers Cathedral, in which they were wed; in the window they kneel at its base and gesture upward to that which their generosity has provided. Another image of Eleanor and Henry made shortly after their marriage comes from the church of Langon, near Bordeaux, and pairs them on a figured capital. The capital displays what several authors have observed to be distinctly individualized features, thus a portrait (Kelly, p. ix; now in the Cloisters, New York).

62. Kelly, *Eleanor of Aquitains*, p. xi and photo facing p. 276.

63. Reproduced in *The Plantagenet Chronicles*, ed. E. Hallam (New York, 1986), p. 257.

64. Reproduced in S. Halliday and L. Lushington, *Stained Glass* (1976), p. 74, and in P. Cowen, *Rose Windows* (San Francisco, 1979), p. 6, and E. Mâle, *Chartres* (New York, 1983), figure 123. While the iconography of the entire Cathedral of Chartres was carefully worked out over several generations through the collaborative efforts of the church canons on the one hand and the sponsoring aristocracy and local guilds and confraternities on the other, the iconography of the North windows and portal—culminating as they do, both in the sculpted jambs and the stained glass, in the figures of St. Anne and the Virgin—is particularly appropriate to the roles of strong queens—Blanche and Eleanor her maternal grandmother—in the intricate political and dynastic claims of the members of the houses of Capet and Plantagenet.

65. Several of these *objets* are reproduced in R. Pernoud, *Blanche of Castille* (New York, 1975), in second photo section: a chalice and paten with the abbey's coat of arms, and a hanap and a statue of the Virgin and Child, as well as a renowned rock-crystal bishop's crozier.

66. Robert Branner, *Manuscript Painting in Paris during the Reign of St. Louis* (Berkeley, 1977), pp. 3–4 and p. 4, n.11, with further references on pp. 6, 48, and 50. Branner suggests other manuscripts which might be attributed to Blanche's instigation: Appendix VA, p. 204, entry on Arsenal 1186, for example.

67. Ibid., pp. 49–50.

68. Pierpont Morgan Library, M.640, fol. 8. One need note here, however, that the identity of the two royal figures is not secure; Branner, *Manuscript Painting*, sees them as "symbolic," p. 4, n.12, and the identification as not critical, although qualifying his opinion by concluding "the work might easily have been commissioned by Blanche for the household and been completed only under Saint Louis."

69. Branner, *Manuscript Painting*, p. 4, n.11.

70. It should be noted that this particular theme finds reflections in iconography of the early fifteenth century when we find a number of genrelike images of the Virgin instructing Christ. See E. Panofsky, *Early Netherlandish Painting* (Cambridge, 1953), vol. 1, pp. 99–100, on the *Spieghel der Maeghden* manuscript in London, of ca. 1415, "a manuscript which once belonged to the Convent of Our Lady in the Vineyard at Utrecht and may well have been illuminated by an art-loving nun rather than a professional" as well as the numerous images adduced by S. G. Bell, "Medieval Women Book Owners: Arbiters of Lay Piety and Ambassadors of Culture," *Signs: Journal of Women in Culture and Society*, VII, 4 (1982), pp. 742–68, with illustrations, in her discussion of the Virgin as a model for the female reader and teacher.

71. Bell, "Medieval Women Book Owners," pp. 742–68.

72. J. Harthan, *The Book of Hours* (New York, 1977), provides an excellent sampling of some of the more famous of these manuscripts, with both descriptions of some of the folios reproduced and very useful historical and genealogical settings within which to appreciate the bibliophilic activities of each donor. See also the many citations in Bell, "Medieval Women Book Owners," passim.

73. F. Unterkircher and A. de Schryver, eds., *Gebetbuch Karls des Kühnen vel potius Stundenbuch der Maria von Burgund, Codex Vindobonensis 1857*, 2 vols. (Graz, 1969); see also O. Pächt, *The Master of Mary of Burgundy* (London, 1948).

74. A. M. Roberts, "The Chronology and Political Significance of the Tomb of Mary of Burgundy," *Art Bulletin*, LXXI, 3 (1989), pp. 378–79.

75. Ibid., pp. 389–95.

76. Berlin (West)-Dahlem, Staatsbibliothek, Stiftung Preussischer Kulturbesitz, ms. germ. quart. 42, fol. 19v; K. Keller, *Zwei*

Stundenbücher aus dem geldrischen Herzogshause. Das Stundenbuch der Herzogin Maria und das ihres Gemahls (Geldern 1969).

77. E. Panofsky, *Early Netherlandish Painting* (Cambridge, Mass., 1953), vol. 1, pp. 100–101.

78. Harthan, *The Book of Hours,* p. 81.

79. Oxford, Lincoln College, Ms. Gr. 35. The fullest recent treatment of the miniatures concerned is by A. Cutler and P. Magdalino, "Some Precisions on the Lincoln College Typikon," *Cahiers archaeologiques,* XXVII (1978), 179–98, with earlier bibliography. Cutler and Magdalino spend a portion of their article refining the dating of this manuscript, which they conclude was probably made early in the period 1327–42 (p. 194). The text of the typikon is transcribed in full in H. Delehaye, *Deux typica byzantines de l'epoque des Paléologues* (Brussels, 1921), and, with other surviving typika for convents, is discussed for its insight into roles for women in Byzantium by A. Laiou in "Observations on the Life and Ideology of Byzantine Women," *Byzantinische Forschungen,* IX (1985), pp. 59–102.

80. For the precise identification of the figures in this manuscript, see Cutler and Magdalino, "Precisions," esp. section I by Magdalino (pp. 179–84) and section II by Cutler (pp. 184–91 and table, p. 193).

81. Magdalino, "Precisions," p. 181. see also A. Laiou, "The Role of Women in Byzantine Society," *Jahrbuch der oesterreichischen Byzantinistik,* XXXI, 1 (1981), p. 259, where the author identifies such self-awareness as manifest in this series of miniatures with the "aristocratisation" of late Byzantine society. Laiou further discusses the dynamics of the relationships made evident in the text of the typikon in "Observations."

82. Cutler, "Precisions," p. 194.

83. Cutler and Magdalino, "Precisions," pp. 194–98.

84. However, Laiou, "Observations," pp. 78–79, points out that the general supervision of the convent was vested in secular males in the family, beginning with Theodora/ Theodule's son.

85. The recent literature for the general topic of women religious in Byzantium includes A. W. Carr, "Women and Monasticism in Byzantium," *Byzantinische Forschungen,* IX (1985), pp. 1–15; D. De F. Abrahamse, "Women's Monasticism in the Middle Byzantine Periods: Problems and Prospects," *Byzantinische Forschungen,* IX (1985), pp. 35–58; and A. M. Talbot, "Late Byzantine Nuns: By Choice or Necessity?" *Byzantinische Forschungen,* IX (1985), pp. 103–17. For women in various roles in the history of Byzantium, J. Herrin, "In Search of Byzantine Women: Three Avenues of Approach," in *Images of Women in Antiquity,* ed. A. M. Cameron and A. Kuhrt (London, 1983), pp. 167–89, and the entry "Women," in the *Oxford Dictionary of Byzantium* (Oxford, 1991), pp. 2201–04.

86. The two most recent studies of Hildegard in English are S. Flanagan, *Hildegard of Bingen, 1098–1179: A Visionary Life* (London, 1989), and B. Newman, *Sister of Wisdom: Saint Hildegard's Theology of the Feminine* (Berkeley, 1987). On Hildegard as a writer, see P. Dronke, *Women Writers of the Middle Ages: A Critical Study of Texts from Perpetua to Marguerite Porete* (Cambridge, 1984), pp. 144–201; K. Kraft, "The German Visionary: Hildegard of Bingen," *Medieval Women Writers,* ed. K. M. Wilson (Athens, Ga., 1984), pp. 109–30 with extensive bibliography; and A. P. Brück, ed., *Hildegard von Bingen 1179–1979: Festschrift zum 800. Todestag der Heiligen* (Quellen und Abhundlungen zur mitterlrheinischen Kirchengeschichte, XXXIII) (Mainz, 1979). For Christine, apart from the many passing references in general surveys and anthologies on women in the Middle Ages, see C. C. Willard, "The Franco-Italian Professional Writer Christine de Pizan," in *Medieval Women Writers,* pp. 333–63, with earlier bibliography.

87. For example, *Illuminations of Hildegard of Bingen* (commentary by M. Fox) (Santa Fe, N.M., 1985).

88. In addition to Flanagan, *Hildegard of Bingen, 1098–1179: A Visionary Life,* and Newman, *Sister of Wisdom: Saint Hildegard's Theology of the Feminine* cited above, note J. Schomer, *Die Illustrationen der hl. Hildegard von Bingen als kunstlerische Neuschopfung* (Diss., Bonn, 1937), C. Meier, *Text und Bild im uberliefelten Werk Hildegarde von Bingen* (Wiesbaden, 1978), and C. Meier, "Die Bedeutung der Farben im Werk Hildegards von Bingen," *Frühmittelalterliche Studien,* VI (1972), pp. 245–355. See also K. Kraft, "Text and Illustration in Hildegard of Bingen's *Scivias,*" in *Literature and the Other Arts,* vol. 3, *Proceedings of the IXth Congress of the International Comparative*

Literature Association (Innsbruck, 1981), pp. 43–49.

89. Wiesbaden, Landesbibliothek, cod. minor. The manuscript is generally believed to date from Hildegard's lifetime but whether illuminated at her Rupertsberg convent or at St. Matthias at Trier has not yet been definitely established (Schomer, *Die Illustrationem der h1. Hildegaard,* p. 17).

90. This same idea is similarly represented, but apart from the process of *recording* it, which our miniature emphasizes, in the first vision of the *Scivias,* where the stream of light descends from God's throne onto the standing Hildegard's head and completely envelopes it (as reproduced in Labarge, *Small Sound of the Trumpet,* figure 30).

91. K. Kraft, trans., in *Medieval Women Writers,* p. 123.

92. For a complete listing of the relevant manuscripts, dates, and proveniences, see Schomer, *Die Illustrationen der h1. Hildegard,* pp. 2–18.

93. Lucca, Biblioteca Governativa, ms. no. 1942, dated by Schomer to ca. 1200; this image prefaces the second of Hildegard's ten visions in this text.

94. The fully illustrated copies of *Scivias* and *De operatione Dei* are the Wiesbaden codex B and the Lucca manuscript, both noted above.

95. Carr, "Women Artists in the Middle Ages," pp. 7–8; earlier bibliography, which is extensive, may be gleaned from G. Cames, *Allegories et symboles dans l'Hortus Deliciarum* (Leyden, 1971); for a facsimile of the drawings made before the manuscript was destroyed in 1870, see A. Straub and G. Keller, eds., *Hortus Deliciarum* (Strasbourg, 1899).

96. See the facsimile edition, fol. 323r. This was also reproduced in Carr, "Women Artists in the Middle Ages," figure 5.

97. Willard, "The Franco-Italian Professional Writer," p. 335.

98. Pizan, *The Book of the City of Ladies,* I.1.1.

99. The *Livre des fais et bonnes meurs du sage Roy Charles V,* written in 1404, was ordered by Philip the Bold for the French dauphin, for example.

100. The *Epistre de la prison de vie humaine,* after 1414, was dedicated to the daughter of the Duke of Berry, Mary of Berry.

101. London, British Library, Harlem ms. 4431, *Collected Works of Christine de Pizan,* fol. 3v. E. J. Richards, "Introduction" in *The Book of the City of Ladies,* trans. E. J. Richards (New York, 1982), p. xxi.

102. L. Schaefer, "Die Illustrationen zu den Handschriften der Christine de Pizan," *Marburger Jahrbuch für Kunstwissenschaft,* vol. 10 (1937).

103. T. Gouma-Peterson and P. Mathews, "The Feminist Critique of Art History," *Art Bulletin,* vol. LXIX, 3 (1987), pp. 326–57, for a thorough, if not exhaustive, summary.

104. L. Nochlin, "Why Have There Been No Great Women Artists?" in *Woman in Sexist Society: Studies in Power and Powerlessness,* ed. V. Gornick and D. Moran (New York, 1971), and copious literature thereafter, most notably R. Parker and G. Pollock, *Old Mistresses: Women, Art and Ideology.* On *topoi* that do not fit, in particular: J. O. Schaefer, "The *Souvenirs* of Elizabeth Vigée-Lebrun," *International Journal of Woman's Studies* (1981), pp. 35–49, and C. Havice, "The Artist in Her Own Words," *Woman's Art Journal,* vol. II, no. 2 (1981/2) 1–7.

105. T. J. Clark, *Image of the People: Gustave Courbet and the 1848 Revolution* (London, 1973); G. Pollock, "Feminist Interventions in the Histories of Art: An Introduction" and "Vision, Voice, and Power: Feminist Art Histories and Marxism," both in *Vision and Difference: Femininity, Feminism, and the Histories of Art* (London, 1988).

106. The most recent example of the latter is H. S. Becker, *Art Worlds* (Berkeley, 1982), who analyzes the complexity of art making in contemporary Western culture and the gray areas of production where collaboration, editing, reproduction, and other processes are involved. Becker, like most contemporary art historians, acknowledges the germinal import for this direction of inquiry of M. Baxandall, *Painting and Experience in Fifteenth Century Italy* (Oxford, 1972).

107. George Kubler, *The Shape of Time: Remarks on the History of Things* (Yale, 1962), chap. 1, esp.pp. 16–30.

108. "Words about Words about Icons: Iconologology and the Study of African Art," *Art Journal,* vol. XLVII, 2 (1988), pp. 75–87, esp. pp. 79–80.

4
Women Architectural Patrons and the Shaping of an Arts and Crafts Culture, 1870–1914

HENRIETTA STARTUP

. . . [T]hough art stirred and trained her, gave her new horizons and new standards, it was not in art that she found ultimately the chief excitement and motive-power of her new life—not in art, but in the birth of social and philanthropic ardour, the sense of hitherto unsuspected social power.[1]

IN THE LATE NINETEENTH CENTURY MIDDLE-CLASS WOMEN SOCIAL REFORMERS SOUGHT TO discover a new sense of identity and a new meaning for women's work through architectural patronage. They participated in and often directed the planning and designing of several urban settlement houses which were formed at the end of the century in ethnically diverse working-class communities. Their pioneering efforts, as I shall show, offered many settlement workers a new sense of selfhood. At the same time their commitment to these projects also provided the impetus for new interpretations of the urban environments in which they had chosen to live and work.

Settlement houses existed, according to their pioneers, to reshape existing meanings of social work and philanthropy and to create social harmony between the classes. As buildings, settlements were important because they represented a "home" outside the private sphere, connecting bourgeois women to the public sphere of the city. Here, middle-class women gained skills and knowledge about the world through their transition to a more public role as social welfare reformers and patrons. But their role was also determined by what had been traditionally asked of them in the home. Privileged women of the period were often encouraged to refine their aesthetic sensibilities, but their pursuits were not considered work. Their accomplishments were intended rather to create feminine virtue and equip them for marriage.[2] In these years before female suffrage was granted in Britain and the United States, the involvement of female social reformers in architectural patronage altered their sense of selfhood as they sought for an opportunity "to do" rather than merely "to be." And the arts of housekeeping and household management along with domestic handicraft skills actually helped women to gain a voice in the urban reform movements.

Many of the women social reformers were freed to pursue more public work because they had access to domestic servants. They also needed access to capital and to other forms of financial and political support. In many cases such support was available largely because of their husbands' financial success and social connections. Thus the kinds of women who acted as patrons, working with or

95

confronting businessmen, management boards, and architects, tended to be wealthy, "born-to-rule," and well-connected women.

These women settlement founders shared a commitment to the Arts and Crafts movement of their time. They read the works of John Ruskin and Thomas Carlyle enthusiastically, and in England, they developed friendships with designers associated with the Art Workers Guild or with disciples of leading arts and crafts designers like Richard Norman Shaw. They had a definite arts and crafts orientation. They believed in the positive influences craft and design could have on urban social problems, such as the plight of working-class children and, in the United States, the well-being of new immigrants. At the core of their passionately held public welfare philosophy was the idea that the relief of urban poverty must involve aesthetic as well as political considerations.

Two of the major social debates from the mid-century on were intertwined. One addressed the "woman question," that is, the status and role of women in society; and the other concerned the impact of industrial society on public and private life, expressed in Britain as "the condition of England" question. The writings of Ruskin and William Morris in Britain, influential on American women settlement founders like Jane Addams, concerned the nature and purpose of work and its relation to art and recreation. Victorian cities in Britain and the United States were indeed full of workers; there were household workers, waged workers, seasonal laborers, and the unemployed; there were places where the paid work of working-class women servants enabled middle-class women to work, too. Domestic-based trades, such as lace-making and weaving, had been mechanized by the mid-nineteenth century. New alignments had taken place in the middle class, forcing women, who had had an important role in domestic production in the eighteenth century back to more restricted domestic role.[3] With this ideology of domesticity, both countries saw the steady underemployment of male hand-loom weavers and the emergence of working-class female workers in textile production.

The arts and crafts designer, May Morris, like her father, William Morris, was a teacher and commentator on the purpose of art in an industrial society. She wrote in her social history of needlecraft about the young women workers who were employed in the "weaving shed, where every hour spent in the hot exhausted air among the clatter and clash of machinery is an undeserved penance to the work-girls."[4] May Morris hoped to strengthen and renew the connection between a worker and his or her craft in her teachings and design work. Her book about needlecraft, *Decorative Needlework* (1893) was one that she bound herself, thus combining her design interests with her political and social commitments (figure 4.1). Arts and crafts designers like May Morris were among those who were critical of the new divisions between home and work created by industrial capitalism, for they knew that with these shifts had come changes in the way work was done and art was made. These concerns were shared with women settlement founders.

The settlement house and arts and crafts movements provided transitional kinds of employment for middle-class women. Despite ideological, social, and political restrictions, the range of middle-class women's public activities was remarkably wide by the 1880s. Women's involvement in public life in the United States can be traced back to the time of the American Revolution when women were formally excluded by men from the conventional political world.[5] Feminist historians have written about nineteenth-century women's involvement in the temperance movement, in charity work for the Charity Organization Society, in abolitionism, prison reform, and nursing, demonstrating the ways women found to compensate for their exclusion from the male public discourse.[6] Work of this kind was sometimes a means of "translating moral authority into political influence."[7] Such work, mostly of a voluntary kind, politicized women of privilege and helped to create selfhood and identity.[8]

Women pioneers in the settlement movement and the arts and crafts movement believed that class conflict could be laid to rest, and that human relationships could be changed by art and design directly through the making of new relationships between classes. Ideas about the possibility of class harmony in settlement houses helped to foster a craft and "folk" revival that extended, in Britain at least,

Fig.4.1.   May Morris. Hardbound copy of Decorative Needlework.

into the 1930s. A female-led heritage preservation and Americanization program, dependent on the organization of settlement houses, had been developed by women in the United States by the 1920s. Although these efforts did not resolve the class conflict as women so earnestly hoped, the work that was accomplished enabled women to play an important role in shaping an arts and crafts culture. This is revealed in women's autobiographies from this period, especially those written by female settlement house founders, as they make reference at times to the close relationships between political, cultural, and artistic work across class lines.[9] As texts, they are interesting narratives of creative political transformation, indicating shifts in the conversion of a "home from home" ideology.[10]

The kind of public life that these women had was obviously influenced by the cities in which they lived, by the choices they made, and by the experience of class itself, which afforded them greater opportunities than those available to many working-class women. It was the experience of living in an ethnically diverse and often poorer section of a city that suggested a new range of alternatives to bourgeois confinement at home; women like Henrietta Barnett and Emmeline Pethick-Lawrence became involved in work with health and welfare movements, with housing policy and housing design. The legal and legislative arms of state government in relation to sweated trades, home industries, and factory inspection were addressed by Florence Kelley, Jane Addams, and, in Britain, by the Women's Cooperative Guild.[11] Significantly many settlement founders, among them Mary Ward (Mrs. Humphry Ward) and Mary Kingsbury Simkhovitch, were to become involved with child labor, child protection and welfare, children's play, and preschool and nursery education.

Two different accounts from autobiographies here will demonstrate the direction and transformation of some middle-class women's patronage and philanthropy in the 1880s. In England in the 1870s, Emmeline Pethick-Lawrence found growing up in the suburbs of Bristol to be very restrictive. Paying calls, going to dances, playing tennis, and "doing" the flowers were what was expected of her and her sisters.[12] She came from a large middle-class family of thirteen children, although five of her siblings had died at or shortly after birth. By joining the ranks of the unpaid voluntary labor force in London, she got away from home and began to work for the West London Mission which she had heard about through a social service agency called "Sisterhood of the People." Working with fellow resident and friend, Mary Neal, these women founded a settlement for working girls called the "Espérance Club" and campaigned with local working women in the neighborhood for the establishment of a minimum wage. As a single woman, Emmeline tried living in a "workingman's flat," paying the rent by starting a cooperative dress-making business with girls from the Espérance.[13]

In 1899 she met Frederick Lawrence, who was teaching at Mansfield House, a university settlement in the East End of London modeled on the most famous of settlement houses, Toynbee Hall. Frederick took her name when they got married in 1901. Emmeline continued to work closely with Mary Neal, starting a folk dancing guild and promoting traditional folk song events at settlement houses.[14] The Pethick-Lawrences were advocates of open-air recreation and education; they wanted to build a seaside hostel on the south coast of England for vacationing working class families. In 1903–4 they approached two arts and crafts architects, Cecil Brewer and A. Dunbar Smith, to design the seaside home called "The Sundial" in Holmwood, Surrey.[15] This young architectural partnership had just finished six years of work in London for Mary Ward, the settlement founder, antisuffrage campaigner, and novelist. They had just designed and built a new settlement for her Unitarian-led University Hall and its companion social settlement, Marchmont Hall, both located in the poorer sections of Bloomsbury.

The desire to intervene in working-class family welfare and to design buildings and services for them was not only a political act for women like Emmeline Pethick-Lawrence. The death of five of her own siblings had left its mark, and this work may have been an attempt at remaking her own family history. Once out of the traditional domestic sphere, middle-class settlement women were clearly keen to identify with the neighborhood, and this often meant, ironically, making a space within it that recreated the design and appearance of a typical middle-class home.

The efforts of social worker Mary Kingsbury Simkhovitch illustrate this phenomenon. Simkhovitch, born in Boston in 1867, traveled to England and Germany on a scholarship from the Boston-based Women's Educational and Industrial Union. At Columbia in the 1890s she decided to combine graduate work with settlement work. Her decision led to her appointment as head caseworker at the female-run College Settlement on Rivington Street, on Manhattan's Lower East Side. In her autobiography, she remembers this neighborhood, "was crowded and noisy, rank with the smell of over-ripe fruit, hot bread and sweat-soaked clothing."[16] It was an environment that contrasted dramatically with her own childhood experiences of growing up in Newton, a leafy suburb of Boston in the 1870s–1890s. She was aware that her own settlement building was influenced by these experiences.

In 1902 Simkhovitch founded Greenwich House Settlement in a New York neighborhood of twenty-six different ethnic groups. She described the settlement as the result of her playing house in Newton with her schoolfriend Josephine Burrage. She writes that the two girls would build a tent in the gardens between their family homes:

> . . . where we got breakfast on the fireplace we made out of stones with slate on top. There we
> made scrambled eggs, ate the berries we had picked . . . and drank the milk we had begged from

my grandfather . . . we instituted another meal called pancakes to which we invited our families at four o'clock as we wished to dispense hospitality. We collected all the local flora and pressed the flowers to keep for our winter inspection.[17]

This mixture of imitative homemaking, combined with the play at household management and nature study, was a framework Simkhovitch used for her own settlement buildings and its programs. Young Russian and Eastern European women, recently arrived in the United States as immigrants, could come to her settlement where they might join the "Good Seed Club" to learn about flowers, and implicitly, the meaning of citizenship. Little children could play on the roof at the settlement kindergarten where they would find opportunities for open-air recreation and supervised play.

Simkhovitch realized that play in her own childhood had provided her with a new model of philanthropy, a unique vision of hospitality toward working-class women and children. By this time she had also discovered that caring for the poor still meant defending class interests. Her church in the 1880s was the landlord for a group of tenants on "Nigger Hill," the east side of Boston's wealthy Beacon Hill area. She discovered as a young church welfare worker conducting home visits to this African-American community that her senior ministers were neglectful property owners, responsible for terrible overcrowding and poor sanitation.[18] Mary Simkhovitch saw her commitment to public work and working-class welfare in terms of the political discoveries she made as an adult, but she drew equally on the memory of childhood delight to plan and design her own settlement.

These stories demonstrate the links women made between creative and political work at the end of the nineteenth century. Women fostered connections between discrete single-issue, seemingly separate organizations campaigning for the relief of urban poverty, overcrowding, and ill health. Welfare work by middle-class women took the many different cultural forms it did for two major reasons. Women were often afraid of the districts where they set up settlements and attempted to shake this off by creating safer middle-class places within districts which were at first unknown and uncharted to them. Founders were clearly prompted sometimes to pursue aesthetic forms of philanthropic work due to their childhood and family backgrounds which were so different from those faced by city neighbors and working-class families. Women settlement founders also attempted to shape and determine the spaces in which their public work was done by the "social power" of philanthropy.

We can see this demonstrated in fiction of the period written by women. In the first chapters of Mary Ward's popular novel *Marcella* the young unmarried heroine Marcella Boyce can be found reading Marx, attending a London art school, and fast becoming a Fabian. Her "Venturist" friends and comrades were designers and decorators, poets, union organizers, and voluntary charity workers.[19] For a short time, Marcella herself becomes a rent collector in London's East End and then a district nurse. Her fortunes change when she discovers that she is to be the heiress of a large country estate in a rural county outside London. The novel is a study of Marcella's personal struggle to unify the conflicting political and creative forces within and around her.

Like Mary Ward herself, Marcella Boyce is a wealthy, well-educated woman confident of her ability to deal with new ideas and challenges to her class position: "But though art stirred and trained her, gave her new horizons and new standards, it was not in art that she found ultimately the chief excitement and motive-power of her new life—not in art, but in the birth of social and philanthropic ardour, the sense of hitherto unsuspected social power."[20] The fictional dilemma was, according to one source, a dilemma for the author herself.[21] Ward was not interested in working, for example, within the new movement for women's suffrage for she believed that conventional political power would not advance the concerns of women. Nor did she think that the settlement work was a way for women to argue successfully for the vote. The "social power" of settlement work and patronage, she believed, functioned best because it was working outside of the state. Settlements were an important way of gaining an independent creative voice for middle-class women but not a vehicle for formal political office.

It is the significant numbers of women in settlement work in the United States that has lead historians to link the settlement movement to wider theories of "social uplift" and "social gospel" practiced during the Progressive Era.[22] In Britain theories of settlement work had ideological roots in neo-Heglian philosophy and liberal political theory. The scholars T. H. Green and Bernard Bosanquet were among those who were allied to the settlement cause. Bosanquet was married to Helen Dendy, whose 1912 book *Social Work in London, 1869–1912,* traced the origins of the settlement movement to the Charity Organization Society and to its many women members.[23] Explanations for the female-led movement in both Britain and the United States have been advanced also by settlement women themselves. Their statements addressed the connections between architectural patronage, self-identity, and the shaping of an "arts and crafts culture."

Jane Addams of Hull House in Chicago spoke in 1892 of the needs young women had for meaningful creative work, and the "desire for action" and the "wish to right wrong."[24] Settlements were social laboratories, which meant that they were places where women largely, instead of men, could provide firsthand knowledge of a city's social, economic, and political problems and offer solutions to them. In the United States records from Hull House demonstrate that sense of purpose and power recently discovered by women reformers. Jane Addams, Ellen Gates Starr, and Florence Kelly organized and refocused what they felt was the political and cultural "uplift" of their chosen city even when the representatives of this power were wealthy and politically well-connected business leaders or members of existing political party machines.[25]

While many historians acknowledge the lasting influence of Toynbee Hall, the first settlement house built in Whitechapel in the East End of London in 1884, the fact that it is an example of female architectural and cultural patronage and of women's emphasis on cultural uplift has not been sufficiently noted. Women played an important role in its establishment and design. Jane Addams had visited Toynbee Hall; Mary Ward had already been to see it before she set up her own settlement. She used Toynbee Hall as the basis for a description of settlement design in her 1889 novel, *Robert Elsmere.*

Toynbee Hall was a university settlement founded for young male graduates from Balliol, one of the Oxford University colleges.[26] These young men were "residents" in the working-class neighborhood of Whitechapel, and were intent on "preaching a religion of service" among the local population. Like Frederick Pethick-Lawrence, who worked at nearby Mansfield House settlement, these young men were interested in shifting attention away from charity organized along the lines of home visiting by women members of the Charity Organization Society, to self-reliance and education, to the "virtues of labour, thrift and self-help."[27]

In her novel *Robert Elsmere,* Mary Ward's hero is a young clergyman. He experiences the "crisis of faith" which had absorbed so many of his mid-Victorian contemporaries and on the advice of a university mentor, Professor Henry Gray (a character modeled on the Wards' Oxford friend, T. H. Green) Elsmere sets up a settlement. The novel parallels to some extent the real-life experiences of Samuel and Henrietta Barnett, the founders of Toynbee Hall whose "crisis of faith" led them to the East End of London away from the safety of a parish in Kensington's Bryanston Square in West London. It was a similar "religion of service" along with the social experiences they felt that art could bring to people of all classes which drove the Rev. Canon Barnett and his wife, the young, wealthy, and socially concerned Henrietta Rowland to Whitechapel.

Toynbee Hall was a new type of building on the streets of Whitechapel. The settlement and its diverse and secularized program of social welfare work, cultural and political activity, and legal service was offered to an ethnically diverse community of Jewish, Italian, and French neighbors. The program of work was soon extended when the Barnetts took in the young arts and crafts architect C. R. Ashbee as a resident. Ashbee set up a Guild of Handicraft at Toynbee Hall in 1890 and helped to get local people's work exhibited at the Arts and Crafts Exhibition Society run by suffragette Emmeline Pankhurst. The Barnetts then commissioned the construction of a popular free art gallery, the Whitechapel Art Gallery, on the main highroad near the settlement building. The art gallery was designed by William Harrison Townsend, an arts and crafts architect, in 1896 with plans for a mural (never to be executed) by the socialist designer Walter Crane. The main elevation for the building carried vigorous bas-relief tree designs which seemed to grow up and connect the twin towers of the building above the entrance to the earth beneath.[28]

By the turn of the century, Henrietta Barnett had extended her role as an architectural patron to include an even larger scheme that she wished to develop for the members of Toynbee Hall Settlement. This was a plan to purchase "a huge estate on which all classes could live in neighborliness together with friendships coming about naturally without artificial efforts to build bridges between one class and another."[29] As the profile of an imagined community, her scheme was determined by her experience as a Poor Law Guardian and her work as a district visitor, working with Octavia Hill in the Charity Organization Society. With the help of male residents at Toynbee Hall, which she needed in order to secure an option on a large, valuable estate in Hampstead owned by the trustees of Eton College (the well known boys private "public" school), Henrietta Barnett set up the Garden Suburb Committee Trust in 1904. Her efforts led her to press for legislation in Parliament for the development, and she made legal history as the first woman to sign the deeds to the property.[30]

Henrietta Barnett commissioned the arts and crafts architectural firm of Raymond Unwin and Barry Parker to proceed with the design of the first cottages.[31] Like a settlement, Hampstead Garden Suburb was intended to be quiet and beautiful, promoting health and welfare, leisure, learning, and worship: it is no coincidence that Mary Ward was one of its earliest supporters. Her description of Elsmere's settlement in *Robert Elsmere* is inspired by the plan of Toynbee Hall and in its requirements anticipates Mary Ward's own Passmore Edwards Settlement:

> Three floors of rooms, brightly furnished, well-lit and warmed: a large hall for the Sunday lectures, concerts, entertainments, and story telling: rooms for the boys club, two rooms for women and girls, reached by a separate entrance, a library and a Reading Room open to both sexes, well stocked with books and made beautiful with pictures, three of four smaller rooms to serve as committee rooms and for the purpose of the Naturalist Club and . . . a gymnasium.[32]

The planning of Toynbee Hall, the Whitechapel Art Gallery, and Hampstead Garden Suburb represent the formation of new building schemes in the Victorian and Edwardian period. Designed partly in reaction to the visible turmoil of urban capitalist society, these schemes drew heavily on nature for their decorative detail and on the countryside as an imagined setting.[33] In order for Toynbee Hall as a settlement building to shape a new relationship between its middle class, professional, and largely male residency and the working-class community of Whitechapel, the design of the settlement drew on domestic arts and crafts architecture for middle-class families. The plan and design recalled the medieval courtyard plan of many of Oxford University's colleges. Significantly Jane Addams adapted an older house, built for a large middle-class family, with servants' quarters and a courtyard for the creation of Hull House. Her settlement house sat on a large site in what had once been a more prosperous middle-class area on Chicago's South Side.

Mary Ward's Passmore Edwards settlement, designed in 1897 by Cecil Brewer and Dunbar Smith, echoes her imaginative creation of a settlement in *Robert Elsmere* (figure 4.2). Recalling domestic arts and crafts country house design by architects such as Philip Webb and Richard Norman Shaw, the Passmore Edwards building was well received in both the lay and architectural press. It is significant that many reviewers refer to the new building as a direct expression of Mary Ward's philosophy. In fact, according to one reviewer the building serves as a metaphor for the settlement movement itself.[34]

Mary Ward was never a resident at her settlement but rather a zealous volunteer. Her own house, a large Georgian town house in nearby Russell Square, was where she lived when she was not at "Stocks," her country estate in Hertfordshire bought in 1892. The building she commissioned to combine the activities of University Hall and Marchmont Hall under one roof, however, was still rather like a spacious well-to-do home. Richard Norman Shaw had been the judge of an architectural competition that the settlements' general committee had held in 1895. Cecil Brewer and Dunbar Smith had been residents of the settlement while Brewer attended the Architectural Association, an

*Fig.4.2.   Passmore Edwards Settlement, Tavistock
Place, Bloomsbury, London, England.*

independent architectural school in nearby Bedford Square. Revised designs for a location on Tavistock Place, just south of Tavistock Square, were under construction by 1896. This was the site of a demolished late eighteenth-century house called "The Grove."[35]

The settlement building Mary Ward commissioned was three stories high and made of brick and stone. White plaster surface treatments were to be found under a mansard roof (intended as a site for murals or bas-reliefs which were never constructed) with chimneys at the gable ends. The roof-line, facing Tavistock Place, was broken by a row of attic windows and twin end towers with low hipped roofs. Massing and design are a more abstract rendering of the Whitechapel Art Gallery.

Smith and Brewer did not try to re-do Norman Shaw's inimitable style and seem to have been aware of the social and cultural statements Ward wanted to make in commissioning the new building. A massive stone porch, looking as if it might have grown organically out of the ground, shaded the main entrance, and two free standing stone eggs crowned the porch at each side. The arts and crafts teacher and theorist William R. Lethaby, in his *Architecture, Mysticism, and Myth* (1892), pointed out that eggs were ancient symbols of rebirth. Lethaby had been influenced by the writings and example of John Ruskin and William Morris.[36] He was also director of the Central School of Art and Design in London where for many years May Morris had taught needlework and embroidery in state-funded technical education classes. Lethaby's book may have been a source for Smith and Brewer's unusual entrance design. The sparing decorative details suggest that Mary Ward herself asked that a sense of renewal in philanthropy be revealed in the design of the building. A side porch for residents on the west elevation led into a generous hall. Georgian revival and free-style design elements define the rear elevation. Here a dining room looked out onto a formally planned garden and Dickens's house, backing onto Tavistock Square.

The original interior furnishings of the settlement were simple while being elegant and finely crafted: oriental carpets, sky-blue curtains, ash and rush "Morris and Co." ladderback chairs. There were designer-named tiles and ceramic fireplaces in the library, classrooms, committee rooms, and in the residents' bedrooms and their dining hall. Large settles and long oval tables (with Voyseyesque heart-shaped details) that folded away to create "friendly gatherings" of people were arranged in the dining and drawing rooms. The library, dedicated to T. H. Green, contained deep recessed wooden bookcases made of deal and oak and a Hopton wood fireplace. Many of the interior furnishings and fittings are still in place today.

A review in *The Studio* written by Esther Wood, one of the first women architects, in collaboration with G. L. Morris tells us that the commission was considered "one of the happiest examples of the influence of the 'arts and crafts' movement . . . upon architecture . . . and gives, according to Mr. Ruskin's demand, something that compensates us for the lost space of light and air."[37] Mary Ward herself stated that the new settlement building was a place for "the building up of that true tolerance which lies in the passionate mutual respect for individuals."[38] Her plan was to bring together different groups of people with conflicting class interests. Their interests would be transformed by the "natural" domestic setting of the settlement building; the business of making "different classes feel differently to each other" was to be achieved through the many cultural and craft-based artistic and recreational activities run by residents at the settlement.[39]

Mary Ward was no May Morris. Her interest in the revival of craft skills was linked to a commitment to rural heritage, to a romanticized view of the beauty of the English countryside, supposedly eternal and immutable. Ward shared with other aristocratic women such as the Countess of Mayo, the Honorable Lily Montagne (a patron of the Pethick-Lawrences), Dame Adelaide Anderson, and the Lady Battersea a commitment to heritage organizations such as the Surrey Garden Village Trust and the Rural Industries Bureau.[40] Nevertheless Ward was an important patron, for apart from a few arts and crafts architects and designers, the male-dominated architectural profession did not value the craft skills she advanced. To an ambitious professional architect the word "craft" was associated with the building trades and workaday traditions.[41] However, to many wealthy women like Mary Ward, craft skills were very important. Ward saw them as a means of "saving" rural heritage. And she also believed that the study of handicraft in classes like those organized for local working-class children and for the young women at her settlement would have not only artistic but also moral benefit.

Independent craftswomen in this period, trying to build up commissions or take on apprentices and pupils, received sponsorship from women like Mary Ward and sometimes found employment teaching in local state schools and in settlements.[42] An example of such a craftswoman is the independent designer Julia Dawson, who was associated with the arts and crafts movement. She lived in the studio and workshop dwellings designed by William Morris's friend, Philip Webb, in Worship Street, Spitalfields in London's East End. Dawson created an independent home for herself and an office in this building where she was secretary of the Clarion Guild of Handicraft.[43] Such craftswomen were able to help the settlement founders with the socially transforming cultural and political revival they envisioned.

In 1898 the Women's Work Committee of the Passmore Edwards settlement set up an invalid school program for "crippled" children currently attending the local schools. Mary Ward's daughters, Dorothy and Janet, helped her to open a "School for Mothers" and a nursery school.[44] In 1902 a new school building, also designed by Smith and Brewer, was opened on a site next to the settlement.

It provided more space for classrooms, clubrooms, a reading room, and games rooms for the physi-cally handicapped children. A vacation school, open in the summer holidays, catered to the local school-age children. Mary Ward had been converted to the principle of organized playground provi-sion and vacation schools for children by Jane Addams during a visit to Hull House in 1894. Craft classes, folk song, folk dancing, and musical drill were important parts of the curriculum.

Mary Ward was clearly influenced by her American counterparts. She actually created an embodi-ment of those American principles of family and child welfare to be articulated later by the Boston feminist Retha Child Door. Door's call to action in *What Eighty Million Women Want* expresses Mary Ward's existing program, "maternal" in scope: "Women's place is Home—but Home is not contained within the four walls of an individual house. Home is the community. The city full of people is the Family. And badly do the Home and Family need their mother."[45]

Although Mary Ward was convinced of the need to promote a new kind of philanthropy and a craft revival, she did not think she could learn from her community of working-class women and their families. It was a middle-class model of loving and efficient motherhood and decent home life that she envisioned in her program of work. She wrote extensively about the "dense" and "dreary" nature of the local children's "street habits." She felt their environment and play was lacking in interest and that their activities were aimless.[46] Cultural activities such as nature study, needlework, singing, and housewifery taught at the settlement may well have been practical and useful, but they were designed by Mary Ward to reform and restructure the behavior, pastimes, and play habits of local city children and young working women. What was good for middle-class children she believed must also be right for working-class children.

The implementing of this craft-based and child-centered instruction gave women like Mary Ward the sense that they had changed the meanings of social obligation in the Victorian and Edwardian city. Mary Ward, Emmeline Pethick-Lawrence, Jane Addams, and Henrietta Barnett accomplished their aims by being "materialist" social reformers.[47] They commissioned buildings and services which they hoped would furnish society with a renewed sense of urban order. But patronage, a dedication to others through privilege, was also a way of devoting time to the pursuit of self-identity. Their actions had the effect of rehabilitating their self-identity and feelings of self-worth. This transforma-tion is very apparent in an article Mary Ward wrote in 1901 describing the building and program of work at the Passmore Edwards Settlement:

> Imagine then that you are arriving at the settlement in the forenoon. You have before you a building very simple but full of charm and beauty; spacious, light, soft in colour, attractive in line, with many rooms of all kinds of shapes and sizes, evidently meant for many and various uses—a House Beautiful, that, as you wander through it . . . might almost set you speculating on its purpose and animating life, like some dainty shell upon the shore. Only the shell is empty and deserted, whereas the House Beautiful is already . . . cheerfully alive. . . . A pleasant Hall opens before you, and broad corridors.[48]

Ward continues in this vein, describing the children's schoolroom, a cheerful atmosphere with many pictures. "To the left you turn a handle—Children! A schoolroom evidently . . . hung with many pictures, and generally gay." She invites us to "peep again" into the room crowded with children where we will find a lady telling the fairy tale of Snow White and Red Rose. Of the story Ward says "on it floats a golden river—and the children with it, out and away, to the great shoreless sea of pure Romance." And finally Ward advises "In that sea we must all dip, for our souls' health."[49] Such passages indicate clearly that she is as concerned about her own soul as she is about those of the children the settlement serves.

Hull House Settlement, like Toynbee Hall and the Passmore Edwards Settlement, had a similar commitment to the social function of art and to "cultural uplift" in Chicago. The founders believed that an important way of reforming society was through what they saw as the emotional power of art. Among the first things that Jane Addams and Ellen Gates Starr did was to fill their converted settlement building with pictures. Reproductions of religious paintings from the Western cultural tradition, especially of madonna and child subjects, filled the walls. Della Robbia statues and "putti" were placed in the children's nursery. Ellen Starr's eagerness to promote classes in art appreciation led her to visit England in 1895 to work with the bookbinder and Art Workers guildsman T. J. Cobden-Sanderson and his wife, Anne Cobden-Sanderson.[50] Hull House, like Toynbee Hall, had its own art gallery by the turn of the century.

Jane Addams also hoped that Hull House could become a place where traditional handicraft skills could be preserved for broader political purposes. Impressed by the weaving and spinning skills of local Russian, Italian, and Bohemian women, Addams opened a Labor Museum. European textiles were exhibited from many different ethnic cultures in the hopes that these traditional skills would be maintained. Classes in handicraft were offered, and spinning wheels, looms, and spindles were worked by local women to demonstrate to local children the work that had been done in the "old country." Ironically, this revival of crafts from the participants' homelands was sometimes a part of settlement-run "Americanization" programs (figure 4.3). Vida Scudder, the founder of Denison House Settlement in Boston, organized an exhibition of native Syrian handiwork, rugs, Bedouin blankets, lace, and inlaid marquetry purportedly so that Syrian children could see how the culture of their homeland could be integrated into American society.

Settlements like Hull House, Dennison House, and the Passmore Edwards Settlement had been designed, in the broadest sense of the word, by women practicing outside the architectural and design professions. Patronage was new to them. It required their acting as planners of urban society *outside*

*Fig.4.3.   Handicraft Class at Hull House Settle-
ment, Chicago, Illinois.*

the statutory and professional institutions whose function from the beginning had been to control those who entered the design professions.[51] Settlements had explicit cultural goals that their founders considered part of a larger social and political revival. Art and design were therefore regarded as social as well as visual experience.

Tensions between different kinds of cultural practice were in evidence at many settlement houses although women patrons and founders themselves did not always acknowledge them. These reformers sometimes recognized that workers' skills had both artistic and social merit. But more often they displayed a lack of respect for different class, race, and workplace experiences; frequently it was the founders' own work and ideas of design that were most valued. Their broad aim of bringing people from different social classes together made settlements function rather like middle-class family parlors. Settlement houses were "safe" places for middle-class women to do significant social work while they tried to combat a real sense of personal exclusion from many aspects of public political life.

From 1900 up to World War I, settlement women found that they were, by default, leaning heavily on the conscience of the state in their efforts to reform city space and relationships between one class and another in poor urban areas. The welfare state in Britain and the branches of the federal and state government in the United States, albeit often reluctantly, had assumed many of the costs and functions of craft and industrial arts training, child and family welfare, and "motherhood" training by 1918. By this time, the arts and crafts revival scorned by professional architectural organizations was perceived to have a positive function in educational welfare work. Theories of the rehabilitative power of craft persisted. This approach proved to be particularly effective in female-led welfare and educational work with nursery-age and physically and mentally handicapped children in the period after World War I. Women continued to practice as architectural patrons in the interwar period, but by this time they had also begun to practice as architects in their own right.

Notes

1. The British novelist and social reformer Mary Ward is here describing the aspirations of Marcella Boyce, heroine of Ward's 1895 novel *Marcella*. For further discussion see below, p. 99.

2. The attitude of the father of painter Susan MacDowell to his three daughters is a typical example of this view. See the account in C. S. Rubinstein, *American Women Artists: From Early Indian Times to the Present*. (Boston: G. K. Hall, 1982), p. 114. In 1879 MacDowell painted *Two Sisters*, which shows graphically the pursuits considered suitable for young and marriageable middle-class women of the time. In the painting one of the sisters dressed in a richly brocaded gown is reclining in a wing chair. An open book rests on her lap while she watches her other sister who is absorbed in her needlework. The painting thus inscribes three acceptable pursuits for women: reading, handicraft, and, by implication, Susan MacDowell's own activity of painting.

3. See Joan Wallach Scott on "The Modern Period," *Past and Present*, no. 101, 1983, pp. 141–57 for a richly detailed and helpful overview of the debates about work and women's work in industrial capitalism.

4. May Morris, *Decorative Needlework* (London: Hughes & Co., 1893), p. 73.

5. Paula Baker, "The Domesticization of Politics: Women and American Political Society: 1780–1920," *American Historical Review*, 89, no. 3 (June 1984), p. 622.

6. Mary Ryan, "The Power of Women's Networks: A Case Study of Female Moral Reform in Antebellum America," *Feminist Studies*, v, (1979), pp. 66–85. See also Carol Smith-Rosenberg, *Religion and the Rise of the American City: The New York City Mission Movement 1812–1870* (Ithaca: Cornell University Press, 1971), Katherine Kish Sklar, *Catherine Beecher: A Study in American Domesticity* (New Haven: Yale, 1973) Barbara Berg, *The Remembered Gate*, (New York: Oxford University Press, 1978), Martha Vicinus (ed.), *A Widening Sphere* (Bloomington: Indiana University Press, 1977),

and more recently Christine Stansell, *City of Women: Sex and Class in New York, 1789–1860* (Chicago: University of Illinois Press, 1987).

7. Baker, "The Domestization of Politics," p. 622.

8. Ibid.

9. Mary Kingsbury Simkhovitch, *Neighborhood: My Story of Greenwich House* (New York: 1938) and Emmeline Pethick-Lawrence, *My Part in a Changing World* (London: Gollancz, 1938).

10. Anne Summers, "A Home from Home: Women's Philanthropic Work in the Nineteenth Century" in *Fit Work for Women*, ed. S. Burman (London: Croom Helm, 1979), p. 52.

11. See Margret Llewellyn-Davies, *Maternity: Letters from Working Women* (London: Virago, 1979). I particularly want to note here Anna Davin's excellent introduction and acknowledge her inspirational role in the development of this work. See also Katherine Kish Sklar, "Hull House in the 1890's: A Community of Women Reformers," *Signs* (Summer 1985), pp. 658–77.

12. Mrs. E. Pethick-Lawrence, "In Women's Shoes," Speech on votes for women, 1913. Pamphlets Collection, British Library, London.

13. Emmeline Pethnick-Lawrence, *My Part in a Changing World* (London: Gollancz, 1938), p. 30.

14. Martha Vicinus, *Independent Women: and Community for Single Women: 1850–1920* (London: Virago, 1985), p. 233–35.

15. For further information about the office of A. D. Smith and Cecil C. Brewer, see the entry by Brian Blackwood in *The RIBA Drawings Collection Catalogue* (London: Royal Institute of British Architects), and the article on their partnership in *Royal Institute of British Architects Journal*, 6 April 1935, pp. 629–38.

16. Simkhovitch, *Neighborhood*, p. 60.

17. Ibid., p. 16.

18. Simkhovitch, *Neighborhood*, p. 60.

19. Mary Ward, *Marcella* (London: Virago, 1984), pp. 16–17.

20. Ibid., p. 15.

21. Tamie Watters, Introduction to *Marcella* (London: Virago, 1984), pp. vii–xvi.

22. J. P. Rousmaniere, "Cultural Hybrid in the Slums: The College Woman and the Settlement House 1889–1894," *American Quarterly,* 22 (Spring 1970), pp. 45–66. See also Allen F. Davies, *Spearheads for Reform: The Social Settlement and the Progressive Movement 1890–1914* (New York: Oxford University Press, 1967); Paul Boyer, *Urban Masses and Moral Order in America* (Cambridge: Harvard University Press, 1978); and David Nasaw, *Children of the City: At Work and at Play* (New York: Oxford Press 1985). I am deeply indebted for these references, along with loving care, child care, and editorial advice to my husband and fellow historian, Robert Macieski.

23. See introduction by C. S. Yeo to *Social Work in London 1869–1912* (London: Harvester Press, 1973), pp. i–xiv.

24. Lecture delivered by Jane Addams to the Ethical Culture Societies as "The Subjective Necessity for Social Settlements" reprinted in *Twenty Years at Hull House* (New York: Macmillan, 1960), p. 93. See also Estelle Freedman, "Separatism as Strategy: Female Institution Building and American Feminism, 1870–1930," *Feminist Studies,* 5, no. 3 (Fall 1979), pp. 512–29.

25. Katherine Kish Sklar, *Hull House in the 1890's,* pp. 658–77, and Helen L. Horowitz, "Varieties of Cultural Experience in Jane Addams' Chicago," *History of Education Quarterly* (Spring 1986), pp. 69–86.

26. See W. Picht, *Toynbee Hall and the English Settlement Movement* (London: G. Bell, 1914), pp. 102–21.

27. Gareth Stedman Jones, *Outcast London: A Study of the Relationship between Classes in Victorian Society* (Oxford: Oxford University Press, 1971), p. 261.

28. It is interesting to note that one of the first exhibits in 1903 at the Whitechapel Art Gallery was not an exhibition of "high art" but instead a show of contemporary British poster art.

29. Kathleen M. Slack, *Henrietta's Dream: A Chronicle of the Hampstead Garden Suburb 1905–1982* (London: private publication, 1982), p. 9.

30. Kathleen M. Slack, *Henrietta's Dream,* p. 10.

31. See M. G. Day, "The Contribution of Raymond Unwin and Barry Parker to the Development of Site Planning Theory and Practice, 1890–1918" in *Themes in Urban History: British Town Planning: The Formative Years,* ed. A. Sutcliffe (Leicester: Leicester University Press, 1981); Mark Swenarton, *Homes Fit For Heroes* (London: Hutchinson, 1983); and Barbara MacFarlane, "Homes Fit for Heroines" in *Making Space: Women and the Man-made Environment* (London: Pluto Press, 1984).

32. Mary Ward, *Robert Elsmere* (London, MacMillian, 1889).

33. Robert MacLeod, *Style and Society: Architectural Ideology in Britain, 1835–1914* (London: Royal Institute of British Architects Publications, 1971), p. 121. See also Alistair Service, *Edwardian Architecture* (London: Thames and Hudson, 1984).

34. *The Cambridge Independent,* November 1898, p. 11.

35. Mrs. E. T. Cook, *Highways and Byways in London* (New York: Macmillan, 1902).

36. Mark Swenarton, *Artisans and Architects: The Ruskinian Tradition in Architectural Thought* (New York: St. Martin's Press, 1989), pp. 96–125.

37. Esther Wood and G. L. Morriss in *The Studio,* 16, no. 71, (15 February 1899), pp. 11–18. See also Anthea Callen, *Women in the Arts and Crafts Movement, 1870–1914* (London: Astragal, 1980), and Lynne Walker, "Design, Class and Gender in Edwardian Britain; Gender and the T-Square," *Fan,* 2, no. 55, pp. 13–16.

38. Letter from Mary Ward and R. G. Tatton, Warden, to members of the Passmore Edwards Settlement General Committee, 5 September 1900. Mary Ward Center Archives, Queens Square, London. I am grateful to the past director, Mr. David Head, for his kind permission to consult these and other records. I also wish to acknowledge the help of Adrian Forty and Mark Swenarton of the Barlett School of Architecture and Design, University College London for first directing me to the information about the Mary Ward Settlement building in 1984–85. See also A. Forty, "The Mary Ward Settlement," *The Architect's Journal,* 2 (August 1989), pp. 28–49.

39. W. Picht, *Toynbee Hall,* pp. 102–21.

40. *The Arts and Crafts Quarterly,* 1, no. 1 (January 1925), pp. 11, 17. See also E. Cumming and W. Kaplan, *The Arts and Crafts Movement* (London: Thames and Hudson, 1991).

41. Henrietta M. Startup, "Institutional Control of Architectural Education and Registration: 1834–1960" (Master's thesis, Thames Polytechnic, The University of Greenwich, London, 1984), pp. 30–33, 60–65.

42. Millar, Fred, "Women Workers in the Art Crafts," *Art Journal,* 1896, pp. 116–18 and *The Art Craftsman; Technical and Handicrafts Yearbook,* vol. 1, 1909, pp. 32–35.

43. *The Art Craftsman,* p. 32. While Julia Dawson is not known to have worked for Mary Ward, she represents the type of independent craftswoman Ward employed.

44. Davin, A., "Imperialism and Motherhood," *History Workshop Journal,* 5 (1978), pp. 9–66.

45. Retha Child Door, *What Eighty Million Women Want* (Boston, 1910; reprint ed., New York, 1971), quoted in Baker, "The Domestization of Politics" p. 632.

46. Ward, Mary, "The Care of the Crippled Child," *The Nursing Mirror and Midwives Journal,* 7 May 1938, p. 114. For an antidote to Mary Ward's assessments about working class "habits," see Ellen Ross, "Fierce Questions and Taunts; Married Life in Working Class London, 1870–1914," *Feminist Studies,* 7 (1982), pp. 575–602. For an insight into the complex family networks in working-class American communities, see Judith E. Smith, *Family Connections: A History of Italian and Jewish Immigrants' Lives in Providence, Rhode Island, 1900–1940* (Albany: State University of New York Press, 1985) and Linda Gordon, *Heroes of Their Own Lives: The Politics and History of Family Violence, Boston 1880–1960* (New York: Viking Penguin, 1988).

47. For an examination of their accomplishments, see Delores Hayden, *The Grand Domestic Revolution: A History of Feminist Designs for American Homes, Neighborhoods and Cities* (Cambridge: Harvard University Press, 1981).

48. Unnamed article by Mary Ward in *The Associate,* the members journal for the Passmore Edwards Settlement, 1901. Mary Ward Centre Archives, London.

49. Ibid.

50. Jane Addams, *Twenty Years a Hull House,* p. 261.

51. Startup, *Institutional Control of Architectural Education* (1984), pp. 30–33.

Part Three
Societal Expectations: Messages about Gender in Painting and Film

5

Moderation and Mutuality: The Dutch Family in Life and Art, 1500–1700

SHERRIN MARSHALL

Historians and art historians are becoming increasingly aware of the ways in which our respective disciplines can support one another. As Theodore Rabb and Jonathan Brown have written in a recent essay entitled "The Evidence of Art: Images and Meaning in History," "the fundamental assumption for both groups [i.e., historians and art historians] . . . is that painters, sculptors, and architects are able to give us clues (and sometimes answers) about the universe that they inhabit that are available nowhere else. In the absence of words, artifacts can point us in directions we could not otherwise imagine."[1] This conclusion seems especially valid for subjects such as family life in the past.

When we study the history of the family and the place and roles of women within the family, we may well be able to imagine the direction in which we are pointed, but we need all the evidence we can muster to get us where we want to go—that is, toward the historical reality of life in the past. The most crucial events and experiences in the life of the family are typically those that take place behind closed doors, particularly as we move into the early modern period (roughly defined as the age of the Renaissance through the coming of the French Revolution) and its new emphasis on privacy.[2] We can hope that artifacts may offer the historian of the family and childhood "a direct mirroring in domestic scenes and family portraits of values and relationships existing in family affairs."[3] Unfortunately, there are several problems inherent in this expectation, and in fact such problems are of crucial importance for art historians at the present time. Should we consider, as one perspective has it, that artists described or "re-presented" what they actually saw around them? Can we believe that when the works of an artist such as Pieter Breugel are described as "naar het leven" (from life), the words are to be taken literally? As one proponent of this theory puts it, "The Dutch present their pictures as describing the world seen rather than as imitations of significant human actions."[4] To take this to its logical conclusion, all works of Dutch art from this period are "re-presentations." None are, or are meant to be, "imitations," that is, "re-creations."

Considering the interpretation of a second school, are we to conclude, rather, that the real meanings are often not immediately understandable to our twentieth-century eyes? This position suggests that most, or even all, of an artifact's meaning is not directly accessible to the viewer without an awareness of the moralistic symbols that are wholly or partially revealed in the work itself, and their meanings. These symbols are termed emblems; the word in Dutch is "sinnebeeld (zinnebeeld)."[5] Whole books of emblems were created in the sixteenth and seventeenth century; this extremely popular genre influenced all the arts, written and visual. Many art historians who look to emblems to enlighten us as to the meaning of an artifact conclude that we can have no way of knowing how "realistic" a work of art is without a careful and informed analysis of the work's iconography, regardless of how the work appears.[6] A given work of art may in fact have little or nothing to do with what could be considered "reality," notwithstanding appearances to the contrary.

It is perhaps already apparent that these questions are significant to historians as well as art historians. If we believe that artifacts can shed light on the history of the family, we need to know in what ways we can rely on the historical validity or trustworthiness of the artifacts themselves. As a historian, I see much of value in both interpretations offered by art historians, and see ways in which they may be reconciled. While each approach offers insights into our subject, other types of historical evidence can be used to demonstrate ways in which each perspective can be examined and evaluated. An overview of early modern Dutch social and religious history will reveal two themes of importance for the historical and artistic interpretation of the family: Moderation and Mutuality express both ideal and reality in Dutch familial relationships. First, these will be revealed from archival, demographic, and literary sources. Then, I will examine selected works of art that reinforce and illustrate the validity of the two themes.

To begin the overview with the arguments of historians, it is possible that art in the north Netherlands of the sixteenth and seventeenth centuries did not so much herald cultural changes through its representation of the family, as Philippe Ariès and other scholars have suggested, but that instead art reflected changes that had already occurred and a mentality that was already in existence.[7] The impact of religious change in the north Netherlands actually dates back to the fourteenth and fifteenth centuries—before the coming of the Reformation in the sixteenth century—and the spread of lay religious movements such as the Devotio Moderna, or "Modern Devotion." Out of these, in turn, came the emphasis on Christian humanism beginning in the late fifteenth century, with the renowned scholar Erasmus of Rotterdam as one of this period's influential spokesmen. The Modern Devotion and Christian humanism affected many people, those of the educated burgher classes as well as the upper classes, women as well as men.[8] With the coming of the Reformation, especially as the sixteenth century progressed, a literate, bible-reading "priesthood of all believers" expanded. The rate of literacy for women (as well as men) in the Netherlands was notably high for the time.[9] More to the point, these movements fostered an atmosphere where religious themes took on meaning and immediacy for the individual. In the Netherlands, at least, a pervasive and eclectic mentality of religious themes and motifs offered practical guidance as to how one could (and should) live a Christian life.[10] That these discussions flourished outside the established church helps explain the coming of the Reformation. Many contempoaries believed that the church failed to provide such guidance, and that the rituals of the church establishment were hollow, removed from the world and the concerns of ordinary Christians.

The religious background provides an important part of the framework necessary for understanding the Dutch family and its representations in art in the sixteenth and seventeenth centuries. There are other pieces to be fitted into that framework, however. Demographic realities were such that husbands and wives in middle-class burgher families, as well as gentry families, were relatively close to one another in age. The mean age for first marriage during the period 1550–1630 in a sample taken from the gentry population was twenty-seven for men and twenty-five for women. This closeness in age fostered different relationships between wives and husbands than would logically occur in a society where brides were much younger than grooms. Moreover, despite the fact that childbearing was a principal cause of death for women, there seems to be some evidence that the mortality rates may not have been so prohibitive for Dutch women, at least in these social classes, as has been established for other countries at this time. Although many women did perish in childbirth, women were as likely to survive men as the reverse. More marriages were long-term than we have guessed, and relationships between husband and wife had the opportunity to be enduring. On the other hand, the survival rate of children, particularly young children, was adversely affected by as yet incurable diseases, such as smallpox, and by accidents such as falls from horseback. Approximately one child of every three reached the age of twenty-one.[11] Rather than regarding children as expendable, parents knew that each child's survival was a crucial element in the survival of the family and lineage. Beyond that pragmatic concern, there is much direct and indirect evidence to indicate that parental love was warm and genuine. Overall, then, parents were just able to reproduce themselves, statistically speaking, and most families did not have large numbers of children who survived to adulthood.

In part because of these demographic realities, in part because of the weight of tradition of Roman and customary law in the Low Countries, women and children in early modern Dutch society had legal rights that made them appear remarkably liberated, at least to many of their European contemporaries. European opinion of the time considered Dutch women overly outspoken and independent, and Dutch children overly indulged.[12] In legal reality, women and children could both inherit and hold property in their own names. In the case of children, this property, which could be inherited from mother as well as father, was legally protected for them until they came of age and could not be alienated. Women typically brought land or other forms of wealth, such as interest-bearing annuities, with them to their marriages as part of a dowry. Men brought similar possessions, often in the form of a *morgengave*, the masculine equivalent of a dowry. Wife and husband thus contributed financially to the creation of a new family, and the economic contributions of each were instrumental in providing fiscal stability for their marriage. If the marriage was without issue, property, especially land, usually reverted to the woman's birth family. Specific terms were spelled out in prenuptial or marriage contracts.[13] In terms of social status and economic werewithal, members of the middle and upper classes were the people with sufficient means and incentive to commission portraits of themselves. Such portraits reflected at least some of the realities of family life. Portraits reified the concept of the lineage, while portraits painted within the landscape or manor of familial holdings demonstrated the family's material substance and status.[14] As will become evident, portraits also aided in the concrete visualization of important religious and social ideals.

Ideals and motifs of Christian life pervaded these realities of family life in many ways. The expression of such ideals aids us in reconstructing the historical reality of family life in sixteenth- and seventeenth-century Holland. In this essay, I will discuss the way in which we can see—in words and in images—the ideals of Moderation, or Balance, and Mutuality, or Reciprocity. Although the Dutch did not use these precise terms themselves, they employed others with meanings parallel to what Moderation and Mutuality connote today. Reciprocal relationships were those in which each member gave something and received something in return. (It is important to note that mutuality is not synonymous with equality: children were not, for example, the "equals" of their parents because they were involved in reciprocal relationships. But mutuality is a meaningful step away from previous historical interpretations that have told us that women and children had no rights in the past, not within the family, and certainly not with respect to the rights of men.[15]) When the Dutch spoke of seeking Moderation, or Balance, in all things, these were characterizing what was regarded as the ideal in every relationship. Passion and emotion were not to be carried to excess, for these feelings could then inspire behavior and conduct detrimental to the individual's own good as well as that of the common good or social order. Throughout the early modern period, the threat of civic disorder, rebellion, riots, and "unruly behavior" appeared as a frightening threat to law and community. To quell these fears and anxieties, and as one important means of social control, social norms maintained that the individual's goal was that of keeping one's emotions and passion in balance.

A sure sign of the significance of principles such as those of Moderation and Mutuality can be seen in their thorough and on-going discussion in codes of domestic conduct, which gained new popularity in the north Netherlands and other European countries in the aftermath of the Reformation and Counter-Reformation in the sixteenth century. Although it is true that these writings drew on a centuries-old tradition dating back to antiquity, the late sixteenth- and seventeenth-century treatises were cast so as to be used by the literate audience for which they were intended. They were a way to transform the ideals of Christian humanism into practice and a number of post-Reformation writers followed in that tradition. The moralist Dirck Volckertsz Coornhert's treatise *Zedekunst, dat is, wellevenskunste (The Art of Morals, That Is, the Art of Living Right)*, published in 1586, emphasized the ways in which the members of households owe duties to one another, and share responsibilities. The father, as head of the household, was responsible for taking a wife comparable to him in background and status, "who is as free and independent as mistress of the house as he is as master."[16] The father had principal responsibility for the material well being of the household, including that of children and servants. Beyond that, the father was to teach his children to fear God, setting a good example for them. The mother was responsible for supporting her husband not only in happiness but throughout any misfortunes, as well as for management of the household.

As Pieter J. J. Thiel points out in his excellent discussion of this subject, Coornhert used exempla to illustrate his principles.[17] For example, the parental love and guidance demonstrated by storks toward their offspring encourage the young, when grown, to treat their parents similarly out of gratitude. This legend of the stork was referred to repeatedly in "sinnebeelden" and explanations of allegorical detail in paintings. Coornhert also utilized historical examples from antiquity: one of these was the story of the Greek hero, Hippothous, who was "so young when he perished before Troy that he was unable to repay his parents for their care."[18] In all of these instances, the exempla were written, not visual, but the messages lent themselves well to either medium. Thiel continues his discussion with the Dutch edition of 1563 of Heinrich Bullinger's sermons, entitled the Huysboeck. Although he points out that the book does not deal with the family or household as such, but rather with explanations of Reformed doctrine, Bullinger's explication of the fifth commandment—"Honor thy father and thy mother"—emphasized that obedience was to be offered to parents and "all who bear rule over us."[19] This signified that parents were to be honored as well as obeyed, and that children were never to forget or disdain their parents. Bullinger, like Coornhert, approvingly cited the example of the stork. What rewards would accrue to children for their right behavior? Since Bullinger's work is replete with biblical and classical examples, it is only logical that he details the story of Joseph, who was raised high "because from his childhood he honored God and reverenced his father Jacob." Children would live long if they upheld this commandment; concomitantly, they could expect to be punished by death for failure to do so.[20]

The Walloon Jean Taffin's work *Grondigh beright vande boetveerdicheyt des levens (A Close Examination of the Repentance of Life)* appeared in 1595. Taffin's book embodied a call to believers to embrace their faith more diligently and to "strive for an inner experience of their faith."[21] In this work is a precursor of seventeenth-century tracts such as the *Oeffeninghe der Christelycke deuchden,* or, in later editions, *Practycke (Practice of Christian Piety)* by the minister Godefridus Udemans; both works remind us that the purpose of these tracts was to inculcate right living.[22]

Taffin's and Udemans's emphasis on the duties which each member of the family owed to the others recalls our principle of mutuality. Parents have duties and responsibilities toward their children, as we have already seen. They are to teach, themselves, or have their children taught "an honest science, art, occupation or trade, in part that they may serve their family and, in time to come, provide for themselves." Children, in turn, have responsibilities toward their parents, particularly their aged parents. "If their parents are reduced to poverty they must assist them in word and deed, with comfort and material support, as Joseph did for his father. . . . If they are rich in the eyes of the world, they must be content with that which the parents give them, and not waste or squander it like the prodigal son." Once again, the credo is based on the fifth commandment.[23]

Petrus Wittewrongel, the conservative minister of the Old Church in Amsterdam from 1638 until his death in 1662, published the *Oeconomia christiana (Christian Economy)* in 1655. Wittewrongel's interpretation of the fifth commandment was that "Everyone shall fear his mother and his father." Thiel states that from this Wittewrongel "derived the concept of 'dutiful fear' or 'dutiful respect.'" Since the child's fear is mixed with love, a loving respect will be nurtured, again with the reward of a long life. Wittewrongel then elaborated in three chapters on the aspects of dutiful treatment, obedience, and gratitude.[24] As he moves into the body of his text, Thiel concludes this section on theological treatises tellingly:

It seems to me that the above are enough to show that the prints and their inscriptions, to which we will now turn, derive from this genre of doctrinal writing by Reformed clerics, who laid down the law for the faithful with the Bible in one hand and a clutch of classical maxims up their sleeves. Theirs was not the more universal, humanistic approach of Coornhert, who presented filial love not as a divine duty inspired by the fear of death and damnation but as a natural and self-evident consequence of an upbringing surrounded by love and warmth.[25]

In fact, I am not at all certain that we have moved in a direction where "filial love (is presented) as a divine duty inspired by the fear of death and damnation," despite the more foreboding tone used by Wittewrongel and others. Wittewrongel was an ecclesiastical killjoy who hated the theater to such an extent that he was instrumental in having performances of Vondel's play, *Lucifer*, banned. His near-contemporary, the pietist Willem Teellinck, inveighed in the pamphlet *Philopatris, Ofte Christel-ijck bericht (Philopatris, or Christian News)* in 1608 against all that he felt should be corrected in contemporary society. Teellinck's long list of grievances included the celebration of (formerly) Catholic holidays—"remnants of Idolatry"—such as Carnival or kermesse, "sinful feasts of Bacchus," "drunkenness," as well as "cursing and swearing." As part of his displeasure, he focused on the "Boldness of the Young to their Elders," and the "frightening spectre of the way in which the Young are being reared."[26]

Thiel noted Taffin's "complaint about the misbehavior of modern youth," which he feels "could have been a reaction to a contemporary problem." There is some evidence that economic problems—not to mention the upheaval of a country locked in military conflict for much of the period from 1566–1609, and sporadically thereafter until peace came in 1648—may have resulted in less parental control over children.[27] But Teellinck laid the blame for this state of affairs on many sources, including the schools and the forces of law and order, so-called: "At best, many of . . . the Sheriffs and Officials in the country-side," he wrote, "are no better than hot-tempered drunks themselves."[28] In other words, it seems important to note that ministers have been known throughout history for fulminating against social sins and attempting to hold society to their own high standards. This provides one useful means for societies to establish and maintain social norms, and the fact that disobedient children were discussed from the pulpit does not necessarily imply that all children were unruly or that all parents accepted these clerical strictures. It could be concluded that even Wittewrongel continues to emphasize the reciprocal relations between (in this case) parents and children. The ordinary citizen upheld the "natural and self-evident consequence of an upbringing surrounded by love and warmth," and was, once again, more interested in religious treatises in terms of the guidance they might provide for daily life than in terms of salvation, although to lead a Christian life surely also led to at least the promise of eternal salvation.

To appreciate a different point of view that will add another dimension of understanding for us, we need to examine other types of written documents and evidence. One example is provided by a small pamphlet written by the philosopher and jurist Hugo de Groot, known as Grotius. This pamphlet of 1619 consisted of a rhymed *Tsamensprake over den doop (Dialogue Concerning Baptism)* between de Groot and his daughter Cornelia.[29] De Groot was embroiled in a political and religious controversy at the time, and the pamphlet (which appeared in several editions) is certainly reflective of his religious philosophy, but it is also a fair reflection of another sort of "Christian guideline." The "questions and answers" de Groot considered include the following:[30]

(Q) What is the duty of the child whom God will most reward?
(A) To show Love, Honor, and Obedience to her parents.
(Q) What shall the parents then confer on her, in turn?
(A) Procure [not only] her livelihood for her, but above all the heavenly estate. . . .
(Q) What should a Man do, then, to please God well?
(A) Earn a livelihood, support his Wife in love.
(Q) What is the most honest adornment for a Young Lady?
(A) An unfeigned virtue, with a modest and chaste countenance.
(Q) What is the Woman charged with, to live in a Christly way?

(A) To raise [up] her children; give to her Husband dominion. . . .
(Q) What must those do, who govern a Household?
(A) Order their lot, with just and equitable ways.

In this question-and-answer format, de Groot demonstrates that each individual had his or her responsibilities within the family. Hierarchical principles were certainly important, since words such as "dominion" and "govern" are both prominent and central. After all, a Chistian calling in terms of family life, or "domestic morality," was being advocated, with specific behaviors and moral judgments attached to this way of life. However, such a life embodied meaningful components of mutuality as well. Each made his or her contribution, each received in return. Lest we conclude that de Groot was so atypical, by virtue, perhaps, of his love of learning and involvement in religious questions, that we cannot use him as a fair example, we can examine the private journal kept by an otherwise unknown seventeenth-century gentleman, J. van Teylingen. Van Teylingen's journal begins with an original poem that stresses reciprocal relationships within the family and the reciprocal relationship of God to Man. The title, "Een, Geen Ander," ("One, No Other"), comes from Teylingen's explication of his family's motto (or emblem).[31] As Teylingen put it,

> know that he [the writer] means one GOD alone,
> who will be served according to his commandments,
> If one wishes to be identified as a man, with principled beliefs,
> . . . Further, to have one wife, and bear for her all love,
> For, otherwise, God has a miserable future in store for us.
> But if we serve on this earth in piety, with faith, and trust,
> We can expect an eternal reward in heaven above.
> Thus, love that God alone, and his son,
> And he will grant you a holy life,
> To continue to be, through him, loved and in love,
> and with a fruitful wife.
> . . . the intent of this motto, which each should take to heart,
> Asks that you read, what he of Teylingen writes here:
> ONE, NO OTHER.

Religion was the link in these reciprocal relationships. Through religious beliefs—which were clearly central to Teylingen's life—both spiritual and secular unity could be achieved. Quite clearly, God's rewards for a worthy life are, to Teylingen, both tangible and intangible.[32] The marriage will be blessed with children, and with earthly love. Eternal life will be the ultimate reward.

Emblem books provided explications of proverbs and moral prescriptions in words and pictures, as well as setting down guidelines for living, in a different form than ecclesiastical writings. Since they relied on artistic representation as well as poetic reflection, such works are a valuable source for both historians and art historians. The Calvinist Johan de Brune's popular *Emblemata of Sinne-werck* appeared in the mid-seventeenth century.[33] Emblemata XXIV is entitled "Eygen-min blint ziel en zin" ("Self-love Blinds Spirit and Sense") (figure 5.1). The emblem portrays the sun's beams focused on a mirror, which reflects the beams in turn onto a vase of artfully arranged flowers. As a result of the reflection of the heated rays, the flowers are wilting. The rhymed explication of the emblem states: "When the gaze of the Sun, the wondrous-light . . . is collected in a concave lens, it scorches and sears until it burns that which was green and youthful. . . . Passion, Desire should be neither hot, neither cold in all measures, The golden mean holds. Enough, but not too much."[34] After the engraving and poem, De Brune continues: "To speak clearly: there is no more deceitful or dangerous sin than the excessive love of our own selves. Just as Ammon [Amnon] melted and pined away through love for his own sister Thamar [Tamar]; the narcissist is consumed by the excessive appetite of his own self."[35] The approval of moderation is expressed in another form by Emblemata XXXV, "Haest u langhsaem" ("Make Haste Slowly"). Addressed to a bachelor suitor, it portrays a young man pushing a young woman in a swing: "First (we) will, then not; now behind, then ahead . . .

EMBLEMATA.
XXIV.

Eygen-min blint ziel en zin,

D E Son, *dat wonder-licht, den hemel om kan rijden,*
Dat al verwarmt, en sterckt, en innighlijck ver-
blijden,
   Wanneer zijn lauwe glans verzaemt in 't hol gelas,
   Verzenght, verkrenght en brand, dat groen en jeugh-
   digh was.
De liefde van ons zelf, of 't geen' wy meest aen-hangen,
Zy enckelijck en vry, niet dobbel of geprangen:
   De zucht en sy niet heet, noch koud in allen deel;
   De middel-maet hout staet. Genough, niet al te veel.

Y 3

Uyt-

Fig.5.1.   *"Self-love blinds spirit and sense" from*
Johan de Brune, Emblemata of Sinne-
werk *(Amsterdam, 1661). Folger Shakespeare Library.*

(And) love a little more coolly, or at least not too hot."[36] In the explication, the responsibility for this form of moderation is on the youth: "A Young Man must exercise enormous caution, not to lead them past the limit."[37]

One final emblem can be cited as illustrative of moderation, or balance, namely Emblemata II, "Het Houw'licks bedt zy onbesmet" ("The Marriage Bed [Should Be] Undefiled"). The emblem pictures a group of women counseling a young bride next to what is obviously her "marriage bed," with flowers strewn beside it on the floor. The speaker is an old women; the bride listens attentively. The explicatory poem states: "The marriage bed is no place for ugly, lustful appetites; Rather, there, those who use it well, will each remain virginal."[38] As De Brune further elaborates: "The rule . . . of the Fathers was: If there is one who cannot contain himself, let him marry; for it is better to marry, than to burn. The holy state (of matrimony) should be used, not to blow out our natural warmth, but to cool an intemperate heat; not for wearying our members, but for a measured refreshment; not for the squeezing dry of our birthright's sap, but rather for tempering of the overflow."[39] In this instance, it is the young woman who is being advised. It seems possible that she is regarded as better able to moderate these appetites than her husband, and is thus being encouraged to take responsibility for this moderation within the marriage. The point of the emblem, yet again, is that moderation is the desideratum. Moderation and balance were thus applied to many aspects of daily life, not only the relations between the sexes. Moderation was intended as a guiding force for all human behavior.

The ideals of moderation and balance as applied to child-rearing had a slightly different focus. Peter Baardt's *Deugden-Spoor (Trail of Virtuousness)* was published in 1645; the twentieth emblem dealt with the subject of "Ver-dwaesde Ouderen" ("Misguided Parents" (figure 5.2).[40] In the engraving, a young girl stands between her parents, depicted in a rather domineering, bossy posture with her hands on her hips. Her mother's hand tentatively touches the girl's sleeve; her father is playing a fiddle—while the child calls the tune? The long, cleverly rhymed explication enjoins them to "Look out! how smartly Madam Els [i.e., the mother], puts lice into her Daughter's furs." The poem's summation chides the parents: "So learn from this, Parents, and from what you say, that everything has its time and place: Daily, your daughter, you should assiduously show; The way in which all things must go; Therefore, if you are daily in error; One will learn in haste, and without care." The principal consideration for parents should be the socialization of their daughter. Parental responsibility was foremost in child-rearing, and parents were urged to implement the principle of thoughtful moderation in their behavior. Children learned from the examples they were given: hasty, thoughtless parental actions, repeated over time, had evil, lasting consequences. If these parents spoiled their daughter by acceding to all her wishes, they would pay the price: she would be no fit wife and neither would she be a fit daughter to care for them in their old age.

This issue was specifically raised with regard to girls in two other interesting, complementary sources. One came from an emblem-book that was perhaps the most famous of all: that of Jacob Cats, who wrote an entire book on the subject of *Houwelick,* or *Marriage.*[41] In this preamble, Cats stated his ideal for wives:

> For wife, I'd wish a middling mate
> Not too high born nor low estate . . .
> A wife not rich or mighty grand
> But like to me in goods and land
> A wife not proud nor haughty high
> But modest yet in her own eye . . .
> No slut at home no doll outdoors
> A wife that puts her best step forth
> In virtue fair. . . .[42]

There is also an earlier portion to this protracted poem. That part introduces it and frames the subject:

De Twintichste Ver-Eeringe;

AENDE
Ver-dwaesde Ouderen.

R 2   Ver-

Fig.5.2.   *"Misguided Parents" from Peter Baardt,*
Deugden-Spoor, *(Leeuwarden, 1645)*
Folger Shakespeare Library.

> If someone asks, what sort of woman
> I'd wish to have in my company,
> A Companion; a Partner, should I have my wish.
> I'll wish for one constituted thus:
> Not too sweet, not too sour,
> Not too soft, not too bossy . . .
> Not too insipid, not too salty,
> Not too smart, not too silly . . .
> Not too short, not too tall,
> Not too fat, not too slender,
> Not too nasty, not too good.[43]

And much, much more. Although once again the aim of this section of Cats's advice-book is the socialization of girls, the structure and form follow the pattern of advocating balance and moderation. Additionally, the potential sting was softened by Cats's humor. The Leiden professor Caspar Barlaeus followed a similar pattern when he composed an original poem to commemorate the birth of a friend's daughter in 1636:

> That she should survive her first days of life without any illness,
> That she should cut her teeth painlessly,
> That as a girl she should be pretty, not overly desirable, but not undesirable,
> That as she reaches the age of marriage her beauty should be pure, modest, and pious,
> That when she is married she should not command her husband but should also not serve him,
> That she should not, as mother, either love her offspring to distraction, or neglect them.[44]

Although both Cats and Barlaeus have rigid expectations for women, there is considerable flexibility in the emphasis each places on the ideals of balance and moderation. Cats, at least, who was an extremely popular writer, seems to have been accepted by the reading populace in this spirit. Barlaeus, writing to honor a specific event, created what he deemed appropriate for the occasion. Very likely, this poem also reflected popular sentiment.

As was the case with the ideals of Moderation and Balance, Mutuality in relationships was also reflected in art. Paintings and portraits from the seventeenth century have been used to suggest the advent of a more "companionate" form of marriage.[45] There are documents that exist from far earlier than the sixteenth or seventeenth century that attest to reciprocity in marital relationships. What seems new is the method of depicting such relationships artistically, inspired by innovative modes of humanistic portrayal that emerged with the Renaissance and were enhanced by new uses for emblematic representations. A number of paintings and portraits can serve as illustrations. The famous portrait that Frans Hals made of Isaac Massa—who was almost certainly the painter's personal friend—and his bride Beatrix van der Laen in 1622 provides one example that exemplifies this marital reciprocity (figure 5.3). The contented happiness and affection displayed by each for the other is apparent. Each smiles; additionally, there is an element of shy pleasure in the bride's expression. The relationship between the two is symbiotic, and studies of the iconography involved in this portrait further support that conclusion. They are "entwined," the groom depicted symbolically as "tree," the bride as "vine." Hands are joined, connoting unity, oneness, and physical bonding. Both are realistically portrayed as individuals; however, each in this marriage portrait is also dependent on the other. They are connected, joined, one to the other.[46]

A comparable portrait is that of Bartholomeus van der Helst, completed in 1654, of the married couple Abraham del Court and Maria de Keerssegieter.[47] At the time of their portrait, the couple had been wed for three years; Del Court was thirty-one, his wife either twenty-two or twenty-three. As is the case with the previous portrait, the iconographic imagery adds considerably to our understanding. Maria holds a rose. Religious proverbs and emblems, some of which dated back to the Middle Ages, identified this flower not only as symbol of love, but also as symbol of marriage.

Fig.5.3. *Frans Hals.* Marriage Portrait of Isaac
Abrahamsz Massa; (1586–1643) and
Beatrix van der Laen (1592–1639. *Amsterdam, Rijksmuseum.*

Roses, after all, were not only beautiful, but could prick with their thorns. The fountain in the background behind Maria added to the symbolism of a loving marriage. Abraham holds his wife's wrist in his hand; by holding her "pulse" he was upholding the conjugal bond. Both husband and wife share in the portrait's reciprocal symbols of unity in marriage. The expression on Abraham's face—surely a highly realistic portrayal of a man who is deeply in love—as he gazes at his wife (she looks out of the portrait, toward the observer) is filled with loving longing. They lean toward one another; again, as was the case with the previous portrait, they are one, linked.

The pair portraits of *Albert Fransz. Sonck and His son, Frans,* and Sonck's wife *Elisabeth Claesdr. Walings and Her Daughter, Elisabeth,* reveal a different kind of reciprocal relationship (figures 5.4 and 5.5). The paintings, dated 1602, were completed when Sonck was thirty and his wife twenty-seven, a good illustration of the age differential alluded to earlier in this chapter. According to the portraits'

Fig.5.4.   Albert Fransz Sonck and His Son
Franz. *Hoorn, The Netherlands, West-*
fries Museum.

Fig.5.5.   Elizabeth Claesdr. Walings with Her
Daughter Elisabeth. *Hoorn, The Neth-*
erlands, Westfries Museum.

inscriptions, their little boy was two at the time, their daughter four. Albert Sonck and Elisabeth
Walings were not newlyweds, but two individuals who had already established their own family and
whose marriage was at a different stage. Sonck was a member of the patriciate of the town of Hoorn,
a wealthy merchant and functionary with many positions and much influence. He and his wife are
equivalently portrayed by an unknown artist in an artistic tradition which is once again replete with
meaningful symbols. Each has a serious demeanor of calm confidence, befitting their social position
and status. Their dress is comparable and even similar, as is that of the children. Only touches of
lace, prized possessions of family and household, lighten the somber black. The use of iconography
highlights the family's genealogy; Elisabeth Walings's portrait also includes a ship, which can perhaps
be equated with the frequently quoted seventeenth-century proverb that compared the housewife to
a sailing ship. Several of the writers quoted earlier utilized this aphorism; in Cats's version "She is
like unto a ship, that travels the sea, Filling the whole land with all sorts of useful wares."[48]

In this initial exploration of the subject of "Moderation and Mutuality: The Dutch Family in Life
and Art, 1500–1700," we have seen that various types of artifacts offer new kinds of evidence in
support of a number of conclusions. Archival, demographic, and literary sources have demonstrated
that familial relationships were sustained by principles of mutuality and moderation. Artifacts reveal
these principles visually. Finally, works of art show us that Dutch painters and engravers did portray
life around them "as they saw it," but that what they "saw" included iconographic emblems and

their definitions as an important part of "seeing" and hence of reality. The emblems that were used, verbally and visually, had real meaning in terms of social and religious ideals and realities. The spectator's awareness of the interplay between symbol and meaning gained significance during this period. Multidimensioned relationships were expressed verbally and visually, and must therefore be interpreted on several levels. The same could be said for our heightened awareness of the mutuality and interconnectedness of relationships in sixteenth- and seventeenth-century Holland.

Notes

The author wishes to express her appreciation to Professors Craig Harbison and Theodore Rabb, who encouraged her pursuit of this subject; to the Center for Advanced Study in the Visual Arts, National Gallery of Art, for the award of a Paul Mellon Visiting Senior Fellowship, and to the Folger Shakespeare Library, for the award of a Short-Term Fellowship, both of which aided in the completion of this essay. This is a preliminary study. Many additional works of art could be utilized, as could other emblem books or pamphlets: I chose a few examples that I consider to be exemplary in terms of their genre. All translations are my own unless otherwise specified.

1. Rabb and Brown, in Robert I. Rotberg and Theodore K. Rabb, eds. *Art and History: Images and Their Meaning* (Cambridge, Eng., 1988), p. 2.

2. See, for example, two volumes in the series *A History of Private Life*, ed. Philippe Ariès and Georges Duby: II (Cambridge, Mass., 1988) and III (Cambridge, Mass., 1989).

3. Diane Owen Hughes, "Representing the Family: Portraits and Purposes in Early Modern Italy," in Rotberg and Rabb, p. 9.

4. The words are those of Svetlana Alpers, *The Art of Describing: Dutch Art in the Seventeenth Century* (Chicago, 1983), Introduction, esp. pp. xxiv–xxv, xxvii.

5. Studies of this subject include E. de Jongh, *Sinne-en Minnebeelden in de schilder-kunst van de zeventiende eeuw* (Amsterdam, 1967), Ernst F. von Monroy, *Embleme und Emblembücher in den Niederlanden 1560–1630* (Utrecht, 1964), John B. Knipping, *Iconography of the Counter-Reformation in the Netherlands*, 2 vols. (Leiden, 1974), and Sturla Gudlaugsson, *Ikonographische Studien über die holländische Malerei und des Theater des 17. Jahrhunderts* (Wurzburg, 1938). I owe this last citation to Arthur Wheelock, National Gallery of Art.

6. The extent to which one must consider "symbol and meaning" is scrutinized in a series of recent articles in *Simiolus* 16 (1986, 2/3): James H. Marrow, "Symbol and Meaning in Northern European Art of the Late Middle Ages and the Early Renaissance," pp. 150–69; Craig Harbison, "Response to James Marrow," ibid., pp. 170–72; Peter Hecht, "The Debate on Symbol and Meaning in Dutch Seventeenth-Century Art: An Appeal to Common Sense," ibid., pp. 173–87; Anne Walter Lowenthal, "Response to Peter Hecht," ibid., pp. 188–90.

7. Ariès, *Centuries of Childhood: A Social History of Family Life*, trans. by Robert Baldick (New York, 1962). An important recent exhibition at the Rijksmuseum, and accompanying study, *Kunst voor de beeldenstorm* (The Hague, 1986) [with a separate introduction in English, *Art Before the Iconoclasm*], decisively demonstrates the influx into the Netherlands of new artistic ideas, as well as the ways in which their interpretation responded to the distinctive social, economic, and intellectual milieu in the north Netherlands before and just after the outbreak of the Revolt.

8. On the Modern Devotion in the Netherlands, see R.R. Post, *De Moderne Devotie, Geert Groote en zijn stichtingen* (Amsterdam, 1950), 2d edition; on Christian humanism, a recent study by Margo Todd, *Christian Humanism and the Puritan Social Order* (New York, 1987), sees the influence of Christian humanism following the Reformation as particularly significant, since in her view the "social thought" of Protestants and Puritans was derived from this source. In a review of her book in *Albion* 21 (1) (Spring, 1989), Christopher Hill suggests that there was considerable ideological continuity between the Christian humanists discussed by Todd and the late medieval Catholicism of the Lollards in particular.

9. On literacy in Holland, see Craig E. Harline, *Pamphlets, Printing, and Political Culture in the Early Dutch Republic* (Dordrecht, 1987), pp. 60–62; Simon Hart, "Geschrift en Getal," *Geschrift en Getal* (Dordrecht, 1976), pp. 130–32; A. Th. van Deursen, *Het kopergeld van de Gouden Eeuw: volkskultuur* (Assen, 1978), pp. 57–71. For other areas of Europe, see David Cressy, *Literacy and the Social Order* (Cambridge, Eng., 1980), as well as his essay, "The Environment for Literacy: Accomplishment and Content in Sixteenth-Century England and New England," *Literacy in Historical Perspective*, ed. Daniel P. Resnick (Washington, D.C., 1983), pp. 23–42.

10. For hints of this mentality, see J. Lindeboom, *De confessioneele ontwikkeling der reformatie in de Nederlanden* (The Hague, 1946), p. 109; Lindeboom, *Het bijbelsch humanisme in Nederland* (Leiden, 1913).

11. Sherrin Marshall, *The Dutch Gentry, 1500–1650: Family, Faith, and Fortune* (Westport, Conn., 1987), pp. 36, 15.

12. For opinions regarding women, see Marshall, *Dutch Gentry*, pp. xix–xxi; regarding children, see H.F.M. Peeters, *Kind en jeugdige in het begin van de moderne tijd ca 1500–ca 1650* (Meppel, The Netherlands), 1966); Mary Frances Durantini, *The Child in Seventeenth-Century Dutch Painting* (Ann Arbor, Mich., 1983), p. 73; Simon Schama, *The Embarrassment of Riches: An Interpretation of Dutch Culture in the Golden Age* (New York, 1987), pp. 485–86.

13. For further information on the Dutch family, see, in addition to Marshall, chapters 1–4, H.F.K. van Nierop, *Van ridders tot regenten: De Hollandse adel in de zestiende en de eerste helft van de zeventiende eeuw* (1984), chapters 2–4; Donald Haks, *Huwelijk en gezin in Holland in de 17de en 18de eeuw* (Utrecht, 1985), which contains much pertinent information on the eighteenth century in particular.

14. On the new appearance of genealogy and lineage in portraits (not only of individuals and in pair portraits, as I consider here, but also in family portraits), see Ton Brandenburg, "St.-Anna en haar familie. De Anna-verering in verband met opvattingen over huwelijk en gezin in de vroeg-moderne tijd," *Tussen heks en heilige. Het vrouwbeeld op de drempel van de moderne tijd* (Nijmegen, 1985), pp. 101–27. Brandenburg sees the emergence of this theme occurs during the period 1400–1500; p. 121. On the use of property as "status symbol," see E. de Jongh, *Portretten van Echt en Trouw. Huwelijk en gezin in de Nederlandse kunst van de zeventiende eeuw* (Haarlem, 1986), p. 158, and Faith Dreher, "The Artist as Seigneur: Chateaux and Their Proprietors in the Work of David Teniers II," *Art Bulletin* 60 (1978), pp. 682–703. I owe this last citation to Craig Harbison, University of Massachusetts, Amherst.

15. The identification of reciprocity as a prevailing theme in all relationships in the early modern Netherlands appears throughout Marshall, *Dutch Gentry*. I have also alluded to a work of art as evidence of reciprocity within marriage in "Protestant, Catholic, and Jewish Women in the Early Modern Netherlands," in Sherrin Marshall (ed.) *Women in Reformation and Counter-Reformation Europe: Private and Public Worlds* (Bloomington, Ind., 1989), pp. 126–28.

16. Coornhert, in Pieter J. J. van Thiel, "*Poor Parents, Rich Children* and *Family Saying Grace:* Two Related Aspects of the Iconography of Late Sixteenth and Seventeenth-Century Dutch Domestic Morality," *Simiolus* 17 (1987, 2/3), pp. 92–93.

17. Thiel's discussion considers these tracts, examples of what he terms "domestic morality." As an aid in understanding the iconography he then goes on to discuss: "*Poor Parents, Rich Children* and *Family Saying Grace*," p. 94. For the entire article, ibid., 90–149.

See also Wayne Franits, "The Family Saying Grace: A Theme in Dutch Art of the Seventeenth Century," *Simiolus* 16 (1986), pp. 36–49.

18. Cited by Thiel, p. 94.

19. Ibid., p. 95.

20. Ibid., p. 96.

21. Ibid.

22. On Taffin, ibid., pp. 96–97; Udemans, pp. 97–98.

23. Quoted from Udemans, ibid., p. 97.

24. On Wittewrongel, ibid., p. 98.

25. Ibid., p. 99.

26. Teellinck, *Philopatris, Ofte Christelijck bericht hoemen Staets saecken soude moghen gheluckelick uytvoeren: Dienende tot desen ieghenwoordighen Vredehandel* (Middelburgh, 1608), p. 14.

27. My forthcoming chapter, "Childhood in Early Modern Europe," which will appear in N. Ray Hiner and Joseph M. Hawes (eds.) *Childhood in Comparative and Historical Perspective* (in press), discusses this situation in greater detail.

28. Teellinck, *Philopadres*, p. 14.

29. De Groot, *Tsamensprake over den doop Tusschen Hugo de Groot Ende sijn Dochter Cornelia de Groot Door Vraghen ende Antwoorden* (The Hague, 1619), 2d edition.

30. Ibid., fols. 4–5.

31. Teylingen's poem and journal are discussed in Marshall, *Dutch Gentry*, pp. 69–71.

32. Ibid.

33. Johan de Brune, *Emblemata of Sinne-werck: voorgehstelt. In Beelden, ghedichten, en breeder uijt-legginghen: tot uijt-druckinghe en verbeteringhe van verscheijden feijlen onser eeuwe* (Amsterdam, 1661).

34. Ibid., p. 173.

35. Ibid., p. 174.

36. Ibid., p. 254.

37. Ibid., pp. 257–58.

38. Ibid., p. 9.

39. Ibid., p. 12.

40. Baardt, *Deugden-Spoor; in de On-Deughden des Werelts aff-gebeelde* (Leeuwarden, 1645), pp. 259–66.

41. Cats, *Houwelick, Dat is, De gansche gelegentheyt des Echtenstaets*, in *Alle de Wercken van den Heere Jacob Cats*, 2 vols. (Amsterdam, 1726), taken from "Vrouwen-Voordicht, toegeeygent alle ware Huys-Moeders," p. 284. There is an enormous volume of literature on the controversial subject of women in artistic ideal and reality. See, for example, Ilja M. Veldman, "Lessons for Ladies: A Selection of Sixteenth and Seventeenth-Century Dutch Prints," *Simiolus* 16 (1986), pp. 113–27; Marjan Boot, "Huislykheid is 't Vrouwen Kroon Cieraad," *Openbaar kunstbezit Kunst Schrift* 22 (1978), p. 168 ff.; C. Boekema-Sciarone en T. Loonen, "De vrouw in het werk van Cats," *Visies op Jacob Cats en zijn tijd, Bulletin van de Werkgroep historie en archeologie van het Koninklijk Zeeuwsch genootschap der wetenschappen*, 28 (1978), pp. 26–43. For the complex relationship between gender and artistic symbol, see Jan Baptist Bedaux's reassessment of the connection between "Fruit and Fertility: Fruit Symbolism in Netherlandish Portraiture of the Sixteenth and Seventeenth Centuries," *Simiolus* 17 (1987), pp. 150–68.

42. Quoted in Schama, *The Embarrassment of Riches*, p. 398.

43. Cats, *Alle de Wercken*, p. 284.

44. Quoted in Marshall, *Dutch Gentry*, pp. 26–27.

45. This is a principal argument throughout David R. Smith, *Masks of Wedlock: Seventeenth-Century Dutch Marriage Portraiture* (Ann Arbor, Mich., 1982), and one of the areas where I do not find his perspective informative. Smith and I came to several comparable conclusions, while utilizing different sources from the background of different disciplines.

46. The portrait by Frans Hals is used as a color illustration by E. de Jongh in *Portretten van Echt en Trouw*; illustration 20; text, pp. 124–30. De Jongh's work is important for the iconographical explanation of this and related works. See also, for example, De Jongh and P. J. Vinken, "Frans Hals als voortzetter van een emblematische traditie. Bij het huwelijksportret van Isaac Massa en Beatrix van der Laen," *Oud-Holland* 76 (1961), pp. 117–52.

47. Portrayed and discussed in De Jong, *Portretten*, item 33, pp. 171–74.

48. The paintings are used as illustrations and discussed by De Jongh, *Portretten*, illustration p. 65, text pp. 209–10. See also De Jongh, *Zinne-en minnebeelden*, pp. 50–55.

6
The Voice of the Other: Women in Third World and Experimental Film

LINDA DITTMAR

Women's film production, theory, and criticism have come into their own only recently. Not only has film been a Johnny-come-lately to the sister arts, but it has been a largely masculine preserve. Nonetheless, more women than is commonly known have in fact worked at all levels of production since the turn of the century, and women have been writing film criticism and theory all along. Much of this work has been path-breaking. Probably the very "masculinity" of the field fostered in women an oppositional state of embattled creativity which has especially come to the fore since the 1970s. Given men's control of film production and distribution, and their ideological use of film's thematic, scopic, and auditory capabilities, this does indeed seem to be the case. It is also the case that until recently women's work tended to be invisible. The extent of this invisibility might be measured by one young man's reaction to a college course entitled "Women Film Directors": "All two of them?" he quipped. "This is going to be a breeze." Film study books which aim at inclusiveness (histories, introductions, genre studies, decade surveys, etc.) support this impression. Their indexes alone reveal a shocking dearth of reference to female directors and scholars. For instance, one may find references to D. W. Griffith's actress wife, Linda Arvidson, but no mention of the pioneering Hollywood director Dorothy Arzner. Only with the recent growth of feminist activism, and after the emergence of a new generation of cinema enthusiasts and the resulting development of influential film schools and educated audiences, have women been able to stake out film production, criticism, and theory as increasingly visible areas of autonomous creativity and analysis.[1]

Given this context, it is hardly surprising that much of women's critical work has been focusing on issues of representation: Woman as victim; Woman as plaything; Woman as sex object; Woman as ornament, servant, or sidekick; Woman as debased by the very pedestals on which she has been perched, obliterated by archetypal renditions, and glamorized beyond recognition by a cinematography that panders to the male gaze. The emphasis here is clearly on mainstream cinema, notably Hollywood films, partly because this cinema has been so influential in producing images and dictating values, but also because both its sweeping falsifications on the level of character and plot and its virtuoso use of the apparatus to sustain these falsifications, make such a clear case for feminist resistance. Key here is Woman rendered as "Other"—both in the essentialist sense of women turned into the archetypal entity of Woman, and in the political sense of difference providing a rationale for inequality. In both respects, "rendition" is the focal point. Paralleling feminist literary criticism, this concern with renditions of difference began in the United States with excavating and surveying abuse along the "images" line. But even as books like *Popcorn Venus* and *From Reverence to Rape* were going into print in the early 1970s, other perspectives were emerging—partly out of the American and British feminist left, which has been especially interested in the "use value" of representation as an ideological instrument, and especially under the influence of poststructuralist theory, notably semiotics and psychoanalysis.[2]

Recent feminist film production has been similarly concerned with renditions of difference. The challenge for women working in production has been to find ways of making films question and subvert received notions of gender. Partly for lack of funding and institutional support, and partly because oppositional politics and activist "consciousness raising" goals have been especially open to unconventional modes of representation since the 1960s, feminist cinema has often yielded formally adventurous films. These jolt audiences' habit-bred expectations and, thus, force awareness of the ideological operations of culture on the level of form as well as theme. Participating in a broader effort to reclaim women from patriarchal formulations, including the "ways of seeing" Hollywood in particular has established as the norm,[3] feminist filmmaking has kept pace with feminist scholarship in its interrogation of ways mainstream cinema constructs representations of women and sets up viewing positions which collude in women's assimilation into patriarchal agendas. In direct opposition to this tradition, feminist filmmakers have been experimenting with ways films can construct representations and set up viewing positions that affirm women's autonomy, equality, and power.

The point of this all too brief and necessarily incomplete glance backward is to suggest that rendition is a function of history and ideology. Most obviously, this means that films need to be considered in relation to the particular circumstances affecting their production and reception. But, in addition, this emphasis on rendition as inflected through history and ideology subjects the very work of this essay, too, to self-reflexivity. The following discussion will concern five films made at the margins of mainstream cinema. Three of them were directed by men and produced before the emergence of feminist cinema; two were directed by women during a period of heightened feminist activism. The first three are feature-length and formally conventional; the latter two are short and formally experimental. All five use women as their protagonists and in various ways explore issues of repression and emergence in terms of interactions between gender, race, and class in postcolonial contexts. In particular, all five use women's silences and speech as a trope for these struggles—a trope that will be central to the following discussion. Clearly, then, an essay covering this territory raises questions of rendition about its own goals and practices.

Let me say outright that the following discussion aims to be interventionist in several respects. Most immediately, it enters into the current debate over "canons" and "cultural literacy" by foregrounding little-known work concerning people and issues generally ignored within film studies. In so doing, it reclaims visions that might otherwise be lost to us. It urges attention to what marginal cinema might offer women in particular, and it argues for readings that link gender to other disenfranchisements. The focus on speech in particular is also interventionist in its shift of emphasis from the gaze to the ear and, thus, from Woman as object to women as subjects. Ever since Laura Mulvey's often-cited work on male spectatorship, feminist readings of patriarchal discourse "against the grain" have provided women with invaluable means of extracting themselves from gender mystifications.[4] In this respect, though, voice is the next frontier precisely because it is the site of articulation. The very notion of "difference" gets recast from difference as erasure to difference as presence.[5] Instead of giving male auteurs and male spectatorship top billing, female articulation and reception insert women into subject positions.[6] Finally, then, the following discussion will open up the question of reception to closer scrutiny. Assuming that the capacity to utter is key to social transformation, I will consider women as speaking subjects—notably women of color—and the implications their filmic treatments have especially (but not exclusively) for female reception.

Given the trajectory traced above it seems appropriate to start with the question of silence and its relation to empowerment. In this respect it is important to note that access to voice does not necessarily translate into power, or vice versa. On the whole, women are audible and even fluent in "talking pictures," though often in ways that do not add up to much. The disruption of reason which screwball comedies often lodge in female speakers, the exclamatory excess of melodrama, the frequent subordination of speech to image, ear to gaze, where women are concerned, and the near absence of authoritative female voice-overs—through these and more, mainstream cinema often casts women's speech as corporeal, subjective, and unreliable.[7] In face of such practices, silence can indeed be a positive value. It can signal a holding of one's self apart, a resistance that cherishes one's inviolability. It can provide a generative space, a lacuna that lets the listener insert herself in the blank space, thus becoming an active participant in the production of meanings. When foregrounded, it can displace conventional notions of audibility and fluency and teach audiences to listen in new ways and discover new, hitherto unsuspected, modes of eloquence and assertion. At the same time, the moment one renames "silence" as "muteness," the valuation of this concept changes. What at first seemed precious, a sign of strength in adversity, turns into erasure. Clearly at issue here is not the absence of sound but a value-laden relationship between articulation and presence, notably as it bears on women's position within society. Ultimately, at stake for women is the interaction of silence, speech, and dignity as it might inscribe defeats and triumphs.

This interaction works itself out interestingly across *Black Girl* (Sembene, Senegal, 1966), *Ramparts of Clay* (Bertucelli, Algeria, 1971), and *Salt of the Earth* (Biberman, U.S., 1954), precisely because in them the soundtrack proves key to our understanding of women's repression and emergence. *Black Girl* concerns a young Senegalese woman, Diouana, who works as a governess for a white French family and who decides to accompany her employers when they return to France, leaving her home, culture, and boyfriend behind her. Once in France, the film focuses on the employers' callous indifference to Diouana and on her isolation and increasing depression as these lead to her eventual suicide. *Ramparts of Clay* also concerns a young woman, this time in a North African village which subsists on stone-cutting in the local quarry. Emphasizing this nameless woman's being as an outsider among her own people and embattled against her position as woman within a strictly patriarchal society, the film probes the relation between isolation and freedom. On the one hand, the very fact of marginality frees this woman to help the men who go on strike; on the other, this same marginality drives her to a suicidal flight into the desert. *Salt of the Earth* concerns a miners' strike in New Mexico and a shift in sex-role expectations which begins in this largely Chicano community once women join the picket line and start participating actively in the strike. Central here is Esperanza—a married housewife, pregnant, and mother of two—whose emergence from gendered subservience to personal autonomy is made possible through the reeducation the strike brings to the community as a whole.

A comparative reading of these films reveals various shared characteristics: all three are feature-length films directed by men and focused on female protagonists; all three concern disempowered people (Senegalese, Berber, and Chicano, respectively) eking out a meager living in a racist world marked by the lingering effects of a recent colonial past; all three treat their female protagonists with considerable respect and compassion; and each situates its protagonist's struggle for personal autonomy as a woman within a larger context of economic, territorial, and racial conflict. Especially significant to the present discussion is the fact that, additionally, each film depicts a woman whose voice is muted by social repression. The Berber woman barely speaks, Diouana sinks into silence once in France, and Esperanza only reclaims her voice when she emerges into a world larger than the domestic one. Though *Salt of the Earth* breaks out of verbal and political paralysis in ways that *Black Girl* and *Ramparts of Clay* do not, a comparative reading suggests that the dialectic between silence and utterance works across all three films as a metaphor for a broader investigation of dignity, autonomy, and community, in ways that ultimately empower women.

Diouana's silence in *Black Girl* goes beyond a language barrier caused by exile. In this film, female muteness functions semiotically; it builds a case, scene by scene, against gender exploitation within a postcolonial context that proves merely a variant on colonial power relations. Using a flat black-and-white film stock, plain utilitarian photography, slow-paced editing, and a plot drained of "action," the film makes no concessions to its audience. It engages viewers angrily, sardonically, in Diouana's increasingly intolerable alienation. Clearly this visual bareness parallels her silence, thus inscribing an uncomfortable reception that is short on visual pleasure.[8] Meanwhile the soundtrack interacts with such commentary by introducing lively Senegalese music to affirm Diouana's origins, and it uses callous French talk and jarring urban noises to critique the social order which destroys her. In short, on both the visual and the acoustic levels, the film creates a dissonance that functions as a surrogate for direct speech. Like the mask that Diouana reclaims from her employers in a symbolically eloquent gesture of resistance, the film's stylistic rendition provides the commentary which the human voice is made to withhold. While the plot's progression toward suicide seems inexorable stylistically as well as thematically, the film's treatment of that suicide reinscribes Diouana's anger and, thus, metaphorically reclaims her absent voice from oblivion. Significantly, this suicide is not an act of despair. Though it does reflect a defeat, in terms of African beliefs it also signifies that Diouana is sending her spirit back home to the *omphalo,* the spiritual center.[9]

In *Ramparts of Clay,* too, the protagonist's silence is oppressively noticeable, except that here there is no free and easy past against which to measure it. Depicted as unmarried, poor, and without kin, this woman exists outside those communal rituals which allow adult married women in her society at least a measure of matriarchal power. When other women prepare a bride for her wedding, serve their husbands, visit one another, pray at the Sheikh's tomb, or ullalate ritualistically, she is silenced by exclusion.[10] Still, perhaps because Bertucelli is himself an outsider to the society he films, *Ramparts of Clay* elicits a somewhat contradictory reception in this regard. In contrast with *Black Girl,* which sets up for spectators a thoroughly uncomfortable viewing position, here the plot may be stark and painful but the camera is sensuously mobile and the color photography of the desert and villagers is intimate and breathtakingly beautiful. Visually, the film invokes an ethnographic "orientalism" that tends to mystify, not challenge.[11] It is mainly on the level of sound that dissonance occurs. On the one hand, the film uses minimal desert sounds, sparingly recorded ambient sounds, and the near absence of speech to project acoustic emptiness. Its lacunas elicit a heightened listening that underscores the fact that there is almost nothing to be heard, and that what can be heard is symbolically overdetermined. The distant call to prayer, a monotonous hammering at the quarry, boots crunching on gravel, and especially the protracted shrieks of the unoiled well pulley which function throughout the film as surrogates for the protagonist's voice, signal anguish and desolation.

In these two films female muteness is clearly based in anger. The women's proud bearing and their increasing refusal to play assigned roles within their social order assert resistance. Their inaccessibility to viewers, as well as to those who claim to control them, affirms an inviolable self opposing patriarchal and colonial order. *Black Girl* conveys this through its formal and symbolic operations, as we have seen. It's very apparatus and icons inscribe a reception that resists defeat. While *Ramparts of Clay* is formally more ambivalent, its plot concerns resistance more directly. Though its protagonist's alienation leads to a suicidal "escape," the narrative includes a number of potentially empowering incidents. The woman observes closely the children at school—girls as well as boys—learning about their village's place in a larger world; she, herself, secretly learns to read; she registers the relative freedom enjoyed by nomads and by a team of female social workers; she helps make the stonecutters' strike confrontational and successful; and she eventually rebels against her servant's role when she refuses to keep drawing water from the village well. Other women may see this rebellion as madness (they force on her a ritual cure that leads to her "escape"), but the film casts this rebellion as rational and politically necessary. Moreover, when in the closing shot the camera loses sight of the woman's vanishing body, pulling back from the desert to reveal the airplane from which the running woman is filmed, self-reflexivity inserts itself as an important viewing position. In contrast to *Black Girl*'s counting on audience identification, *Ramparts of Clay* uses this distanciation to foreground didactic address.

Unlike mainstream cinema, which generally gives women a voice but goes on to degrade their use of it, *Black Girl* and *Ramparts of Clay* are honest in denying certain women their voices and constructive in exposing the causes of this silence and in embedding in their cinematography signifiers which go beyond the plot to indicate that the loss is by no means irrevocable. In *Black Girl* Senegalese music, African clothing, Diouana's African mask, and even her suicide, in its traditional meaning, signal the persistence of articulation and self-determination. *Ramparts of Clay* does likewise in its loving treatment of its materials, and when it links its remote village to a larger world, spotlights the schoolhouse as a site for political education, treats the strike as an act of resistance, and quotes Fanon as a frame of reference for a political reading of its narrative.[12] In their different ways, then, both films place their protagonists' silence in a dialectic relationship to the process of social change.

It is especially on the level of language that audiences are made to experience this dialectic most personally. In *Black Girl* the interplay of French and Wolof replicates the relation of the colonized to the colonizer. Forcing a distinction between "them" and "us," the film makes verbal inaccessibility become the arena for the exercise of power on the one hand, resistance on the other. Access to language proves not just a natural gift, a birth right, but an acquisition subject to politics. *Ramparts of Clay* not only shares this view but uses Arabic without subtitles to further defamiliarize language for Western audiences. In so doing, it situates the struggle between the colonized and the colonizer in the auditorium itself. Treating Arabic (itself a conquering language) as a linguistic norm, it casts Western audiences into the role of outsiders.

Lest this dialectic escape audiences, *Ramparts of Clay* incorporates explicit commentary into its footage. It opens with an epigraph from Fanon and, later, inserts periodically into the soundtrack a disembodied female voice whose singing punctuates the narrative with voice-over commentary. The introductory quotation provides a conceptual framework from which to consider the narrative. It establishes the political perspective viewers are to bring to bear on the film and, especially at the time of its original screenings in the early 1970s, but also to this day, it uses Fanon to inscribe militancy:

> In fact, the bourgeois phase in the history of underdeveloped countries is a completely useless phase. When this caste has vanished, devoured by its own contradictions, it will be seen that nothing new has happened since independence was proclaimed, and that everything must be started again from scratch.[13]

While Amrouch, the singer, does not enjoy the same kind of name-recognition, she plays an analogous role in the film, in that her song similarly provides an extraneous framework from which to interpret the narrative. Like the quotation from Fanon, it too extrapolates from the particular to the general. Starkly unaccompanied, rough-timbered, and aggressively unornamented, it inserts inself into the soundtrack as an uncompromising articulation coded as both forceful and female. Its repeated reentry into the film foregrounds female identity. It counters the protagonist's silence with sound, and the threat of erasure with presence.

Though initially akin to *Black Girl* and *Ramparts of Clay* in its treatment of women's silence as a function of their social subordination, ultimately *Salt of the Earth* retrieves women's voices more directly. Here, from the opening sequence onward, it is a woman's voice-over narration that guides us. Moreover, the recollections the film enacts for us, together with the retrospective intelligence it allows this woman, clearly establish that voice as authoritative. In part, this happens because Esperanza recounts an event that is remarkable in its own right. But her account is also compelling because it joins a privately experienced emergence to public imperatives, and because it does so in a direct, factual, and purposeful manner. The force of Esperanza's voice-over is, precisely, that it documents emergence of political analysis and personal authority in women.

Early on in the film, women's voices seem irrevocably set in the traditional mold. Especially when men are around the women are diffident, barely audible, and quick to relinquish their speech and let their voices trail off in unfinished sentences. When they first try to voice their concerns in the union hall, they are easily silenced. Yet once these same women replace men on the picket line, their voices grow in power. They now speak as equals at union meetings, they are vocal and courageous on the picket line, and their protest chant in prison proves a spirited and determined assertion of political cohesion and purpose. In contrast with Diouana's paralysis, Esperanza derives her strength from working actively for change. Unlike Bertucelli's protagonist, she works with other women who share her circumstances, and she is buoyed by the common purpose which unites people normally divided by ethnic and gender inequalities. Her role as a female narrator affirms women's authority, while her being a Chicana further affirms the access of minorities in general, and minority women in particular, to eloquence and self-definition.

That *Salt of the Earth* parts ways with Hollywood's typically derogatory use of foreign culture and speech echoes a linguistic dialectic we have already seen at work in *Black Girl* and *Ramparts of Clay*. While here Spanish is an authenticating device, what is most noteworthy about its use is not just its realism but the respect and clarity the film accords a language and an accent Hollywood normally encodes as "inferior." Unlike Sembene and Bertucelli, who sever their protagonists from their own linguistic communities as well as from ours, Biberman normalizes Spanish, honoring Chicano identity and cultural heritage. Thus, when the soundtrack records heated debates in a Spanish unaccompanied by subtitles, it empowers the speakers and temporarily disables Anglo listeners. The film helps such listeners recover from this lacuna only as it clarifies the context in which the Spanish is spoken— that is, when it lets Anglo characters (and thus English) enter the debate, and when it embeds in the narrative instances where the Chicanos educate their Anglo "brothers" about their Mexican heritage. Here bilingualism signifies, not conveys. It emphasizes the existence of a cultural and political community more than the particular content of a given sentence. In granting Mexican-Americans the gift of eloquence and the right to social exchange, in withholding comprehension from their audience, at least temporarily, and in letting Esperanza's way of speaking seem increasingly accessible and ordinary, *Salt of the Earth* underscores the dignity and rightness of the struggles it depicts.

Clearly Esperanza's way of speaking is central to this process. At first, her voice-over seems laconic, unidiomatic, tentative, and cramped by choppy syntax and limited vocabulary. Yet that same voice-over elicits increasing respect as the speaker moves from self-effacement to assertion, in company with other women and, beyond them, a broadening horizon of neighboring communities. What starts off as a deficiency gradually proves to be a strength. In part, this happens through Esperanza's development *in* language, for she clearly becomes assertive. More importantly, it comes about through the film's repositioning of its audience. Making listeners question and re-form their own relation to language, *Salt of the Earth* argues that barriers to articulation reflect the disposition of economic and political powers; it has its characters, especially women, work to reallocate this power; and it engages the audience in complementary efforts when it forces listeners to reclaim meaning despite their linguistically impeded access to it. In this, *Salt of the Earth* guides as well as depicts the cultural construction of ideology.

Such a recasting of women's silences and voices as the site of political struggle is rare in feature-length narratives, and all the more so in films made by men. That it occurs in *Black Girl, Ramparts of Clay,* and *Salt of the Earth* reflects Sembene's, Bertucelli's, and Biberman's oppositional politics in general, but also reflects, I would suggest, the particular inflection of oppositional politics which occurs when gender functions as a trope or nexus for discourses of race, class, and colonialism.[14] Not surprisingly, feminist films produced at the margin of the mainstream often use articulation centrally along similar lines. Even in *The Smiling Madame Beudet* (Dulac, France, 1923) the position of a woman as an unheard subject within patriarchy is a central concern; for all its being a silent film, it manages to portray the husband as garrulous and the wife as silenced. American avant-garde directors such as Maya Deren and Yvonne Rainer echo this concern in their treatments of gestural eloquence and, in Rainer's case, its relation to vocal excess and suppression. Concern with articulation can also be traced across the work of Marguerite Duras (France) and found in Sarah Maldoror's *Sambizanga* (Angola, 1972), where cries and silences insert themselves oppositionally, as alternative modes of assertion. It is a central theme in Julie Dash's *Illusions* (U.S., 1983), where a black woman's voice gets usurped by a white woman during a Hollywood dubbing session. It is evident in Chantal Akerman's minimalist severings of women's voices from their social and expressive use

(Belgium), in Marleen Gorris's encoding of silence and laughter in *A Question of Silence* (Holland, 1982), in Lizzie Borden's use of women's music, interview, radio announcements, and high volume noise to signify female diversity and revolutionary reciprocity in *Born in Flames* (U.S., 1983), and in Lis Rhodes's use of the female voice to push off-screen Woman's overfetishized image, as she does in *Light Reading* (England, 1978).[15]

This survey of oppositional practices aiming to free female voices from their traditionally acquiescent roles is hardly exhaustive. An overview of recent women's film production, notably since the 1970s, reveals a concerted effort to validate personal recollection and opinion; to endow female voice-overs with new authority; to insert dialectically into the soundtrack songs, interviews, commentary, and monologues as supplementary content; to experiment with shifting distances and attributions of disembodied voices; and to explore new relations between the seen and the heard. Often this formal experimentation concerns relations of power and diversity. Its emphasis is on dispersal and on dynamic interaction. Using a problematized soundtrack, a reduced spectacle, and an embattled counter-pointing of images and sounds, such films urge audiences to relinquish their Hollywood-trained viewing expectations in favor of a more actively deciphering and reasoning relationship to the issues at hand. Reclaiming the soundtrack as a particularly important site of meaning, they put in crisis the very notion of norm and its "Other." Seen in aggregate, they have audiences reconsider the terms on which women are to be seen and, more importantly, heard.

Two films whose treatment of emergence depends on such a polemic rendition of the female voice are Sally Potter's *Thriller* (England, 1979) and Sara Halprin's *For a Woman in El Salvador, Speaking* (U.S., 1985). Directed by women, narrated by women, focusing on women, and using women of color as particular vehicles for meaning, these films link female self-determination to other kinds of emergence. Though they are not strictly "Third World," in that both were directed by white women living in prosperous "First World" countries, they make for an interesting comparison to *Black Girl, Ramparts of Clay,* and *Salt of the Earth* precisely because they are more explicit and challenging in their casting of language as a site of conflict. In this respect, they are at once representative and especially clear examples of the feminist practices sketched above. Moreover, considered in light of their historic moment, including feminist activism and a growing understanding that "difference" is susceptible to inegalitarian appropriations, their attention to race, gender, and postcolonial conflict carries over into the eighties the thinking evident in the preceding three films.

Thriller is a short film (thirty-four minutes) that uses Puccini's *La Bohème* to initiate an inquiry into the use of operative melodrama, and by extension other cultural artifacts, to assist in the suppression of women. Dismissing the libretto's claim that *La Bohème*'s female protagonist, Mimi, dies of tuberculosis, the film unravels such alternative "murder" scenarios as social marginality, economic exploitation, and male egoism as likely causes of death (cf. *Black Girl* and *Ramparts of Clay*). Focusing on the fact that these are socially produced causes of death and therefore avoidable ones, *Thriller* encodes them as "murder." In particular, it focuses on the working conditions under which seamstresses like Mimi would have labored in nineteenth-century Paris, inserting documentary stills and commentary to add information the opera obviously suppresses. The film also unmasks the romance of bohemian carousing, showing it to offer a sense of community and pleasure only to those who can afford it financially. A self-supporting, working-class woman's relation to this milieu is necessarily lonely and exploited.[16]

That *Thriller* assigns the investigation of Mimi's murder to a woman (acted by Colette Lafonte) positions Woman as the central interpreting intelligence. Ascribing to her both the power of voice-over inquiry and a participant's role as a person engaged in unraveling *La Bohème*'s deceptions and eventually assisting Mimi, the film narrates this woman's growth in ways that echo Esperanza's emergence. At issue here is not the coming-of-age typical of masculine first-person narratives, but a coming into one's self and one's power. From the opening shots, where Lafonte's harsh, mirthless laughter signals a derision whose cause is not yet available to her audience, to her growing solidarity with Mimi and action on her behalf, this woman's rejection of patriarchal renditions of female destiny

Fig.6.1.   *The silenced speaker emerges as a disrup-*
             tive force, from Thriller. *Women Make*
             Movies.

guides the audience toward a similarly impatient anger about inegalitarian gender relations.

In contrast to *Salt of the Earth, Thriller* conveys all this through a treatment that insists on a symbolic, not literal, reading. *Salt of the Earth* depends on identification, while *Thriller*'s organization and narrative procedures call for analysis. Its narrator-protagonist enters the audio-visual tracks as a disruptive force right off (figure 6.1). Not only does she inhabit a bare set and wear plain dance clothes clearly coded as blank and, thus, stripped of mimetic reference, but her opening laughter disrupts reason. Its initially unexplained presence asserts power and menace as forces beyond discussion. Only gradually does the film situate that initial derision in what turns out to be a reasoned condemnation of *La Bohème* and similar artifacts. At issue are, finally, analysis, anger, and intervention, not just the empathy that is key to *Salt of the Earth*. Progressing as an inquiry that dismantles patriarchal renditions of female destiny, *Thriller* has its protagonist move toward solidarity with a symbolic "Mimi." Instead of Hollywood-style sutured coherence on the level of plot and its representations, *Thriller* puts forth exposition as a model for understanding and social change, and it gives control of that exposition to a woman whose role as a voice-over narrator and filmed participant models for audiences a reception committed to analysis and action. Enacting the process of "reading against the grain," it has her unmask Puccini's misrepresentation of Mimi's life and concludes that "Mimi" as a collective entity must be rescued before her life turns into yet another "thriller."

Still, especially important to the present discussion is the fact that this film's protagonist-narrator is also a black, and one whose English is obtrusively French-accented. In this respect Potter clearly embeds her film's oppositional feminism in additional layers of conflict. Lafonte's task is partly to guide her audience through a gendered struggle to reclaim from invisibility the actual conditions of women's lives, but also to challenge the colonizing hegemony sanctioned by dominant constructions of racial and national difference. Seen through the lens of racial ideology and colonial history, the black speaker is "Other" to the two white women the film has stand in for Mimi and to the white women who are her primary audience.[17] At the same time, as a commentator arguing the case for womankind in general, she is not "Other" to the universal "Mimi" the film posits. Quite the contrary, through her the film gathers women into a solidarity based on recognition of difference. Thus, while Lafonte's color and accent bear the unmistakable marks of colonial and postcolonial politics, her role as the film's governing intelligence, together with her capacity for reasoned compassion, anger, and humor, cast her "Otherness" as a norm and all those who resist her as "Other." Clearly in full possession of her authority as an informed thinker whose words are compelling, for all their acoustical blockages on the level of accent, this woman at once puts us on notice and beckons us toward a matter-of-fact view of difference that is egalitarian and affirming.

As must be obvious from the above, *Thriller*'s address is intellectual in the extreme. Its expository operations dismantle conventional expectations of narrative unity and visual pleasure and provide, instead, a deconstructive reading of *La Bohème* that addresses an audience familiar with poststructuralist thought and avant-garde film practice. Though equally unconventional in terms of its audiovisual operations, *For a Woman in El Salvador, Speaking* addresses a different audience, and it does so to different ends. Instead of *Thriller*'s highly educated, cineaste, feminist left, British and broadly Western, *For a Woman in El Salvador, Speaking* posits especially a Yankee audience and is conceived as an agit-prop consciousness-raising tool. Given this function, the film is accessible to a broad audience despite its determined rejection of conventional narrative and formal procedures. Its address is direct, and it insists on accessibility by having its account unfold through several language-systems at once— Spanish, English, Sign-Language, and body-language. As we shall shortly see, the interaction of these languages turns out to be a central signifier in its own right here, and a much more complex one than the above suggests, but for the moment the point is that this film insists on intelligibility as key to reception.

This intelligibility is evident most directly in relation to the theme of *For a Woman in El Salvador, Speaking*. Centering on a mother's account of her young daughter's disappearance, and on her own torture once she tried to inquire about her daughter's fate, the film concerns the horrendous use of "disappearances" and torture by repressive regimes, notably in Latin America. The story is simple and, in its rough outline, not unknown, though the extent of this knowledge depends on the viewer's political awareness.[18] The compassion and indignation it provokes are immediate and unqualified. While the film is not the usual feature-length realist rendition of this event, its brief seven-minute reading of the mother's account is readily graspable. Visually, the film's simplicity also provides clarity. Much of its eight minutes go to a woman "signing" the mother's account. Shot against the background of a bare stage and wearing the kind of pants and top anyone in her audience might wear, the woman's hand-signing and expressive motion and facial expression are what stands out as eloquent. The framing of this sequence in shots of portraits representing the women whose story is being told, assigns the narrative further immediacy. The film starts and concludes with the still picture of a mother holding her daughter's framed portrait in the icon of inquiry and protest that has come to represent mothers-of-the-disappeared (figure 6.2).

The anguish of absence haunts this film: the daughter's literal disappearance; the mother's loss of voice (her tongue was cut out by the prison guards) and visual absence from the screen; the disembodied Spanish and English female voice-overs which stand in for her; the English subtitles which echo an original language listeners cannot grasp; and the excess visibility of the female sign narrator whose gestures address the deaf audience our society renders invisible. In this layering and withholding of discourse, the horror of the events narrated gets transmuted into an epistemological wrenching audiences cannot flee. Each speaker and each utterance is in some way disabled. Foregrounding a surplus of languages, the film problematizes each of them. The plenitude of discourse as a theoretical possibility gets erased by the political repression of its speakers and by the conflicted reception the

Fig. 6.2.   *The silenced protagonist holding a portrait*
              of her "disappeared" daughter. San Fran-
              cisco mural used in opening sequence of For
              a Woman in El Salvador, Speaking.

film forces on its audience. That *For a Woman in El Salvador, Speaking* nonetheless recovers from this disjunction is made possible partly because audiences do have access to at least one readable or audible account, and partly because, for all their linguistic differences, these languages tell the same story.

This fact of translation makes the interweaving of languages in *For a Woman in El Salvador, Speaking* serve a unifying as well as conflictual role. On the one hand, audiences are clearly made to experience conflict concerning their ability to choose and follow a linguistic system and, underlying this choice, concerning their politically inflected favoring of Anglo or Latino speech. In this respect, the film clearly foregrounds issues of political and cultural hegemony as they come into play in the context of reception. Especially given the immediate life-and-death issues this film raises—issues much more pressing than *Thriller*'s deconstruction of *La Bohème*'s relatively abstract ruminations about labor, race, and solidarity—some self-criticism in this respect seems inevitable. The question of whose voice one hears involves politics as well as epistemology. At the same time, running counter to this dialectical use of language as the site of conflict, is the integrating process built into the film's use of female speakers and especially translation as organizing principles. Not only do all these speakers and languages tell the same story, but the fact that they are all unified by a common purpose, and a purpose so clearly life-affirming and resistant to tyranny, acts as a trope for community and solidarity. Translation, then, functions as a site of order. In this respect, *For a Woman in El Salvador, Speaking,* resembles *Thriller* and, before that, *Salt of the Earth*. In all these films audiences are given the means by which to recover from linguistic dissonance, and in all of them recovery posits reciprocity, unity of purpose, and an expanded understanding of one's community.

In *Thriller* the vehicle for this emergence is a character clearly coded as "Other." In *For a Woman in El Salvador, Speaking* the vehicle is a community of "Others." Each film uses its speakers to induce in its audience states of linguistic and political crisis, and each privileges the heterogeneity and multiplicity of meanings it inscribes in ways that challenge hierarchical notions of difference. *Thriller* derides the operatic rendition of "human"—that is, male—redemption as based on female sacrifice.[19] *For a Woman in El Salvador, Speaking* protests the cheapness with which governments hold human lives. Both have us examine our notions of "Self" and "Other" as inflected through colonizing renditions of human worth, and both do so by making us hear women whose voices have traditionally been treated as inaudible.

The reception called for by *Thriller* and *For a Woman in El Salvador, Speaking* foregrounds a solidarity based on people's ability to hear one another and speak for one another. The impulse here is clearly utopian, imbued as it is with various strains of feminist politics as these evolved in the wake of the counterculture and the New Left as well as subsequent developments. As the preceding discussion suggests, there are important differences in the communities each of these two films address and in the social function each aims to fulfill, but the overall drift of both is to affirm women as empowered speakers and to anchor this empowerment in the interaction between feminimisn and other egalitarian struggles. In all these respects *Salt of the Earth* clearly anticipates *Thriller* and *For a Woman in El Salvador, Speaking*, though the community it addresses is quite different (considering that it was produced during the height of the "Red Scare" which tore Hollywood apart and destroyed the careers of many involved in this film's production). Seen together, these three films respond to the very disempowerment *Black Girl* and *Ramparts of Clay* inscribe across their plots. They argue for solidarity based on understanding, they locate the capacity for such understanding in ordinary women, and they affirm that this capacity must be informed by an inclusive view of human good in ways that transcend single-issue politics.

Of course, utopian visions are particularly vulnerable to totalizing views of humanity. For women, the danger has been that they will adopt an overly inclusive view of themselves as a "class" or as a "colonized" group—a view that has at times encouraged unrealistic notions of "sisterhood" and an ahistorical essentialism which disregards women's diverse and changing inscriptions within their respective societies. This caveat is meant to highlight the importance of noting the historically specific origin and use of culture in general and of the films under consideration in particular. Of the five films discussed here, *Ramparts of Clay* and *Thriller* come the closest to an archetypal perspective. *Ramparts of Clay* achieves this effect through its episodic structure, through a photography and soundtrack whose operations exceed narrative function to the point of fetishizing their material, and through Amrouch's singing. *Thriller* does so by draining its set, costumes, and action of specificity, and by linking its exposition to the obtrusive artifice of an opera, and a melodrama by Puccini, at that. In contrast, *Black Girl, Salt of the Earth,* and *For a Woman in El Salvador, Speaking* are anchored in historic specificity. Still, ultimately these differences are a matter of degree only. Both films are careful to avoid a totalizing essentialist perspective. Bertucelli's quoting Fanon situates his narrative in a debate over current politics; he disrupts the illusion of pristine timelessness with episodes which exemplify Fanon's thinking, and his concluding airplane shot signals the film's crafted origin. Potter's historic documentation functions similarly, and her citing of Freud and Marx, together with her frankly symbolic renditions of narrative, avoids essentializing female experience.

At issue in all these films, and in many others besides them, is the interaction they set up between analysis and compassion, and the ways that interaction guides reception. Given the political motivation of such work, this interaction is important precisely because it guides reception and inscribes the terms of spectatorship. That in this group of films reception derives from a combination of analytic and identifying processes is my central concern, precisely because I find the respect these films accord their audience and the trust they evince in the possibility of social transformation at once moving and empowering. In all these films language itself becomes the territory through which struggles for emergence get enacted. It is the arena where lived linguistic and cultural codes clash, reflecting the hierarchies of power which motivate them.[20] But in all these films language is also the site of dialogism, the place where diversity can involve discursive configurations and reciprocations that allow for strategies of coherence.[21] In this respect, language invokes the process of passage, or a coming-into-being, that links articulation to understanding.

The process I have in mind is less concerned with speech as a mark of absence (in the psychoanalytic and deconstructive sense) than it is with speech as a mark of presence. It is not motivated by a yearning for a fundamentally elusive *logos,* that phantom of being that humanity is forever doomed to pursue much like Keats's lover pursues his maiden on his Grecian urn.[22] At issue is emergence— emergent understanding, self-respect, and power—as these can actually affect people's tangible as well as intangible place in society. The films under consideration here at once represent this process (by ascribing it to characters and by having the plots work it out) and insert it into the very process of reception. Most importantly, they concern the construction of social relations, and they use the very duration of the medium—the fact that film necessarily unfolds over time—to suggest that emergence is something that can happen in the auditorium, too. Highlighting what Teresa de Lauretis describes as the "constitutive presence" of language, they link the critique of culture to the possibility of change.[23]

Notes

1. At this point publications in this area require a bibliography, not a footnote. Books and anthologies of special importance include work by Annette Kuhn, E. Ann Kaplan, Teresa de Lauretis, Mary Ann Doane, Kaja Silverman, Charlotte Brunsdon, Constance Penley, and quite a few others. The journal *Camera Obscura* has been committed to publishing only feminist work, and other leading journals have encouraged such submissions. For an overview of these and related developments in production, see Laura Mulvey, "Film, Feminism and the Avant-Garde," *Visual and Other Pleasures* (Bloomington: Indiana University Press, 1989), pp. 111–26.

2. Marjorie Rosen, *Popcorn Venus: Women, Movies, and the American Dream* (New York: Coward, McCann and Geoghegan, 1973) and Molly Haskell, *From Reverence to Rape: The Treatment of Women in the Movies* (1973, reprint; Chicago: University of Chicago Press, 1987).

3. My analysis here uses John Berger's discussion of ways artifacts engage audiences ideologically and, especially, the materialist underpinnings of such engagement. In *Ways of Seeing* (New York: Penguin, 1981).

4. This point is central in Laura Mulvey's essay, "Visual Pleasure and Narrative Cinema," *Screen* 16, 3 (Autumn 1975), pp. 6–18. (Republished in *Visual and Other Pleasures.*)

5. Cf. the evolution of feminist literary criticism from Tillie Olsen's discussion of the systematic suppression of women's writing in *Silences* (New York: Delacorte Press, 1971) to Patricia Yeager's celebratory analysis of women's disruptive and self-pleasing articulation in *Honey-Mad Women: Emancipatory Strategies in Women's Writing* (New York: Columbia University Press, 1988).

6. Note especially Kaja Silverman, *The Acoustic Mirror: The Female Voice in Psychoanalysis and Cinema* (Bloomington: Indiana University Press, 1988). Though not specifically focused on women, note also Sarah Kozloff's *Invisible Storytellers: Voice-Over Narration in American Fiction Film* (Berkeley: University of California Press, 1988), and Mary Ann Doane, "The Voice in Cinema: The Articulation of Body and Space," *Yale French Studies* 60 (1980), pp. 6–18.

7. Especially germane to this discussion is Silverman's chapter, "Body Talk" (*The Acoustic Mirror*, pp. 42–71). Note also Kozloff's "Gender" (*Invisible Storytellers*, pp. 99–101), and Doane's "The Voice in Cinema" (YFS) and her chapter "Paranoia and the Specular" in

The Desire to Desire: The Woman's Film of the 1940s (Bloomington: Indiana University Press, 1987).

8. "Visual pleasure" in the sense the phrase has had since Mulvey's 1975 essay (op. cit.), especially as elaborated by Teresa de Lauretis in *Alice Doesn't: Feminism, Semiotics, Cinema* (Bloomington: Indiana University Press, 1984; chapter 5, "Desire in Narrative"), and Stephen Heath in *Questions of Cinema* (Bloomington: Indiana University Press, 1981).

9. My point is indebted to Clyde Taylor's essay, "Two Women," in *Journey Across Three Continents*, ed. Renee Tajima (New York: Third World Newsreel, 1985). Cf. also Robert Stam's and Louise Spence's discussion of this film in "Colonialism, Racism, and Representation: An Introduction," *Screen* 24, 2 (1983), pp. 21–31.

10. *Ramparts of Clay* is a filmic interpretation based on segments from Jean Duvignaud, *Change at Shebika: A Report from a North African Village* (Austin: University of Texas Press, 1977). Duvignaud's *Report* is based on a ten-year sociological study of the Tunisian village, Shebika. Bertucelli's protagonist is a composite of two unmarried women Duvignaud describes—a nineteen-year-old orphan who disappeared in the desert and another young woman who was subject to "the fevers."

11. Edward W. Said, *Orientalism* (New York: Vintage, 1978). Also Assia Djebar, "Forbidden Sight, Interrupted Sound," in Special Issue: "She, The Inappropriate/d Other," *Discourse* 8, Winter (1986/87), pp. 39–56.

12. Cf. *Sugar Cane Alley* (Palcy, Martinique/France, 1983), where education is identified as "the key that opens the second gate to our freedom."

13. Frantz Fanon, *The Wretched of the Earth* (New York: Evergreen, 1968; First French edition 1961). Bertucelli credits Fanon but does not cite a precise source.

14. Given the concerns of this essay and this volume, my discussion gives special attention to gender. The larger political interconnections can be traced through Sembene's *oeuvre*, through interviews with Bertucelli, and in Michael Wilson and Deborah Silverton Rosenfelt's *Salt of the Earth* (Old Westbury, N.Y.: The Feminist Press, 1978).

15. There is a growing body of feminist theory and criticism concerning these and related films. In addition to *The Acoustic Mirror*

(loc. cit.), see also Teresa de Lauretis, *Technologies of Gender* (Bloomington: Indiana University Press, 1987); *Films for Women,* Charlotte Brunsdon, ed. (London: British Film Institute, 1986); E. Ann Kaplan, *Women and Film: Both Sides of the Camera* (New York: Methuen, 1983); Annette Kuhn, *Women's Pictures: Feminism and Cinema* (London: Routledge and Kegan Paul, 1982); also *Heresies* 16 (4, 4, 1983) Special Issue: *Film Video Media*—especially Nina Fonroff and Lisa Cartwright, "Narrative is Narrative; So What is New?" and Lis Rhodes and Felicity Sparrow, "Her Image Fades as Her Voice Rises," pp. 52–56 and 63–66 respectively.

16. Cora Sandel's "Alberta" trilogy describes this in painful detail. Adding to the economic issues Potter sketches out the problem of unwanted pregnancies and irresponsible men. See especially *Alberta and Freedom* and *Alberta Alone* (Athens: Ohio University Press, 1984). Cf. also *The Song of the Shirt* (England: Susan Clayton and Jonathan Curling, 1979).

17. Here, as in *Ramparts of Clay,* the issue is the film's implied audience. Potter identifies hers most clearly with the citation of Marx and Freud, further inflected through the Anglo-French intersection in Lafonte's speech.

18. Though more accessible than *Thriller,* Halprin's implied audience is also circumscribed, as signaled by her film's taking an informed reception for granted, by its use of sign-language—notably Holly Near's signer—as a mark of current feminist/activist practice, and in its use of a political mural from San Francisco as the original of its missing woman's portrait.

19. "In every opera that deals with redemption a woman is sacrificed in ACT V," Kluge inscribed in the film, *The Power of Feeling.* Kaplan suggests a different but complementary reading of female sacrifice in her discussion of *Camille:* "Classical narratives of this kind require that the heroine die . . . because she offers a threat to the patriarchal order," *Women and Film,* p. 48.

20. Ella Shochat and Robert Stam, "The Cinema After Babel: Language, Difference, Power," in Special Issue: "Other Cinemas, Other Criticisms" *Screen* 26, 3–4 (May–August 1985).

21. This emphasis on the generative aspect of discursive configurations and reciprocation is central to de Lauretis's chapters, "Strategies of Coherence" and "Rethinking Women's Cinema" (*Technologies of Gender* pp. 107–26 and 127–48). Especially relevant to my discussion is her analysis of *Born in Flames,* which would have been highlighted in my essay, too, were it not for considerations of space.

22. This discussion at once acknowledges and strains against Silverman's psychoanalytic reading of the voice as a sign of absence ("Body Talk").

23. My concern here with women's language, film, and the possibility of change is part of an ongoing investigation. Ideas developed in this essay were originally pursued in presentations I made at two Annual Meetings of the Modern Language Association: "Unsounded Utterances" (1984) and "From Image to Voice: The Inscription of Emergence" (1987).

7

Genre and Gender: The Subversive Potential

JULIE LEVINSON

THE PRIMARY AIM OF THE CULTURE INDUSTRY, LIKE ALL INDUSTRIES, IS TO SELL ITS PRODUCT. This has been a truism among popular culture theorists since the likes of Walter Benjamin and Theodor Adorno confronted the phenomenon of art works as consumer goods, mass produced and mass marketed.[1] Marketers and movie makers alike know that the surest way to sell your wares is to create or cater to a perceived need and then to fill that need, expediently and efficiently, by routinely turning out a product that appeals to the largest number of consumers. The need, in the case of the culture industry, is for escape from the doubts, difficulties, and disappointments of the outside world. For the movie business, the resultant product is designed to reassure us that the world on the screen (and, by extension, the one out there) is comprehensible and tractable. The mass-mediated culture product does not rock the boat and makes no waves as it floats calmly above the flotsam and jetsam of ambiguity or irony.

The Hollywood studios in their heyday fabricated what they called product by a system of industrial production. The quantity of films was great, by contemporary standards, and the method of manufacture was quick and standardized. As the staple of the studios, genre movies—by definition iterative and codified—established themselves as easily (re)produceable and salable items. Since Westerns, gangster movies, musicals, horror films, etc., followed already established patterns, they were proven commodities. A ticket to a genre movie bought its holder the assurance of a predictable narrative line, familiar characters and conventions, and, in most cases, a happy ending that provided closure and complacency for characters and audiences alike.

Genre upon genre, film after film gave us contemporary myths which, on the surface, consistently reaffirmed our beliefs in a stable social order and in an America where, by the final reel, good is rewarded, evil is routed, God's in his Heaven and all's right with the world. For many years, these routine genre films were widely considered to be ideologically identical and disposable, like any other product designed to sell fast and big. As cultural products that packaged ideas for mass consumption, they had a persistent critical reputation as essentially conservative blandishments for the masses.

Robert Warshow, in his justly famous essays on the Western and on gangster films, was one of the first critics to rebut the notion of genre movies as nothing more than reactionary guardians of the status quo. Writing in the late 1940s and early 1950s, he claimed that the best of these films were capable of encompassing a potentially complex contemplation of American myths and obsessions. As manifestations of the mass psyche, genre movies offered up collective self-images which, according to Warshow, often challenged rather than reinforced its audience's values and verities. He recognized in select works of mass culture the presence of what he called a current of opposition; although "likely to be disguised or attenuated," this insurrectionary stance towards cultural smugness could be found in a form as seemingly simple as the gangster film, which Warshow deemed nothing short of "a consistent and astonishingly complete presentation of the modern sense of tragedy."[2]

Shortly after Warshow wrote about the subtexts of genre films, the auteur theory lobbied for recognition of a singular artistic sensibility capable of stretching, overriding, or contradicting the putative artlessness of standard movie fare. By insisting that film discourse, however seemingly routine, always contains ideology, the auteurist approach helped to legitimize select studio movies as complex artistic enterprises whose agenda, far from acculturating us to societal norms, actually rebels against prevailing ideologies. Having made their case for a movie's ability to interrogate the clichés of the very genre it represents, Warshow and the auteurist critics paved the way for the idea of the deviant text which, working within the familiar strictures of its form, nonetheless confronts and subverts conventional generic—and societal—codes.

It is a commonplace, in considering film genre in relation to gender typology, that masculine and feminine lineaments tend to be drawn with broad strokes. The consistency of gender representations in a given genre allows us to generalize about archetypal male and female characters. The Westerner, for instance, is a strong, silent loner who speaks with his gun and who disdains the trappings of domesticity. Women in *film noir,* to take another example of facile gender portraiture, are *femmes fatales* who lure the male leads to their doom. A casual survey of each genre upholds these stereotypes.

But at second glance, there are a few films which, while ostensibly following the canons of their individual genres, implicitly question axiomatic assumptions about gender. Rather than upholding and endorsing prevalent attitudes toward such monolithic American institutions as motherhood, the family, and the success myth, insurgent genre films reveal fissures in the foundations of these mythic structures. The characters in these movies are frequently conflicted about or defiant toward gender constraints; the films themselves often mutiny against hackneyed modes of gender representation.

Many such films date to the classical era of Hollywood cinema and undermine gender dogma from within standard genre structures.[3] Against all odds, these movies manage to be ideologically progressive while remaining aesthetically conservative and true to the contours of their form. Later, more self-conscious works overtly manipulate and redefine gender orthodoxies while simultaneously investigating the workings of genre mythopoeia. These revisionist films play against their generic forebears through exaggeration of or ironic distanciation from the genre's methodologies and strategies.[4] In both classical era genre films and generic transformations, the narratives embody ideological contradictions and tensions which, implicitly or explicitly, call into question sexual representation within popular culture as well as sexual stereotyping in the society at large.

In an article titled "Ideology, Genre, Auteur," Robin Wood succinctly outlines the four main gender norms found in classical Hollywood cinema. The ideal male is a virile man of action; an adventurer and wanderer, he neither needs nor really wants a settled home life. The ideal female, on the other hand, is the embodiment of the domestic idyll: a sexless (or postsexual) good girl who aspires only to wife- and motherhood. Obviously, these two together comprise what Wood calls, "an ideal couple of quite staggering incompatibility."[5] So each has an opposite number: the reliable but lackluster husband/father, and the erotic but treacherous bitch goddess. Run-of-the-mill genre movies (and, for that matter, most popular culture fare) at best work only minor variations on these four types. But the occasional savvier entry complicates and contradicts these formulae and their implications.

Two prime representatives of this more manifold approach to gender representation are King Vidor's *Stella Dallas* (1937) and Howard Hawks's *Bringing Up Baby* (1938). Both date to the glory days of the studio system and of their respective genres: the woman's film and the screwball comedy. Furthermore, both initially locate themselves within highly conventionalized generic traditions and then proceed subtly but unmistakably to undermine the bedrock convictions about gender that their genres usually espouse. John Ford's *The Man Who Shot Liberty Valance* (1962) is a more self-conscious transformation of the central genre myth of Hollywood movies: the Western. Made when the studio system was all but defunct, this film deliberately manipulates and reexamines established generic elements. In distinctive ways, all three films resist the tyranny of gender stereotypes. Although they share little in the way of characterization or narrative milieu, together they represent a subtle but durable minority strain in the vast procession of genre movies.

The woman's film or "woman's weepie," as it was perjoratively dubbed, was the soap opera of its day. It was designed to cater to the moviegoing demographics of the 1930s and 1940s, an era when adult females formed the crux of cinema audiences. Films such as *Daisy Kenyon* (1947), *Dark Victory* (1939), *Now Voyager* (1942), *Angel* (1937), *Letter From an Unknown Woman* (1948), *Back Street* (1932, remade in 1941 and 1961), *Mildred Pierce* (1949), *Madame X* (1937, remade in 1966 and 1981), and *When Tomorrow Comes* (1939) mercilessly played on the spectator's identification with the main character's frustrations, miseries, and obsessions.

Generally speaking, the action of the weepies involves the heroine's struggle against the restrictions of her world; more often than not, she loses the struggle and valiantly capitulates to the forces that thwart her. Male characters are relatively insignificant in these films, present as prods to the suffering and self-sacrifice of the female character or as foils to her lack of self-determination. In film after film, she is the odd woman out in a love triangle, or she is done wrong by her man, or she is saddled with children who betray her or sap her energies, or she is impregnated out of wedlock, or she is stricken with a deadly illness just as she finds true love. Whatever the situation, she is perpetually an other-directed victim: defined and fulfilled solely through her relationships with husbands, lovers, or children, and inevitably disappointed by them. With her choices and possibilities painfully circumscribed, she is, ultimately, tyrannized by the entire infrastructure of middle-class American life.

In *From Reverence to Rape,* her landmark study of women in Hollywood movies, Molly Haskell defines the function and technique of the most banal entries in the genre:

> At the lowest level, as soap opera, the "woman's film" fills a masturbatory need, it is soft-core emotional porn for the frustrated housewife. The weepies are founded on a mock-Aristotelian and politically conservative aesthetic whereby women spectators are moved, not by pity and fear but by self-pity and tears, to accept, rather than reject, their lot."[6]

In spite of their melodramatic conventions, the weepies' grounding in the social sphere offers the potential for a radical critique of society. And so there are, in Haskell's words, a "rare few that used the conventions to undermine them."[7]

Enter *Stella Dallas,* all gussied up in the outer trappings of the genre and bathed in enough tears to inspire the most sublime suffering in its audience. King Vidor's film is a woman's weepie with a vengeance; it belongs to an especially lachrymose subcategory of the genre known as the maternal melodrama. The mother in these films sacrifices all for her child, a creature who is usually either ungrateful for or unaware of this supremely unselfish act. The intensity of mother's devotion to child is so excessive that it must be construed as a sort of reaction formation: a method of disguising unacceptable feelings through behavior patterns that are directly opposed to them. The woman's total masochistic immersion in her motherhood masks her resentment and frustration that this is the one acceptable role available to her.

Stella (Barbara Stanwyck) begins the film with other ambitions besides motherhood. She intends to better herself beyond her working-class origins so that she can succeed in the only fashion open to a woman of her era, by marrying well. She manages to do just that, and, although husband Stephen Dallas initially tells her to "stay the way you are," she embarks on a campaign of self-improvement so that she can become "like the people in the movies." A year later, Stella is still unrefined and vulgar, ripe with sexual vitality that, in Hollywood's moral universe, always bars a woman's entrance into the rarefied reaches of the upper class. Prim and prosperous Stephen has, however, changed his tune and demands that Stella tone herself down, reminding her that, "You're my wife now."

Stella is also now newborn Laurel's mother, an occupation in which she initially has little interest. But a couple of years later, after Stephen has moved to New York for his career and Stella has chosen to remain behind with her daughter, she tells her low-life friend Ed Munn that she seems to be interested in little else. Thus begins her trajectory into the stratosphere of mega-motherhood, an ascent which is, not incidentally, concommitant with her steady descent in class, wealth, taste, and happiness. The narrative continues on its inevitable cataclysmic course. After a series of defeats and humiliations, Stella commits the ultimate act of martyrdom and self-abnegation: she severs her bond with Laurel—the one thing that she cares about and the only thing that defines her—by giving her up to Stephen and Helen, his new upper-class wife. In so doing, Stella achieves at least vicarious fulfillment in seeing her daughter accomplish what she could not do or, as the case may be, what she chose not to do.

Stella does make choices, and this is one thing that sets her apart from many of the heroines in woman's films, who passively accept their plight. It is she who sets her cap for Stephen, she who opts to stay behind when he goes to New York, she who shapes Laurel into a lovely young woman, and she who elects to give her daughter up. And, most importantly, it is she who decides that the price of conformity to accepted norms is too high. It is not that Stella can't be the wife that Stephen wants her to be. Rather, at some point early in their marriage, she realizes that she doesn't want to be. From her raucous enjoyment at the country club dance to her increasingly outré outfits, Stella's behavior is unabashedly defiant.

In women's films, clothing is rife with semiotic significance, and Stella's garb from scene to scene

Fig.7.1.   Stella Dallas in flamboyant attire, from
Stella Dallas (1937). Museum of Modern
Art, Film Stills Archive.

speaks volumes. When she is trying to woo Stephen, both before their marriage and after their separation, or when she goes to visit his new wife, she dresses conservatively and demurely. But when she aims to please herself, she pulls out all the stops, concocting get-ups that are positively inspired in their tawdriness. Clearly, she knows the difference in effect. But Stella's gaudy attire, especially in the latter part of the film, is one of the few expressive outlets for her otherwise suppressed creativity, sexuality, and vitality (figure 7.1). At least intermittently, she chooses to indulge herself. In a culture where acceptable standards of female appearance and comportment are stringently upheld, her frills and furbelows are downright heretical.

Throughout the film, Stella is repeatedly punished for her breaches of etiquette and taste. Every time she is with Ed Munn who, like her, just wants to have some fun, her behavior offends one of the representatives of the buttoned-down bourgeoisie. The disapproving party is usually Stephen; when Stella and Munn cut a rug at the country club dance, when they are rowdy in young Laurel's presence, or when down-and-out and drunken Munn pays Stella a surprise visit, Stephen is there to look askance. But he is not the only one who scowls at Stella's heterodox behavior. In one scene, Laurel's revered teacher Mrs. Phillibrown sees Stella and Munn having a rollicking good time on a train ride to Boston. Her disapproval is strong enough to rally Laurel's friends to renege, at the last moment, on invitations to Laurel's birthday party.

This is the first, but not the last, time that Laurel is stigmatized because of her mother's lack of decorum. She has an inchoate awareness that she is victimized by association with her mother so, although her love for Stella is strong, she, too, is sometimes cast in the role of castigator. The most obvious example of this is the soda fountain scene where a grotesquely garbed Stella is the laughing stock of Laurel's new, in-crowd friends. But even before this scene, Laurel is unhappy with her mother's sense of style (or lack thereof!); she obliquely lets Stella know that, compared to proper Helen Morrison, Stephen's new love interest, Stella is embarrassingly uncouth. It should be noted that Stella's social transgressions get no worse than laughing unself-consciously in public, dressing ostentatiously, or enjoying herself while dancing. That these actions should incur such stern disapproval suggests how intolerant and narrowly defined the society's standards of behavior are.

In each of the above instances, the audience's perspective and sympathies are manipulated so that we initially share Stella's emotion but then—often through point-of-view camera placement—are placed in the position of the people watching her. This shift in outlook is a shrewd directorial strategy. It works against our total identification with any one character by aligning the audience first with Stella, enjoying her self-expression, and then with the person casting a disapproving eye. By playing our sympathies in this manner, the film sets up a dialectic between the main character and the patriarchal codes that dominate and define her. The scene in which Stella calls on Helen to ask her, in effect, to adopt Laurel works in a similar manner; since neither woman is privileged in terms of camera placement, mise-en-scène, or editing, both come off sympathetically. There are, in fact, no real villains in the film (unless Stephen's and Helen's deadly dullness qualifies as villainy). Rather, Vidor implies that the problem resides in a rigid and unrelenting social order that does not allow for any deviation from strict social norms—particularly for women.

The film's excruciating final scene again yields a dual perspective for the audience, thereby complicating the meaning of the movie's ending. From a distance, Stella watches Laurel marry into the upper class, presumably because Stella has removed herself from her daughter's life. On the one hand, we weep with and for Stella as she watches her daughter, now lost to her, having made the leap to the other side and achieved what Stella did not. But, for a number of reasons, we are also alienated both from Stella's exultant victimization and from the assurance that Laurel has arrived at a happy ending. Romantic myths to the contrary, a wedding is a beginning rather than a final achievement, and, on the evidence of the film, the state of marriage that follows is fraught with disappointments. The brief glimpse that we get of Stella's working-class parents (her mother is played by the ever-haggard Marjorie Main) makes "The Honeymooners" look like lovebirds. And from the start, Stella's own marriage—although, like Laurel's, a step up the class ladder—is steeped in unhappiness. Given these examples, it is difficult for the audience to view Laurel's wedding as the *ne plus ultra* accomplishment for a woman.

Vidor emphatically (and literally) frames the wedding and the desired happy ending as an ideal to be examined and dismantled. The scene is internally framed by the window through which Stella gazes, so that it appears as if Stella is watching a movie. The ceremony is ogled by a group of rapt spectators, Stella among them, standing on the street in the pouring rain. Having spent the entire film making an all-too-visible spectacle of herself, she is now one more anonymous spectator. Light from the window falls on her face while she gazes upward; as the spectators are shooed away by a policeman, she begs to be allowed to stay so that she can see the final kiss.

Stanwyck displays a telling gesture in this scene; as she gazes absorbedly at the proceedings, she puts fingers to mouth and cocks her head to one side. She has performed this gesture elsewhere in the film each time she beholds a creation of fantasylike perfection: when Laurel first models the dress that Stella has made for her, again when she sees Laurel off at the train station for what she believes will be the last time, and, most significantly, when she and Stephen go to a movie for their first date, and Stella confides that she wants to be like the people on the screen.

With this gesture—along with the internal framing, the lighting, and the mise-en-scène—Vidor purposely invokes, in the final scene, the experience of watching a film. The implication is that Laurel's perfect wedding and the perfect future that it promises are as unrealistic as the ending of movies. Like all of us, Stella fervently wants to believe that the romantic ideal is achievable, but Vidor seems to be saying that it is as elusive and illusive as the world on the screen. This is a reflexive comment on the woman's weepie genre and on all fictions which promise us redemption and relief from our lives. Stella's dewy-eyed, masochistic rapture cannot help but make us aware of our own response to such fictions. This awareness is crucial since it enables us, in Linda William's words, "to resist the only way we can by struggling with the contradictions inherent in these images of ourselves and our situation."[8]

The final shot of the film shows Stella walking away from her spectator's perch. She begins the walk tentatively, still lost in thought, but as the camera tracks backward, she picks up speed and purpose, finally smiling to herself as she strides exultantly into the night. This is an exceedingly disturbing shot, since Stella seems to be revelling in her own self-effacement. But there is a sense in which she has, after all, triumphed. Since the patriarchal apparatus permits women only one role— that of mothering—she has played this role to the hilt, channeling all of her creative energies into the creation of her daughter. Like an obsessed artist who sacrifices all for her art, she sees Laurel as the fulfillment of her life's work, her pièce de résistance.

Additionally, the Stella who marches toward the camera is victorious in that she has managed to avoid transforming herself into the woman that society expects her to be. Her fierce determination to be who she wants to be is intact; from the moment that she refuses to change herself for the sake of her marriage to Stephen, she becomes what E. M. Forster called a round character: one whose personality and motives are complex. And because *Stella Dallas*'s ending makes us simultaneously ashamed of her degradation and proud of her stalwart resistance to remodeling herself, Vidor's film, too, is round, with complex motives and strategies. For both character and film, subverting the norm is a notable accomplishment.

The heroines of screwball comedies rarely have to concern themselves with bucking the status quo since the behavioral norm in these films is anything but normal. As the genre's name implies, these movies depict a world run amok where everyone is daft and nothing is as it seems. These films usually deal with the romantic trials, tribulations, and ultimate triumph of a young couple. One feature that distinguishes screwball comedy from classic comic form is that here, rather than being the ciphers they usually are, the leads as well as the subsidiary characters all engage in the high jinks. Since everyone is wacky, we begin to question the whole concept of normality. In many of the prototypical examples of the form, the woman is a daffy heiress who has been sheltered by her riches. Conversely, the man is a down-to-earth working-class type who educates the heroine in the ways of the world. Along the way, he also liberates her latent sexuality and spontaneity.[9] There are many variations on and varieties of this formula, but the screwball comedies invariably comment on the opposition between the upper and lower classes (the former revealed to be at least as zany and generally less capable than the latter) and between men and women. The films' resolutions serve to mute these polarities, as opposing forces come together for a happy ending.

One of the hallmarks of the screwball comedies is their rapid-fire repartée; the verbal wit and verbosity proceed with breakneck speed. Most of the major ones date to the 1930s, when Hollywood was blessed with the presence of some of the finest writers of that generation, so it is not surprising that the dialogue in these films is good and plentiful. But their prolixity serves a dramatic purpose, too. Since talk is so important in the screwball universe, he or she who talks best (not to mention most) gains the advantage. A character's verbal ability is a prime indicator of his or her control of the situation. The tongue-tied or inarticulate person is actually in peril of losing sovereignty over his or her identity.[10] In the realm of screwball comedy, the crucial thing is to keep talking, keep moving, and keep up with the action.

In spite of their particularities, the classic screwball films follow many established precepts of comic form. Like all romantic comedies, the plots involve an initially thwarted relationship between two young lovers; the challenge for the star-crossed pair is to overcome the obstacles to their union. Typically, these obstacles involve either the hindrance of a blocking character who tries to prevent the coupling or the initial antipathy of one or both of the lovers toward the other. A number of oppositions recur in comedies ranging from the Greeks through Shakespeare to the screwball era. Apart from the aforementioned male/female and upper-class/lower-class dichotomies, there are several other thematic antipodes including old versus young, urban versus rural, responsibility versus fun, and, most importantly, reason versus passion. Further, the comic universe is one where appearances are deceiving, so determining the true identity of things and people is a major undertaking (hence the prevalence of disguise and mistaken identity in comedy). Exposing the essences underlying the surface and debunking the foibles and folies of the society at large is the major intention of the comic form.

Howard Hawks's *Bringing Up Baby* both demonstrates and deviates from the characteristic screwball comedy. Hawks was a prolific director who worked across many genres but who nonetheless imbued all of his films with the same recurring themes. The Hawksian universe is a male world where men are defined by their capability. In his gangster films, Westerns, adventure pictures, and comedies alike, women are threats to the male group's solidarity a well as to the male hero's independence. The Hawks female tends to be "a man's woman"; once she proves that she is as tough and self-reliant as the hero, she is accepted by him and he agrees, often ambivalently, to compromise his solitary state.[11] Particularly in the comedies, women challenge not just the male character's self-reliance, but also his professionalism, his dignity, his sexuality—indeed, his very masculinity. When these ongoing Hawksian concerns are brought to bear on the screwball form, what emerges is a film that is *sui generis:* undeniably part of its genre but also in a class by itself, particularly in regard to gender roles and reversals.

Bringing Up Baby revolves around absent-minded Professor David Huxley (Cary Grant), who is one step—that is, one bone—away from reconstructing a brontosaurus skeleton. We first see him in a museum and learn that he is engaged to marry his assistant, Miss Swallow. She reminds him that their marriage will entail "no domestic entanglements of any kind," that the dinosaur will be their child, and that he has a date to play golf with one Mr. Peabody, who represents a client considering a million dollar contribution to the museum. On the golf course, David meets Susan (Katherine Hepburn), a madcap heiress. For her it is love, of a sort, at first sight; for him it is vexation and bewilderment. The remainder of the plot defies neat synopsis; suffice it to say that David and Susan keep crossing paths, usually through some stratagem of Susan's. The extended middle section of the film takes place at the Connecticut country home of Susan's aunt who, it turns out, is the potential donor to the museum. Things get progressively screwier: David's bone gets lost, the million dollars seems lost. After repeated complications and setbacks, the bone gets found, the million gets donated and, in the final shot, Susan and David end up together, if hanging for dear life onto the scaffold of the now-collapsed brontaurus. In the midst of all this lunacy is a tame leopard named Baby, as well as a man-eating leopard who gets mistaken for Baby.

Role reversals and shifting identities abound in *Bringing Up Baby*. The most consistent and significant of these involve gender, since both Susan and David display characteristics usually associated with the opposite sex. In spite of her flighty ways, Susan is always self-possessed and independent (with Hepburn in the role she could hardly be otherwise). David, on the other hand, is perpetually helpless: utterly reliant on other people—usually women—to steer his course. Susan is not the only female to control David's fate. At the beginning of the film, it is clear that Miss Swallow keeps the distrait professor on track. And Aunt Elizabeth holds the purse strings and, therefore, the power to make or break David's museum. In many of Hawks's films, the male character takes pride in having no strings attached, but David is repeatedly bound to (as well as gagged by!) his more capable female companions. Miss Swallow has to tie actual strings around his fingers to get him to remember his appointments.

Whereas Susan is athletic and purposeful in her movements, David is klutzy and bumbling. She is openly sexual and at ease with her body; he is up-tight and repressed, always moving as if his

Fig.7.2.   *Cary Grant in a negligee, from* Bringing Up Baby. *Museum of Modern Art, Film Stills Archive.*

torso were in a splint. En route to Connecticut, she drives the car; he rides in the passenger seat, being transported against his will to the next of Susan's escapades. She is singleminded, knowing from the first time they meet that she will snare him; he is absentminded, never knowing why he is doing what he is doing, or what will happen next. Susan usually wears pants or businesslike suits (although she is clearly not employed). The first time we see him, David wears a lab coat that looks like a cross between a dress and a straight-jacket; his later get-ups include a too small livery outfit, complete with knickers, and a flouncy negligee.

David dons this latter costume after Susan has stolen his clothes in order to keep him from returning to New York and to his fiancée (figure 7.2). He greets the aunt in the negligee and, when asked why he is wearing it, leaps in the air and proclaims, "I just went gay all of a sudden!" The ensuing scene is typical in its revelation of gender reversals. After sputtering and stuttering his way through his first meeting with the aunt, he sits and sulks as Susan takes charge. She concocts a new identity for him ("Mr. Bone") and a nervous breakdown in his recent past. Never at a loss for words, she is, as always, resourceful and quick on her feet, as loquacious as he is lock-jawed.

Throughout the film, Susan is inventing stories, situations, and identities, all designed to help her hang on to David. For her, life is a series of games for which she makes up the rules as she goes along. Creative and spirited, she embodies the forces of the id: a childlike, unrepressed glee and a guilt-free faith in impulse and instinct. David, governed by the super-ego is, alas, a sorry specimen of adulthood. Here, as in other Hawks's films, there resides the suggestion that the state of adulthood exacts too high a price; maturity and dignity are no fun. But unlike many of the screwball comedies, in *Bringing Up Baby* it is the female character who teaches the male this lesson.

The point of enumerating these gender reversals is not simply to demonstrate that the male and female characters swap traits. Popular culture narratives offer us any number of tough women and feminized men, but these portrayals are often at least as insulting as the usual stereotypes; gender reversal is not, of itself, necessarily progressive. Rather, what is significant about *Bringing Up Baby* is that it questions the very notion of systematically classifying certain attributes as emblematic of or appropriate for either men or women. As Hawks reminds us again and again in the film, normality is simply a matter of perspective. Certainly Hepburn's character represents an appealing commixture of qualities normally thought to belong to one or the other gender. Just as her personality is enhanced by her malelike vigor and self-assertion, the movie suggests that David's would be improved by a dose of such putatively female qualities as silliness and spontaneity.

Further, far from devaluing those qualities that are usually labeled feminine or asserting the superiority of those considered masculine, the film emphatically comes down on the side of the female character's disposition. The male world of professionalism, decorum, and discipline is revealed to be a sham, and the foundations of David's identity and alleged sanity are fragile indeed. By asserting the triumph of impulse over protocol, of nature over civilization, of enjoyment over responsibility, and of passion over reason, *Bringing Up Baby* casts its vote for forces that, at least in the film's universe, are associated with the female temperament.

This valuation carries through to the end of the film. Up until the final scene, the movie has faithfully followed the movement of a green world comedy. In this ancient form, the beleaguered couple moves from the normal world into a dreamlike natural setting, the green world. Here, away from the constraints of civilization, natural desires come to the fore as enemies are reconciled, lovers are joined, and problems are solved. In the final scene of classic green world comedies, the couple is back in their usual habitat. Having made their peace with each other and with the forces that would oppose them, they are now ready to unite and dwell in the civilized world.[12]

Bringing Up Baby follows this schema up to a point. But in the coda of the film, there are some significant departures from the typical green world conclusion. David is back on his scaffold in the museum. He is ready to complete his life's work now that Susan has recovered the missing bone. Susan breezes in, and he haltingly admits that he had fun with her and that he thinks he loves her—and that he is scared of her. Despite his typically garbled and futile protestations, she scurries up a ladder to embrace him. In the process, she destroys the hapless dinosaur: David's dry, dead alter ego. Far from restoring order or reaffirming the values of the workaday male world, this ending asserts the supremacy of Susan and her outlook. In the first shot of the film, we saw David posed as Rodin's "The Thinker"; the final image recalls that artist's sculpture "The Kiss." Rationality has ceded to instinct. David mutters one last, "Oh dear, oh my, oh well . . ." and then capitulates, quite literally, to Susan's charms and all that they represent.

The portrayal of a definitive masculine ideal is the mainspring of the Western genre. In the classic Western, male and female dynamics are clearly delineated and irreconcilably opposed. As in the screwball comedy, these contrasting values are represented by a series of antinomies around which the action revolves: the book versus the gun, the church versus the saloon, the homesteader versus the rancher, the community versus the individual, civilization versus nature, the garden versus the wilderness, and, indeed, the East versus the West. The first of each of these pairs is associated with femininity and domesticity which, in the world of the Western, ultimately encroach on and supplant the emblematically male wild west.

The Western hero is as tough and stony as the landscape that he inhabits. His identity is not dependent on his relationships or his possessions, since he has few of either. Rather, he defines himself through his ability with a gun and through his understanding of Western codes of behavior, particularly those pertaining to violence. He is a man who does what he has to do, sometimes reluctantly but always with a sense of duty that borders on fatalism.

Usually what he has to do is rid the community of savage forces (generally Indians or outlaws) to make way for the ineluctable coming of civilization. He has, however, a profoundly ambivalent attitude toward the settling of the once primeval West. Although he commits the necessary act of violence, thereby clearing the way for the march of progress, in so doing he helps to bring into being a world that has no place for him. By definition, civilization eschews violence; he, who is defined by violence, cannot exist in the settled, tamed West, so, of necessity, he ends up a loner and a nomad, riding off into the sunset to avoid the trappings of civilized society. The Westerner is, in many ways, a tragic figure. By his nature ineligible for domesticity or matrimony, he is unable to accommodate himself to the modern West and is thus doomed to be a creature of the past. For this reason, the purest instances of the genre have an unmistakably elegiac tone; from *The Virginian* (1929) through *Shane* (1954), they are rueful requiems for the death of a world in which real men were untainted by the forces of femininity and civilization.

Archetypal Western women come in two varieties. First, there is the transplanted Eastern woman who, by profession or personality, is a school marm. Educated, chaste, and proper, she represents all of the forces that threaten to displace the world of the wild West. The Western hero respects and protects her and often courts her. But she is his polar opposite, embodying as she does the seeds of progress. She also disapproves of his violent means and her opposition contributes to his own misgivings about violence and, therefore, about himself. For a female soul mate (not to mention for sex), he turns to the other type of Western woman. Euphemistically referred to as the dance hall girl or the good-time gal, she is, in actuality, the town whore. As tough and independent and self-sufficient as the hero, her fate is generally even sorrier than his. Things inevitably end badly for the Western bad woman. At best, she is jilted in favor of the virtuous woman or shunned by the town's self-appointed guardians of morality. At worst she is gunned down or she dies, presumably of some unnamed but fatal moral malady. The details vary from film to film but, in routine Westerns, the women fall into one of these camps, with little latitude for movement between the two. Although unlike the male characters they do not wear black hats or white hats to signal their moral status, as symbols they are equally readable.

Due to its manichean moral vision and its preoccupation with key American conflicts, the Western was one of the earliest and most durable of Hollywood genres. Its prevalence and popularity have oscillated since it first appeared around the turn of the century. The late 1950s and early 1960s saw the last great efflorescence of the genre. During that time a number of directors, most notably John Ford, Howard Hawks, Anthony Mann, Sam Peckinpah, and Bud Boetticher, made what have come to be referred to as mature Westerns: films that varied and complicated the basic formula in order to confront its fundamental moral questions. Often, their films were self-conscious genre transformations that integrated a fondness of the Western's conventions with a purposeful reexamination of those conventions and their implications.

John Ford's *The Man Who Shot Liberty Valance* is one such mature Western. In fact, its maturity borders on jadedness as Ford gazes back on the genre that he helped to create and finds it riddled with moral confusion and fallibility. This is a Western that cross-examines the very foundations of the genre: its inherent racism, its essentially conservative world view, its glorification of violence, its apotheosis of a flawed hero, and its rigidly circumscribed gender delineations. With its account of the making of a hero and its depiction of contrasting—and equally problematical—male ideals, *Liberty Valance* takes on the whole process of myth-making. In so doing, it becomes a film about, among other things, the very workings of story, legend, and genre, and how they indoctrinate us into certain ways of viewing the world.

Liberty Valance begins as an elderly Senator Ransom Stoddard (James Stewart) and his wife Hallie (Vera Miles) return, for the first time in many years, to Shinbone for the funeral of a now long-forgotten rancher named Tom Donovan (John Wayne). Stoddard has built an impressive political career on his legendary status as the man who shot Liberty Valance, a ruthless gunman who for years terrorized the territory's settlers. At the prompting of a local newspaper reporter, Stoddard recounts the events that followed his long ago arrival in Shinbone; these events are shown to us in flashback.

The flashback comprises the central portion of the movie. In it we discover that Tom has been in love with Hallie for some time when Ranse comes to town armed with a new law degree, a satchel of books, and a determination to clean up the area and impose upon it the civilized values of the East. Ranse wins Hallie over in spite of, or perhaps because of, his lack of typically Western manly qualities. Bullied by Liberty Valance, he eventually has to face a showdown with this nemesis of law and order. Local lore has it that, against all odds, he shoots Valance dead, and, thus ensconced as a hero of legendary proportions, goes on to elective glory. In a flashback within the flashback, however, we learn that it was actually Tom who killed Liberty. Recognizing in Ranse the unavoidable face of the future, Tom reluctantly but inevitably saves him from certain death, cedes Hallie to him, and allows the lie about Liberty's death to remain intact. Whereas Ranse achieves international eminence, Tom languishes in obscurity. Having rid the community of Liberty Valance, he finds that, as a man with a gun and without any civilized ways, he is now an anachronism in the world that he helped to bring about.

In the film's finale, the reporter who has dutifully recorded Stoddard's story rips up his notes declaring, "When the legend becomes fact, print the legend." Apparently, legend is more palatable than fact; we embrace its simplicity and purity and choose to overlook its lies. From the title through the last line of the film, Ford probes the legend and the lies of Western manhood and heroism. He gives us conflicting exemplars of manhood so that, in it, unlike most models of the genre, it is difficult to decide who is actually the hero. It could be either Ranse, the man whom everyone believes shot Liberty Valance, or Tom, the man who really did the vaunted deed.

If the identity and quiddity of the film's hero is in question, however, the claim to villainy is undisputed. Liberty Valance is Western maleness gone psychotic. He has no ambivalence about violence; in fact, he gets a sexual charge out of his sadism. Flaunting black hat and whip, he is the unremitting scourge of civilization. At the town meeting called to elect representatives to the territorial convention, he is brutally frank about his opposition to the values of community, to statehood, and, for that matter, to the entire democratic process. In classic films, the Western hero is something of an *übermensch* who subscribes to a sort of holy moral law which, for him, supersedes the laws in the books. His self-sufficiency, ability with a gun, and opposition to change are couched as positive values. But these putative virtues are so distorted in Liberty Valance that he represents vice writ large: Western manhood run amok.

Fig.7.3.   Jimmy Stewart in an apron, from The
Man Who Shot Liberty Valance. *Museum of Modern Art, Film Stills Archive.*

Ranse is his opposite number. A century later than the film's time period, he would be called a new male. At first look, he is sensitive and sensible: unequivocally opposed to violence and determined to introduce legal process to the lawless West. When he arrives in Shinbone, he is promptly humiliated and nearly murdered by Liberty Valance. He vows to see this enemy of the people behind bars, but no one takes him very seriously. Liberty calls him "dude," Tom dubs him "Pilgrim," and both consider him a laughable specimen of manhood. That he spends a good deal of time in an apron, helping out in the kitchen, does little to dispel the impression of fecklessness (figure 7.3). But Ranse does make good on his promise of vengeance, if not on his method. Having schooled himself in the use of a gun, he proves his mettle by facing Liberty Valance in a classically posed Western showdown.

It is hard to know how to respond to Ranse's abandonment of pacifism. We do not know whether to cheer because he finally takes up the gauntlet of manhood or to deplore the lapse of his nonviolent ways. He is canonized throughout the territory as the man who shot Liberty Valance and his subsequent meteoric ascendancy to the highest reaches of national politics is predicated on this bogus claim. Is he then a new sort of hero whose reluctance to resort to violence excuses his eventual capitulation to it? Is he an old style Westerner who proves himself—however falsely—by being a man with a gun? Or is he a self-serving sham who, having achieved his fame not as a peace bringer but as a gunfighter, allows the legend to prevail over the truth?

On close reading of the film, Ranse's heroic status is dubious even before he does (or supposedly does) the fateful fatal deed. Ford paints the young Stoddard as a naive idealist who is full of abstract principles but not very adept in dealing with what is. He brings to Shinbone a sort of white man's burden attitude as he insists on enlightening the natives by replacing their values with his own. When Hallie admires the cactus rose that Tom has given her, Ranse insensitively asks if she has ever seen a "real" rose. In the schoolroom where he presides, he bullies grown men and children alike (and it is, of course, significant that, in this film, Ranse is the school marm). Pedantic and arrogant, he patronizes all of the townspeople by regularly pointing out their ignorance and provincialism. In the latter-day scenes, the elderly Stoddard is a hammy, pat-em-on-the-back politician, laying on the charm for everyone from the feeble sheriff to the train conductor. When the conductor says to him at the end of the film, "Nothing's too good for the man who shot Liberty Valance," Ranse's expression makes it clear that he is more embalmed in than ennobled by his legend. Ultimately, in spite of his larger-than-life reputation, Ford characterizes him as an unsatisfactory candidate for hero in either the old or the new West.

This leaves Tom Donovan, played by John Wayne, that icon of Western manhood. Stolid and stalwart, and the only man faster with a gun than Liberty Valance, he is the film's closest thing to an old style hero. But, revisionist Western that this is, Tom embodies not just the mythic but also the defective aspects of the cowboy figure. Pulled in two directions, he personified the schizophrenia of a society poised between the old and the new. He is a symbol of the mythic past, a man's man who relies on violence to settle his scores and boasts about his prowess with a gun. Still, he longs to settle down; at the beginning of the flashback he is building a house for Hallie on the assumption that they will be married. His instant antipathy for Ranse is not just jealousy toward a rival for Hallie's attentions. He recognizes in his educated, Eastern competitor the new version of desirable manhood. Tom knows early on that he is about to become obsolete. So, doomed to extinction, he performs one last act of Western valor and violence: he kills Liberty ("cold-blooded murder," he deems it, knowing that by ambushing his prey he has violated a basic code of gunfighter's law). Later he tells Ranse that he did so for Hallie because she clearly loves him rather than Tom and wants him alive.

For his part, Tom seems to prefer Valance—like him a gun-toting man of action—to Ranse. But he is smart enough to know when he is licked. It is Tom who reveals the truth about who really fired the fatal shot, thus enabling Ranse to be rid of his guilt and to represent his people. After the killing and the inevitable forfeiture of Hallie, Tom, in effect, ceases to exist. With Hallie lost to him, there is no reason to tame himself and settle down. And once the town is rid of Valance, who was the last impediment to civilization, there is no longer any need for an old style gunslinger. Liberty is both Tom's foil and the mirror of his darker side. It is not just the old West that dies along with him. It is also a whole pedigree of hyper-masculine Westerners, Tom among them. Thus emasculated, he tries, unsuccessfully, to commit suicide by immolating himself in the house that he has been building. But he need not bother since, atavistic and alone, he is already a nonentity in the new West.

Having internalized the tensions of a society in flux, each of the three male characters is profoundly neurotic in his attitude toward violence and its bearing on his manhood. Each is in limbo between the past and the future, unable to situate himself on a shifting set of gender coordinates and expectations. Hallie, the major female character, is likewise caught between the old and the new but, in her case, this tension resolves itself not in neurosis but in strength. She is an unsual Western woman, falling somewhere between the two generic female stereotypes and incorporating the best of both. A native of the West, she is unschooled and independent. But like the typical good-girl heroine, she is virtuous and nurturing.

Hallie is, in many ways, the pivotal character in the movie since, unlike either Ranse or Tom, she is able simultaneously to accept the value of civilization without renouncing the vitality of the old West. She alone acknowledges without guile that something is both lost and gained in the sweep of progress. With equal measures of sensitivity and stability, she might be the most heroic character in the film. Long after she becomes Ranse's wife and a worldly Eastern lady, she continues to love

Tom and the old West that defined him. At the end of *Liberty Valance,* Ranse promises her that they can come back and live in Shinbone. But the West is not the same. The beauty and epic grandeur of the wide open spaces has been replaced by pasteboard towns. And, in transporting the East westward, the new transcontinental train has symbolically polluted this once pristine landscape.

The characters' ambivalence toward their changing world is parallel to Ford's own seeming vacillation between the values of old and new. He is demonstrably nostalgic for, if not a better time, then a purer myth where conventions—among them those pertaining to gender—are simple and understood. But he also recognizes this purity as simplistic and reductive. The film's brilliance lies in its sophisticated presentation of the allure as well as the danger of sureties with regard to both gender and genre. In this most categorical and unequivocal of genres, the film's irresolution about the nature of heroism is its great strength.

By eschewing closure and consensus about the fate of its characters, each of the foregoing genre films refuses the common Hollywood convention of what director Douglas Sirk once called the emergency exit: an improbably happy ending tacked on to an otherwise problem-ridden narrative. The eleventh hour *deus ex machina* is a convenient way of blunting whatever social critique has preceded it by reassuring us that the characters' difficulties (and, by implication, ours as well) are, after all, solvable within and by existing systems. The resolution provided by these happily-ever-after endings sends us out of the theater convinced that all's well that ends well. But *Stella Dallas, Bringing Up Baby,* and *The Man Who Shot Liberty Valance* each end with a question mark. Rather than bestowing on us the luxury of complacency, they leave us with a lingering and profound ambivalence about their characters' positions vis-à-vis the social systems that contain them and about the futures that those social systems allow. Alas, the characters in these films generally remain benighted about this tension between themselves and the culture's patriarchal structures. It is up to the director to attitudinize, and it is left to the audience to contend with this dialectic.

The generic traditions represented by these three films are not very prominent anymore.[13] As movie audiences have grown younger and more preponderantly male, the genres of choice have changed. Nowadays, instead of classic Westerns, screwball comedies, and women's weepies, we have space Westerns, action films, and troubled teen pictures. But if the forms have changed, the ideologies that they endorse have remained strikingly similar. Despite the utter upheaval of gender assumptions which has taken place in the society at large over the past few decades, most genre films (and most popular culture forms from advertisements to pop music) continue to tell us that men are men, women are women, never the twain shall meet, *vive la différence.*

Genre films thus have a bad name among those committed to social progress. A typical screed comes from Judith Hess Wright, writing in the film journal "Jump Cut":

> Genre films produce satisfaction rather than action, pity and fear rather than revolt. They serve the interests of the ruling class by assisting in the maintenance of the status quo, and they throw a sop to oppressed groups who, because they are unorganized and therefore afraid to act, eagerly accept the genre film's absurd solutions to economic and social conflicts. . . . Genre films address these conflicts and resolve them in a simplistic and reactionary way.[14]

For the most part, she is right. But, thankfully, she is wrong in some cases. There exist, in the history of movie genres, a few anomalous rebel texts which, albeit conventional in form, are idiosyncratic in attitude. Such films not only dissect and debunk the status quo but they do so from within familiar and easily digestible narrative structures. This is a cunning, bait-and-switch technique in which we are lured to the theater with the promise of generic familiarity and are then, subtly but surely, challenged to rethink ideologies that had seemed so thought-proof and monolithic.

Cloaked in conventional vehicles, these divergent points of view are serendipitous discoveries—particularly noteworthy and powerful in their unexpectedness. As frankly commercial, ostensibly conventional products of the mainstream cinema, *Stella Dallas, Bringing Up Baby* and *The Man Who Shot Liberty Valance* are provocations rather than radically subversive calls to action. Still, in locating the problems and leaving it at that, these aberrant genre films go one step further than most popular culture narratives which do our thinking for us by giving us the problem and then the convenient solution, all wrapped up neatly by story's end. Unlike most popular culture products, which are oppressive and insidious in their uniformity of perspective, these works encourage us to ponder the implications of what we have seen. That a movie as seemingly light and innocuous as *Bringing Up Baby* can, in the guise of a classic screwball comedy, still challenge us to consider the wrongheadedness of strictly assigned gender roles suggests genre films' real potential for reaching broad audiences who might otherwise shy away from reflecting on the absurdity of gender stereotyping.

It is pointless to decry or dismiss generic forms of popular culture. They are here to stay and to shape, however surreptitiously, our attitudes and opinions. At least it is encouraging to realize that the popular culture is not a looming, hegemonic monster who always insists on conformity and consistency of thought. Rather, even so codified a form as genre films can, in rare cases, accommodate a pluralism of perspective. As consumers of mass media images and ideas, the best we can do, is ferret out and celebrate those genre films with a difference. *Vive la différence* indeed!

Notes

1. See, for example, Walter Benjamin, *Illuminations,* trans. Harry Zohn (New York: Schocken, 1969) and Theodor Adorno, *Prisms,* trans. Samuel and Shierry Weber (Cambridge: MIT Press, 1981).

2. Robert Warshow, *The Immediate Experience: Movies, Comics, Theatre and Other Aspects of Popular Culture* (New York: Doubleday, 1946), p. 129.

3. "The classical era" and "the studio era" are common if inexact terms for that period in Hollywood history when the studios controlled virtually all movie production. The terms roughly encompass the years from the beginning of talking pictures (the late 1920s) through the gradual demise of the studios (the late 1950s to early 60s). In *From Reverence to Rape: The Treatment of Women in the Movies* (New York: Holt, Rinehart, Winston, 1974), Molly Haskell claims that women characters were actually more rounded and independent in classical era films than in the later, supposedly liberated films of the 1960s and 1970s. In making her case for the heroines of the classical era, Haskell thus belies the notion that the movies have progressed in recent decades in their treatment of gender stereotypes.

4. See John Cawelti, "Chinatown and Generic Transformation in Recent American Films" in *Film Theory and Criticism,* eds. Gerald Mast and Marshall Cohen, 2d ed. (New York: Oxford University Press, 1979), pp. 559–79. Cawelti outlines a taxonomy of types of generic transformations. He attributes the rise of self-conscious genre films to "the feeling that not only the traditional genres, but the cultural myths they once embodied, are no longer fully adequate to the imaginative needs of our time" p. 579.

5. Robin Wood, "Ideology, Genre, Auteur," *Film Comment* 13, no. I (January–February 1977), p. 47.

6. Haskell, *From Reverence to Rape,* p. 155.

7. Haskell, *From Reverence to Rape,* p. 154.

8. Linda Williams, "'Something Else Besides a Mother': *Stella Dallas* and the Maternal Melodrama," *Cinema Journal* 24, no. I (Fall 1984), p. 22.

9. Such popular screwball comedies as Frank Capra's *It Hap-* pened One Night (1934), Gregory La Cava's *My Man Godfrey* (1936), and George Cukor's *Holiday* (1938) all follow this essential formula.

10. For example, actresses such as Diane Keaton and Jill Clayburgh often play characters who are putatively feminist, but their vocal patterns give them away as, ultimately, stereotypically flighty women. In films including Clayburgh's *An Unmarried Woman* (Paul Mazursky, 1978) and *Starting Over* (Alan J. Pakula, 1979) and in Keaton's *Manhattan* (Woody Allen, 1979) and *Baby Boom* (Leonard Nimoy, 1988), their characters' stuttering and groping for words constantly undercut their supposed control and work against the films' claim to strong, secure female leads.

11. For a sampling of these themes across genres, see such Hawks films as *Scarface* (1932) for the gangster genre, *Only Angels Have Wings* (1939) for the adventure genre, *Ball of Fire* (1941) for the comedy genre, and *Red River* (1948) for the Western.

12. For a complete discussion of the green world comedy, see Northrup Frye, "The Mythos of Spring: Comedy," in *Anatomy of Criticism: Four Essays* (Princeton: Princeton University Press, 1957(, pp. 163–86.

13. All three genres have, however, turned up on television wearing their readily recognizable generic raiments. The TV Western is no longer much in favor, but the woman's weepie has survived in the afternoon soaps, where the good woman still suffers and sacrifices. Vestiges of screwball comedy can be found in situation comedies such as *Cheers* and in such intentionally allusive shows as *Moonlighting.* The latter has been hailed as a backward-looking but forward-thinking romantic comedy, but it is actually all too familiar in its depiction of gender issues. In this show as well as in *Cheers* the female character is still upper crust and uptight; her male foil is a middle-class regular guy with one thing on his mind, and most of their interplay involves his attempts to get to her and loosen her up. In genre land, the more things change, the more they remain appallingly the same.

14. Judith Hess Wright, "Genre Films and the Status Quo," *Jump Cut,* no. I (May–June 1974), p. 1.

Notes on Contributors

NATALIE HARRIS BLUESTONE teaches philosophy at the Radcliffe Seminars, Radcliffe College. She received her Ph.D. from The Johns Hopkins University and has taught epistemology, ethics, and aesthetics in the United States and England. Recently she was a guest professor at The Center for the Arts in Vero Beach, Florida. She has published articles on literature and film and is the author of *Women and the Ideal Society: Plato's* Republic *and Modern Myths of Gender.*

LINDA DITTMAR is a professor of English at the University of Massachusetts/Boston. She holds a Ph.D. from Stanford University and has written extensively on film and literature. Dittmar chaired a conference on "The War Film: Images and Context" and coedited and contributed to *From Hanoi to Hollywood: The Viet Nam War in American Film.* She is also a co-editor and contributor to the forthcoming *Multiple Voices in Feminist Film Criticism.*

NANCY FINLAY holds a Ph.D. from Princeton University, and is the author of *Artists of the Book in Boston, 1890–1910.* She was a contributor to *American Art Posters of the 1890s* and a participant in the symposium *Breakthroughs: Women in the Visual Arts* at Skidmore College. She has long been interested in animal imagery, particularly that of the French Romantics. Formerly assistant curator of printing and graphic arts at the Houghton Library of Harvard University, she is now print specialist at the New York Public Library.

CHRISTINE HAVICE is associate professor, medieval art and architecture, at the University of Kentucky. She received her Ph.D. from Pennsylvania State University and has published widely in art history and women's studies. She has written many reviews and been guest curator for exhibits of illuminated manuscripts and of feminist art. She is a former president of Women's Caucus for Art and serves on the Editorial Board of the *Women's Art Journal.*

JULIE LEVINSON teaches film at Babson College in Wellesley, Massachusetts. She holds a Ph.D. from Boston University in Film and Literature. She has been film curator and programmer for several institutions including the Institute of Contemporary Art/Boston, The Boston Film and Video Foundation, the Flaherty Film Seminar, and The Celebration of Black Cinema. She is currently working on a book about the success myth in American cinema.

SHERRIN MARSHALL works for the U.S. Department of Education. She formerly taught history for many years and has edited and contributed to *Women in Reformation and Counter-Reformation Europe: Private and Public Worlds* and coedited and contributed to *The Process of Change in Early Modern Europe: Essays in Honor of Miriam Usher Chrisman.* She is the author of *The Dutch Gentry 1500–1650: Family, Faith, and Fortune* and is presently working on a study of Protestants, Catholics, and Jews in the Dutch Republic.

HENRIETTA STARTUP was educated in England and holds an advanced degree from University College, London, in Architectural History. She has published in the journal of the Royal Institute of British Architects and written reviews for the *Journal of the Oral History Society.* In England she also worked on the Whitechapel Art Gallery and Island History Project. She has been a museum educator at the Children's Museum of Rhode Island, the Slater Mill Historic Site, and the Providence Preservation Society. Currently she teaches at The Rhode Island School of Design. At Brown University she was guest curator of the exhibit, "A Matter of Simple Justice: One Hundred Years of Women's Higher Education in Rhode Island, 1892–1992."

Index of Names and Works of Art